D1556268

The Cumulated Indexes
to the
Public Papers of the Presidents
of the
United States

Herbert Hoover
1929–1933

With the Index
from
Proclamations and Executive Orders
Herbert Hoover
March 4, 1929 to March 4, 1933

Kraus International Publications

A U.S. Division of Kraus-Thomson Organization Ltd.
Millwood, New York
1979

ISBN 0-527-20755-1

Composition by Vance Weaver Composition, Inc., New York

First Printing
Printed in the United States of America

PREFACE

Although the words spoken by a president during the course of his administration are directed to the citizens of his own time, they become invaluable to future generations of Americans who look to the past for help in understanding their present world. *The Cumulated Indexes to the Public Papers of the Presidents of the United States* provide, for the first time in one volume, full access to the papers of each presidential administration published in the government series, the *Public Papers of the Presidents*. The *Public Papers* offer a remarkable view of the American presidents and of American history. The character of a president, the individuals with whom a president interacts, the historical events that are shaped by a president and that, in turn, shape his presidency, are all to be found within the pages of the *Public Papers*.

A resolution passed by the United States Congress on July 17, 1894, provided that a compilation of "all the annual, special, and veto messages, proclamations, and inaugural addresses" of all the presidents from 1789 to 1894 be printed. The publication was to be prepared by James D. Richardson, a representative from Tennessee, under the direction of the Joint Committee on Printing, of which Richardson was a member. The official set was issued in two series of ten volumes each. A joint resolution of May 2, 1896, provided for the distribution of the set to members of Congress, with the remainder to be delivered to the compiler, James Richardson. An act passed about a year later provided that the plates for *A Compilation of the Messages and Papers of the Presidents* be delivered to Richardson "without cost to him." Representative Richardson then made arrangements for the commercial publication of the set. Several other compilations of presidential papers were commercially published in the first half of the nineteenth century; these usually contained only selected documents.

The Richardson edition of the *Messages and Papers*, however, was the only set authorized by Congress and published by the government until 1957, when the official publication of the public messages and statements of the presidents, the *Public Papers of the Presidents of the United*

States, was initiated based on a recommendation made by the National Historical Publications Commission (now the National Historical Publications and Records Commission). The Commission suggested that public presidential papers be compiled on a yearly basis and issued in a uniform, systematic publication similar to the *United States Supreme Court Reports* and the *Congressional Record.* An official series thus began in which presidential writings and statements of a public nature could be made promptly available. These presidential volumes are compiled by the Office of the Federal Register of the General Services Administration's National Archives and Record Service.

As might be expected, the "public papers" vary greatly in importance and content; some contain important policy statements while others are routine messages. They include, in chronological order, texts of such documents as the president's messages to Congress, public addresses, transcripts of news conferences and speeches, public letters, messages to heads of state, remarks to informal groups, etc. Unlike other volumes in this series compiled by the Office of the Federal Register, Hoover's proclamations and executive orders, required by law to be published in the *Federal Register* and *Code of Federal Regulations,* instead appear in their entirety in two companion volumes, *Proclamations and Executive Orders: Herbert Hoover.* These volumes had been published simultaneously with the volumes of the *Public Papers of the Presidents: Herbert Hoover.* The Index for the volumes of the *Proclamations and Executive Orders* has been reprinted here, for the use and convenience of the user. This index appears at the end of this volume, pages 89 through 134.

The *Public Papers of the Presidents* are kept in print, and are available from the Superintendent of Documents, United States Government Printing Office. The *Papers* of each year are published in single volumes, with each volume containing an index for that calendar year. *The Cumulated Indexes to the Public Papers of the Presidents* combines and integrates the separate indexes for a president's administration into one alphabetical listing.

References to all of the volumes of a president's public papers can thus be found by consulting this one-volume cumulated index. *See* and *see also* references have been added and minor editorial changes have been made in the process of cumulating the separate indexes.

References in *The Cumulated Indexes to the Public Papers of the Presidents* are to item numbers. Individual volumes are identified in the *Index* by year, as are the actual volumes of the *Papers.* The year identifying the volume in which a paper is located appears in boldface type. When page references are used, they are clearly noted in the entry.

Other volumes in the set of *The Cumulated Indexes to the Public Papers of the Presidents* include Harry S. Truman, 1945–1953; Dwight D. Eisenhower, 1953–1961; John F. Kennedy, 1961–1963; Lyndon B.

Johnson, 1963–1969; and Richard M. Nixon, 1969–1974. Forthcoming volumes will index the papers of Gerald R. Ford, as well as those of future presidents when their administrations are completed.

Kraus International Publications

HERBERT HOOVER
1929-1933

Abbeville, La., **1932–33:** 86
Abbott, Charles F., **1929:** 278n.; **1930:** 344
Abbott, Julia Wade, **1932–33:** 145
Abelman, Max, **1932–33:** 355
Accounting Office, General, **1932–33:** 423
Adams, Charles F., **1929:** 104, 178; **1930:** 11n., 145, 267, 395; **1931:** 218, 219n., 324, 327, 435n.; **1932–33:** 34
Adams, Lucy C., **1931:** 414
Adams, Raymond, **1932–33:** 369n.
Adams, T. S., **1931:** 314
Adams, Gov. William H., **1932–33:** 5
Addams, Jane, **1931:** 165
Addresses and remarks of the President
  See also News conferences; Preinaugural addresses.
  American Bankers Association, 56th annual convention, **1930:** 311
  American Bar Association, **1932–33:** 335
  American Federation of Labor, **1930:** 315
  American Institute of Architects, **1929:** 51
  American Legion, **1930:** 314; **1931:** 318
  American National Red Cross, **1930:** 89, 149
  American Public Health Association, **1932–33:** 348
  American Society of Mechanical Engineers, **1930:** 108
  American Society of Newspaper Editors, **1930:** 119
  Armistice Day, **1929:** 275
    District of Columbia War Memorial, **1931:** 404
  Arms reduction and peace efforts, **1929:** 206
  Associated Press, **1929:** 47
  Association of National Advertisers, **1930:** 363
  Aviators Wiley Post and Harold Gatty, welcoming ceremony, **1931:** 253
  Battle of Kings Mountain, 150th anniversary, **1930:** 319
  Boy Scouts of America, 20th anniversary, **1930:** 81
  Brazilian President-elect Julio Prestes, visit, **1930:** 185

Addresses and remarks — *continued*
  Buchanan, James, dedication of statue, **1930:** 207
  California and Nevada, rear platform and other informal remarks, **1932–33:** 394
  Cardinal Gibbons, memorial statue, unveiling, **1932–33:** 263
  Census schedule, exchange of remarks with census taker, **1930:** 99
  Chamber of Commerce Conference, **1929:** 297
  Chamber of Commerce of the United States, **1930:** 144
  Charleston, W. Va., **1931:** 223
  Christmas greeting to the Nation, **1929:** 323; **1930:** 426
  Christmas seals campaign, **1932–33:** 408
  Collier Trophy, presentation ceremony, **1931:** 142
  Columbus, Ohio, **1931:** 229
  Commerce Department, cornerstone laying, **1929:** 115
  Community Chest workers, **1930:** 43
  Conference on the Crisis in Education, **1932–33:** 442
  Conference of Governors, **1932–33:** 137
  Congress.
    See Congress, communications to.
  Cornell University War Memorial, **1931:** 199
  Cornerstone laying ceremonies
    Justice Department Building, **1932–33:** 472
    Labor Department and Interstate Commerce Building, **1932–33:** 427
    National Archives Building, **1932–33:** 471
    Post Office Department Building, **1932–33:** 307
  Curie, Madame Marie, ceremonies honoring, **1929:** 266
  Currency hoarding, **1932–33:** 73
    Denver, Colo., **1932–33:** 383
  Danville, Ill., **1931:** 234
  Daughters of the American Revolution, **1930:** 115
  Decatur, Ill., **1931:** 235
  Disabled war veterans, **1932–33:** 365

[References are to items except as otherwise indicated]

Addresses and remarks — *continued*
Distinguished Flying Cross, presentation ceremony, **1932–33:** 247
Eckener, Dr. Hugo, exchange of remarks, **1929:** 189
Edison, Thomas A., tribute to, **1929:** 245, 246
Elections.
See main heading, Elections.
Federal Farm Board, first meeting, **1929:** 150
Federal Reserve District Banking and Industrial Committees, conference, **1932–33:** 272
Fifth International Oratorical Contest, **1930:** 340
4-H Clubs, **1930:** 389
French aviators, remarks welcoming, **1930:** 287
Governors' Conference, **1930:** 215
Greenburg, Ind., **1931:** 225
Gridiron Club, **1929:** 35, 314; **1930:** 133, 408; **1931:** 155, 439; **1932–33:** 120, 424
H. J. Heinz International Radio Banquet, **1930:** 358
Harding Memorial, Marion, Ohio, **1931:** 228
Herbert Schiff Memorial Trophy, presentation ceremony, **1930:** 398; **1931:** 435
"Hoover Day," Madison County, Va., **1929:** 180
Howard University, **1932–33:** 191
Huntington, W. Va., **1931:** 224
Illinois State Legislature, **1931:** 232
Inaugural address, **1929:** 1
Incandescent electric lamp, 50th anniversary, **1929:** 245, 246
Indiana Republican Editorial Association, **1931:** 226
International Association of Chiefs of Police, **1931:** 355
International Chamber of Commerce, **1931:** 168
International Christian Endeavor Societies, **1931:** 262
Interstate Conference of Legislators, **1932–33:** 461
John Fritz medal, presentation ceremony, **1929:** 52
Joint National Planning Committee to Get Out the Negro Vote, **1932–33:** 318
Liberal Arts Colleges Association, **1931:** 409
Lincoln's Birthday, **1931:** 58; **1932–33:** 46, 465
Lincoln's Tomb, Springfield, Ill., **1931:** 233
London Naval Treaty, remarks on deposit of articles of ratification, **1930:** 341
Medal of Honor, presentation ceremony, **1930:** 354; **1932–33:** 270
Memorial Day
Arlington National Cemetery, **1929:** 94
Gettysburg Battlefield, **1930:** 170
Valley Forge, Pa., **1931:** 205
Methodist Ecumenical Congress, **1931:** 372
National Advisory Council on Radio in Education, **1931:** 198
National Association of Broadcasters, **1931:** 376

Addresses and remarks — *continued*
National Automobile Chamber of Commerce, **1931:** 8
National Commission on Law Observance and Enforcement, first meeting, **1929:** 92
National Education Association, **1932–33:** 57
National Geographic Society gold medal, presentation ceremony, **1930:** 196
National Recreation Association, **1931:** 134
New Mexico and Kansas, rear platform remarks, **1932–33:** 397
Ohio River improvement project, completion, **1929:** 250, 253
Pan American Commercial Conference, **1931:** 347
Pan American Union, **1931:** 135
Pennsylvania's unemployed, representatives, **1932–33:** 7
Pioneer Woman, statue unveiling, **1930:** 129
Porto Rico, visit, **1931:** 108, 109
Radiotelephonic service
Argentina, exchange of remarks with President Irigoyen, **1930:** 111
Chile, exchange of remarks with President Ibáñez, **1930:** 100
Uruguay, exchange of remarks with President Campisteguy, **1930:** 101
Renunciation of War, General Pact for the, **1929:** 161
Special Congressional Medal, presentation ceremony, **1930:** 267
Third National Conference on Street and Highway Safety, **1930:** 166
Tuskegee Institute, **1931:** 136
Unemployment relief, **1931:** 360
Union League, Philadelphia, Pa., **1931:** 204
Waldorf-Astoria Hotel, **1931:** 328
WCAU Radio building, dedication, **1932–33:** 463
Welch, Dr. William Henry, ceremonies honoring, **1930:** 107
Welfare and Relief Mobilization of 1932, address, **1932–33:** 338
Welfare and Relief Mobilization Conference, remarks, **1932–33:** 294
White House Child Health Conference Planning Committee, **1929:** 164
White House Conference on Child Health and Protection, **1930:** 376
White House Conference on Home Building and Home Ownership, **1930:** 302; **1931:** 425
Women's Conference on Current Problems, **1932–33:** 311
Women's International League for Peace and Freedom, **1931:** 351
World Alliance for Friendship Through the Churches, **1930:** 365
Yorktown, Va., **1931:** 364

[References are to items except as otherwise indicated]

Addresses and remarks — *continued*
  Yorktown Sesquicentennial Commission, **1931:** 365
  Young Men's Christian Association, **1931:** 286
Advertisers, Association of National, **1930:** 363
Advertising Association, International, **1929:** 103
Advertising Federation of America, **1931:** 227; **1932–33:** 41n.
Advisory Commission on Unemployment Statistics, **1932–33:** 135
Advisory Committee for Aeronautics, National, **1932–33:** 422
Advisory Committee on Education, **1932–33:** 135
Advisory Committee on Illiteracy, **1932–33:** 135
Advisory Committee on Shipping Board Sales, **1930:** 176, 177, 190, 231
Advisory Committee on Unemployment Statistics, **1930:** 244, 247
Advisory Committee on Veteran Preference, **1932–33:** 135
Advisory Council of the National Arboretum, **1932–33:** 423
Advisory Shipping Committee, **1932–33:** 135
Aerial Carnival, Gordon Bennett International Balloon Races and, **1930:** 280
Aeronautic Association, National, **1930:** 275; **1931:** 142; **1932–33:** 105
Aeronautical Chamber of Commerce, **1931:** 131
Aeronautics.
  See Aviation.
Aeronautics, National Advisory Committee for, **1929:** 298; **1930:** 391, 394; **1931:** 397; **1932–33:** 422, 423
Affiliated Better Business Bureaus, **1932–33:** 281
Afghanistan, **1929:** 161
Agricultural Association, Illinois, **1930:** 272
Agricultural Commodities Act, 1930, Perishable, **1930:** 182
Agricultural credit corporations, **1931:** 43, 44, 45, 50, 121, 181; **1932–33:** 347, 377, 380, 419
Agricultural Economics, Bureau of, **1929:** 221
Agricultural Marketing Act of 1926, **1929:** 221
Agricultural Marketing Act of 1929.
  See Farm relief.
Agriculture.
  See also Farm relief.
  State of the Union message, **1929:** 295
  Statement by agricultural representatives, **1929:** 285n.
  White House conferences, **1929:** 280, 281
Agriculture, Department of
  Appropriations, **1930:** 72, 390, 391, 395n.; **1931:** 6, 432
  Bureau of Biological Survey, **1932–33:** 423
  Bureau of Chemistry and Soils, **1932–33:** 423
  Bureau of Public Roads, **1931:** 453; **1932–33:** 423
  Committee to study the disposition of U.S. Army posts, **1931:** 181

Agriculture, Department of — *continued*
  Cooperative Marketing Division, **1929:** 219, 221
  Crop production loans, **1932–33:** 187, 251, 309
  Drought relief.
    See main heading, Drought relief.
  Economy conference, **1931:** 211, 213
  Executive branch reorganization, **1932–33:** 423
  Export debenture plan, **1929:** 46n.
  Farm land use, study, **1932–33:** 322
  Farm products, prices, **1932–33:** 322
  Forest Service, **1931:** 189, 190
  Muscle Shoals development, **1931:** 88
  Secretary of (Arthur M. Hyde), **1929:** 46n., 61, 128, 136, 155, 241, 281; **1930:** 253, 255, 258, 259, 259n., 265, 265n., 266, 271, 272, 276, 331, 332, 390, 395, 417; **1931:** 15, 45, 50, 120, 121, 181, 189, 190, 211, 213, 275, 324; **1932–33:** 76, 77, 78, 92, 186, 251, 264, 309, 313, 380, 449n., 470
  Unemployment statistics, development, **1930:** 244, 247
  Weather Bureau, **1930:** 391
Agriculture and agricultural programs
  American Farm Bureau Federation, **1932–33:** 194
  Commodities and commodity markets, **1931:** 122, 210n., 256, 257, 303, 318, 350, 358, 387, 389, 412, 426, 430; **1932–33:** 186, 187, 208, 209, 221, 251, 259, 264, 267, 295, 347, 377, 380, 449
  Conference on hoarding of currency, **1932–33:** 36
  Credit, **1931:** 43, 44, 45, 50, 121, 147, 181, 334, 343, 350, 407, 408, 425, 430, 432, 436, 437, 446, 447; **1932–33:** 1, 36, 38, 175, 234, 259, 264, 267, 272, 322, 347, 380, 419
  Crop production loans, **1932–33:** 187, 251, 309, 322, 377
  Des Moines, Iowa, campaign address, **1932–33:** 322
  Drought relief.
    See main heading, Drought relief.
  Export debenture plan, **1930:** 147
  Farm cooperatives, loans, **1932–33:** 259, 371, 377
  Farms
    Mortgages, **1932–33:** 1, 272, 313, 322, 328, 358, 371, 377, 380
    Taxation, **1932–33:** 137, 259, 292, 322, 377
  Federal expenditures, **1930:** 65, 238, 422; **1931:** 147, 148, 214
  Federal land and intermediate credit banks, **1932–33:** 1, 28, 29, 66, 226, 234, 251, 259, 272, 313, 322, 334, 343, 347, 366, 377, 380, 407, 408, 419, 430, 436, 437
  Federal Reserve District Banking and Industrial Committees, **1932–33:** 264, 267, 272, 295
4-H Clubs, **1930:** 389
Grasshopper infestations, **1931:** 275

Agricultural programs — *continued*
  Indiana Republican Editorial Association, address, **1931:** 226
  Land use, **1932–33:** 322, 370, 377, 420, 470
  Legislation, **1930:** 182, 390
  Loans, **1930:** 72, 76, 77, 144, 265, 311, 357, 390, 418
  Muscle Shoals, **1931:** 79, 82, 88, 260, 416, 430, 440
  Reconstruction Finance Corporation loans, **1932–33:** 76, 78, 92, 94, 175, 186, 187, 208, 209, 221, 233, 238, 239, 251, 295, 313, 322, 347, 377, 378, 380, 419
  State of the Union message, **1930:** 390
  Tariff protection, **1930:** 188
  Tariffs, **1931:** 122, 412; **1932–33:** 155, 322, 344, 346, 358, 371, 377, 380, 384, 385, 386, 387, 388, 457
Air Express, Western, **1930:** 273n.
Air Races, National, **1930:** 275; **1931:** 306
Air rights, construction, **1929:** 146
Air Show, National, **1931:** 131n.
Air Transport, Transcontinental, **1930:** 273n.
Aircraft.
  See also Aviation.
  Antarctic flights, **1929:** 244, 292, 293
  Budget message, **1929:** 296
  Round-the-world flights, **1929:** 174, 188, 189
  State of the Union message, **1929:** 295
  Transatlantic flights, **1929:** 110, 119, 137, 148
Airmail service
  Argentina, **1929:** 234
  Rates and routes, **1929:** 237
  South American service, **1929:** 8, 295
Aishton, Richard H., **1929:** 281n., 285n.; **1930:** 130n., 271, 272
Aitken, James, **1931:** 323
Akerson, George E., **1929:** 6, 41, 67, 218, 282, 307; **1930:** 64n., 157; **1931:** 1, 2, 24
Akron, Ohio, **1932–33:** 336
Alabama, **1929:** 8
  Education, **1931:** 136
  Muscle Shoals Commission, **1931:** 88, 260, 416, 430, 440
Alaska Highway Commission, **1932–33:** 135
Albania, **1929:** 161
Albert, King of the Belgians, **1929:** 30, 100, 329; **1930:** 171; **1931:** 125, 209; **1932–33:** 115, 185
Alderman, Edwin Anderson, **1931:** 164
Aldrich, Chester, **1931:** 105
Alexander, Archibald S., **1932–33:** 416
Alexander, Magnus W., **1932–33:** 41n.
Alexander, Vance J., **1931:** 260, 440
Alexander I, King of Yugoslavia, **1930:** 415; **1931:** 441; **1932–33:** 430
Alfaro, Ricardo J., **1931:** 393
Alfonso XIII, King (Spain), **1929:** 247
Alien enemy property, **1929:** 295

Alien Property Custodian, **1932–33:** 423
Aliens, **1930:** 135, 390
Allen, Cleveland G., **1930:** 186n.
Allied Forces for Prohibition, **1932–33:** 268n.
Allied Jewish Relief Campaign, **1930:** 80, 151n.
Almazán, Gen. Jésus M., **1929:** 10
Almon bill, **1932–33:** 146ftn.
Alpine, John R., **1931:** 101, 277n.
Ambassadors.
  See under Appointments and nominations; Resignations and retirements; *country to which assigned.*
Ambassadors and Ministers, U.S., Canada, **1932–33:** 273
  Czechoslovakia, **1932–33:** 210
  Mexico, **1932–33:** 477
  United Kingdom, **1932–33:** 3n., 37, 38, 39, 44
American Academy of Arts and Letters, **1930:** 375n.
American Arbitration Association, **1929:** 76
American Artists Professional League, **1932–33:** 369
American Automobile Association, **1930:** 130n.
American Bankers Association, **1930:** 250, 311; **1931:** 66, 314; **1932–33:** 41n.
American Bar Association, **1929:** 25, 203; **1930:** 276, 277, 292; **1932–33:** 335
American Battle Monuments Commission, **1930:** 89n.
American Bible Society, **1931:** 427; **1932–33:** 362
American Braille Press, **1932–33:** 478
American Brown Boveri Electric Corporation, **1929:** 193n.
American Chemical Society, **1929:** 200
American Child Health Association, **1929:** 14n.; **1930:** 204, 361
American Civic Association, **1930:** 250; **1931:** 314
American Civic Association's Committee of One Hundred on the Federal City, **1929:** 52n.
American Classical League, **1930:** 375
American Conference of Institutions for the Establishment of International Justice, **1932–33:** 141
American Electric Railway Association, **1929:** 285n.; **1930:** 130n.
American Engineering Co., **1932–33:** 41n.
American Engineering Council, **1932–33:** 41n.
American Farm Bureau Federation, **1930:** 250, 259n.; **1931:** 260, 314, 440; **1932–33:** 194
American Federation of Labor, **1930:** 29, 30n., 244, 247, 250, 315, 383, 384; **1931:** 101, 314; **1932–33:** 41n., 389, 390
American Game Protective and Propagation Association, **1930:** 388
American Gas Association, **1929:** 285n.
American Hebrew, The, **1929:** 249
American Hebrew Medal, **1931:** 417; **1932–33:** 406
American Home Economics Association, **1930:** 250; **1931:** 314

American Indians, **1931:** 65, 75; **1932–33:** 136, 458
American Institute, **1931:** 127
American Institute of Architects, **1929:** 51; **1930:** 250; **1931:** 314
American Institute of Electrical Engineers, **1929:** 52n.
American Institute of Mining and Metallurgical Engineers, **1929:** 52n.; **1930:** 57
American Institute of Steel Construction, **1929:** 278; **1930:** 344, 345; **1932–33:** 180n.
American Iron and Steel Institute, **1932–33:** 257n.
American Jewish Congress, **1931:** 167; **1932–33:** 72
American Jewish Joint Distribution Committee, **1931:** 107, 157; **1932–33:** 98
American Legion, **1929:** 166, 275n.; **1930:** 200, 202, 203, 222, 314; **1931:** 64, 171, 225n., 318, 324, 325
  Bonus loans for veterans, **1932–33:** 101, 102, 293
  Crosscup Pishon Post, Boston, Mass., **1932–33:** 256
  Employment drive, **1932–33:** 38, 40
  Grand Street Boys' Post No. 1025, **1932–33:** 51
American Medical Association, **1930:** 206
American Museum of Safety, **1932–33:** 179
American Mutual Alliance, **1930:** 130n.
American National Red Cross, **1932–33:** 121, 249, 294, 398
  Addresses, **1931:** 29, 133, 195, 310
  Annual convention, **1930:** 149
  Central Committee, **1930:** 406
  Chairman, **1930:** 33n., 265n., 271, 272; **1931:** 15, 26, 29, 44n.
  Chapter House, dedication, **1930:** 89; **1931:** 396
  Christmas seals program, **1930:** 392
  Drought relief.
    See main heading, Drought relief.
  Membership drive, **1930:** 362
  Mission to Russia, 1917, **1930:** 214n.
  New Jersey chapters, regional conference, **1931:** 326
  Nicaragua, disaster assistance, **1931:** 116
American Newspaper Publishers, **1929:** 43
American Newspaper Publishers Association, **1930:** 118; **1931:** 139, 405
American Olympic Committee, **1931:** 241
American Opera Company, **1930:** 69
American Palestine Campaign, **1931:** 90n.
American Palestine Committee, **1932–33:** 19
American Peace Society, **1932–33:** 141
American Petroleum Institute, **1929:** 25
American Printing House for the Blind, **1932–33:** 423
American Public Health Association, **1932–33:** 348, 358
American Railway Association, **1929:** 285n.; **1930:** 130n., 265, 271, 272
American Red Cross, **1929:** 108, 279
American Relief Administration, **1930:** 204n.

American Revolution, Daughters of the, **1932–33:** 301
American Revolution, National Society of the Sons of the, **1932–33:** 164
American Road Builders Association, **1932–33:** 14
American Samoan Commission, **1931:** 10
American Society of Civil Engineers, **1932–33:** 175
American Society of Engineers, **1929:** 52n.
American Society of Mechanical Engineers, **1929:** 52n.; **1930:** 108
American Society of Newspaper Editors, **1931:** 139
American Society for the Promotion of Aviation, **1929:** 187
American Trade Association Executives, **1931:** 160; **1932–33:** 41n., 296
American War Mother magazine, **1932–33:** 479
Americanization Committee of the Newspaper Post, No. 1955, of the Veterans of Foreign Wars, **1931:** 419
Ames, Joseph S., **1930:** 394
Amundsen, Roald, **1931:** 23n.
Anderson, Harry G., **1931:** 83
Anderson, Henry W., **1931:** 27
Angell, R. H., **1929:** 135; **1930:** 272
Anslinger, Harry J., **1930:** 299; **1931:** 103
Antarctic, **1929:** 137, 244, 292, 293
Antarctic expeditions, **1930:** 196, 208, 211, 220
Anthracite coal industry, **1930:** 133, 260
Anti-Hoarding Committee.
  See Citizens Reconstruction Organization.
Antitrust laws, **1931:** 430
Appeals, Court of, **1932–33:** 15, 418
Appendix A—Additional White House Releases, **1929:** p. 663; **1930:** p. 591; **1931:** p. 685; **1932–33:** p. 1093
Appendix B—Messages to the Congress, **1930:** p. 596; **1931:** p. 693; **1932–33:** p. 1101
Appendix B—Presidential Proclamations and Executive Orders, **1929:** p. 666
Appendix C—Presidential Proclamations and Executive Orders, **1930:** p. 614; **1931:** p. 701; **1932–33:** p. 1117
Appendix C—Presidential Reports to the 71st Congress, 1929, **1929:** p. 680
Appendix D—Presidential Reports to the 71st Congress, 1930, **1930:** p. 635
Appendix D—Presidential Reports to the 71st and 72nd Congresses, 1931, **1931:** p. 723
Appendix D—Presidential Reports to the 72nd Congress, During 1932–33, **1932–33:** p. 1141
Appendix D—Reading Copies of Selected Addresses, With Holograph Changes, **1929:** p. 681
Appendix E—The President's Calendar, **1930:** p. 637; **1931:** p. 725; **1932–33:** p.1143
Appendix E—Rules Governing This Publication, **1929:** p. 783

[References are to items except as otherwise indicated]

Appendix F—Radio Addresses by the President, **1932–33:** p. 1275
Appendix G—Rules Governing This Publication, **1930:** p. 790; **1931:** p. 827
Appendix G—Rules Governing This Publication, **1932–33:** p. 1281
Appleton, Robert, **1929:** 87
Appointments and nominations
  Advisory Committee on Shipping Board Sales, **1930:** 190
  Advisory Committee on Unemployment Statistics, **1930:** 244, 247
  Ambassadors and Ministers, United States
    Canada, **1930:** 158
    Ecuador, **1930:** 25
    Hungary, **1930:** 303
    Peru, **1930:** 34
    Uruguay, **1930:** 303n.
  Budget, Bureau of the, Director, **1929:** 128
  Cabinet Committee on Unemployment Relief, **1930:** 331, 332
  Commerce Department, Assistant Secretary, **1929:** 41
  Commerce Department, Secretary, **1932–33:** 257
  Commission for the Celebration of the Tercentenary of the Founding of the Colony of Massachusetts, **1930:** 233
  Commission on Conservation and Administration of the Public Domain, **1929:** 241, 242
  Commission to attend the ceremonies in Iceland, **1929:** 270
  Committee to examine statements of President of Navy League, **1931:** 392
  Committee to study the disposition of U.S. Army posts, **1931:** 181
  Conference on the Limitation of the Manufacture of Narcotic Drugs, U.S. delegation, **1931:** 103
  Corps of Engineers, Chief, **1929:** 204
  Court of Appeals, 7th Circuit, judge, **1932–33:** 15, 418
  Court of Claims, **1929:** 237
  District of Columbia, Commissioners, **1930:** 45, 45n.
  District of Columbia Public Utilities Commission, **1929:** 75
  European Broadcasting Conference, Chief of American delegation, **1929:** 8
  Federal Farm Board, **1929:** 136, 140; **1931:** 92, 106, 283
  Federal Farm Loan Board, **1929:** 177; **1931:** 303
  Federal Farm Loan Bureau, **1930:** 258
  Federal Power Commission, **1930:** 195, 218
  Federal Radio Commission, **1929:** 12
  Federal Reserve Board, **1930:** 284, 285; **1931:** 173
  General Accounting Office, **1931:** 92
  General Disarmament Conference
    Chairman, **1932–33:** 23, 25

Appointments and nominations — *continued*
  General Disarmament Conference — *continued*
    U.S. delegation, **1931:** 446, 449, 453
  Hawaii, Governor, **1929:** 48
  Indian Affairs, Bureau of, Commissioner, **1929:** 37
  Interdepartmental Committee on Marine Mail Contracts, **1929:** 104
  Interior Department, Bureau of Indian Affairs, **1930:** 3, 5
  Internal Revenue Collector, 1st district of New York, **1929:** 304
  International Joint Commission, United States and Canada, **1929:** 84
  Interoceanic Canal Board, **1929:** 125n.
  Interstate Commerce Commission, **1929:** 315; **1930:** 6n., 249
    Withdrawal of prior nomination, **1930:** 3, 6
  Justice Department, **1930:** 36
    Assistant Attorney General, **1929:** 270; **1931:** 211
    U.S. Attorney, Southern District of Florida, **1929:** 248
    U.S. District and Circuit judges, **1929:** 37n.
  Labor Department, **1930:** 383, 384
    Bureau of Immigration, **1931:** 348n.
  London Conference of Ministers, U.S. delegation, **1931:** 263
  Muscle Shoals Commission, **1931:** 260
  National Advisory Committee for Aeronautics, **1931:** 397
  National Drought Relief Committee, **1930:** 265, 271, 272
  National Guard Bureau, Chief, **1929:** 209
  Naval Advisory Committee, **1929:** 241
  Naval Aeronautics, Bureau of, Chief, **1929:** 6
  Navy Department, **1930:** 145, 146, 253
    Assistant Secretary, **1929:** 6
  Pensions Bureau, Commissioner, **1929:** 41
  Philippine Islands, Governor-General, **1929:** 77
  Philippines, Governor-General, **1932–33:** 11
  Post Office Department, Third Assistant Postmaster General, **1929:** 108
  Porto Rico, Governor, **1929:** 84
  President's Commission for the Study and Review of Conditions in the Republic of Haiti, **1930:** 50, 51
  President's Emergency Committee for Employment, **1930:** 347
  President's Organization on Unemployment Relief, **1931:** 295, 299
  Reconstruction Finance Corporation, Board of Directors
    Chairman, **1932–33:** 23, 24, 243
    Directors, **1932–33:** 31n.
    President, **1932–33:** 23, 24, 31n., 243n.
  Special Ambassador to Japan, **1929:** 308
  State Department
    Assistant Secretary, **1931:** 189

Appointments and nominations — *continued*
  State Department — *continued*
    Under Secretary, **1929:** 84; **1931:** 116
  Supreme Court of the District of Columbia,
    1931: 173
  Supreme Court of the United States, **1930:** 92
    Associate Justice, **1932–33:** 16n.
  Treasury Department
    Assistant Secretary, **1929:** 256
    Bureau of Narcotics, **1930:** 299
    Collector of Customs, Los Angeles, **1931:** 218
    Collector of Internal Revenue, **1930:** 266
    Secretary, **1932–33:** 38, 39
    Under Secretary, **1932–33:** 38, 39
  United Kingdom, U.S. Ambassador to, **1932–33:**
    37
  United States Commission on Education in
    Haiti, **1930:** 51n.
  United States Customs Court, **1930:** 299
  United States Employment Service, **1931:** 101
  United States Shipping Board, **1930:** 176
  United States Tariff Commission, **1930:** 195, 273,
    276, 293; **1931:** 420
  U.S. attorneys, Oklahoma, **1931:** 211, 277
  U.S. circuit judge, 4th circuit, **1931:** 173
  U.S. district judges
    Maryland, **1931:** 177
    Minnesota, **1931:** 46, 70
  Veterans' Administration, **1930:** 226, 227
  Vice Governor of the Philippines, **1930:** 244, 245
  Virgin Islands, Governor, **1931:** 39, 41
  War Department
    Army Reserve Corps, **1931:** 31, 32
    Assistant Secretary, **1929:** 6; **1930:** 126
    Chief of Staff, U.S. Army, **1930:** 253, 254
    Secretary, **1929:** 304
    Surgeon General, **1931:** 181
  White House Conference on Child Health, Ex-
    ecutive Secretary, **1929:** 140, 142
  White House Conference on Home Building and
    Home Ownership, **1930:** 249, 250
  Yellowstone National Park Boundary Commis-
    sion, **1929:** 31
Apportionment, **1930:** 373, 374, 390, 396
Appropriations.
  See also Appendix B—Messages to the Congress;
    Budget.
  Agriculture Department, **1930:** 72, 390, 391,
    395n.; **1931:** 6
  Budget message, **1930:** 391; **1931:** 432; **1932–33:**
    421
  Chicago World's Fair Centennial Celebration,
    Federal participation, **1930:** 417
  Children's Bureau, **1932–33:** 358
  Claims by and against the United States, **1931:**
    35, 36
  Conference on the Limitation of the Manufac-
    ture of Narcotic Drugs, **1931:** 28, 87

Appropriations — *continued*
  Congressional leadership, meetings with the
    President, **1930:** 55, 65n., 368
  Deficiency and supplemental appropriations,
    veto of bill, **1932–33:** 456
  District of Columbia, **1930:** 183, 218, 391; **1931:**
    21
  Executive branch, **1932–33:** 459, 482
  Executive Office, **1930:** 410
  Federal Farm Board, **1930:** 78, 391, 401, 423
  Federal land banks, **1932–33:** 29
  Fiscal year 1933, reductions, **1931:** 397, 398
  Fiscal year 1934, reductions, **1932–33:** 287, 402,
    450, 451, 452, 453
  Foreign claims, **1930:** 22, 28, 31, 37, 83, 90, 136,
    138, 139, 152
  General Disarmament Conference, **1932–33:** 441
  Haitian Commission, **1930:** 38, 39
  Interior Department, **1930:** 3, 391; **1932–33:** 133
  International Conference for the Codification of
    International Law, **1930:** 86
  International Fur Trade Exhibition and
    Congress, **1930:** 18
  International Geological Congress, **1931:** 25
  International Monetary and Economic Confer-
    ence, **1932–33:** 207, 441
  International Water Commission, United States
    and Mexico, **1931:** 11
  Joint United States-Canada dam investigation,
    1930: 42
  Justice Department, **1930:** 395n.
  Labor Department
    Bureau of Immigration, **1931:** 9, 53
    Bureau of Labor Statistics, **1931:** 60
    United States Employment Service, **1931:** 61
  Law enforcement, **1930:** 142, 193, 209, 210
  National Council of Intellectual Cooperation,
    1931: 52
  Navy Department, **1930:** 65, 66, 67, 238, 395n.
  Navy Department, controversy, **1931:** 327, 358,
    359, 385, 387, 390, 392, 406
  Permanent International Association of Road
    Congresses, **1930:** 49
  Porto Rican Hurricane Relief Commission,
    1930: 20
  President's Organization on Unemployment Re-
    lief, **1932–33:** 215
  Public vs. private financing of relief efforts,
    1931: 43, 44
  Public works, **1930:** 55, 58, 127, 128, 132, 158n.,
    357, 391, 395, 397, 406; **1931:** 45, 67, 101;
    1932–33: 282, 283
  Reconstruction Finance Corporation, **1932–33:**
    26
  River and harbor works, **1932–33:** 83
  Second Polar Year program, **1931:** 56
  State Department, **1930:** 86, 181, 391
  Treasury Department, **1930:** 128, 193, 391, 395n.

Appropriations — *continued*
  Veterans' Administration, **1932–33:** 225
  Veterans' Bureau, **1930:** 140, 391
  War Department, **1930:** 58, 65, 66, 67, 238, 391,
    395n.
Arapahoe Indians, **1931:** 65
Arbitration treaties, **1930:** 365, 390; **1931:** 433
Arboretum, Advisory Council of the National,
    1932–33: 423
Architect, Office of Supervising, **1931:** 453; **1932–
    33:** 423
Architects, American Institute of, **1929:** 51; **1930:**
    250; **1931:** 314
Archives, National, **1932–33:** 471
Ardmore, Okla., **1931:** 221
Argentina, **1929:** 3, 86, 234, 322
  Agricultural exports, **1932–33:** 385
  Communications development, **1930:** 111, 312
  Natural resources, **1930:** 311, 390
  President Augustin P. Justo, **1932–33:** 177
  President José Francisco Uriburu, **1931:** 201
  Revolution, **1930:** 390
  Wheat production, **1931:** 303
Arias, Harmodio, **1932–33:** 373
Arizona, **1929:** 132, 133, 134, 185n., 286n.
  Boulder Dam, **1930:** 326, 328
  Lincoln's Birthday, message, **1932–33:** 45n.
Arizona, U.S.S., **1931:** 102
Arkansas
  Child health and protection conference, **1932–
    33:** 5n.
  Drought relief, **1930:** 258, 259, 265n.; **1931:** 121
  Thanksgiving Day celebration, **1931:** 422
Arkansas Railway Co., Louisiana and, labor dis-
    pute, **1931:** 196
Arkansas Traveler, **1930:** 372n.
Arlington Memorial Bridge Commission, **1932–33:**
    423
Arlington National Cemetery, **1932–33:** 393
Armed Forces, United States
  Army, troop ratios, **1932–33:** 3
  Army·Air Corps, maneuvers, **1931:** 211, 212
  Army Day, **1932–33:** 67
  Contract public works, **1930:** 347
  Disarmament, **1932–33:** 111, 112, 206
  Haiti, U.S. withdrawal, **1930:** 38, 39, 85, 92, 97,
    390; **1931:** 433
  Herbert Schiff Memorial Trophy, **1931:** 415
  Memorial Day, **1932–33:** 185
  Military force, use of, **1931:** 138, 140, 141, 433
  Navy Day, **1931:** 380
  Nicaragua, U.S. withdrawal, **1930:** 92
  Pay, **1932–33:** 119
  Pay increase, **1930:** 55, 65, 66, 67
  Shanghai, China, International Settlement, de-
    ployment of troops, **1932–33:** 34
  Tomb of the Unknown Soldier, dedication cer-
    emonies, **1932–33:** 393

Armed Forces, United States — *continued*
  U.S. Army of Occupation, Germany, **1930:** 74
  U.S. Navy, reduction in force, **1930:** 112, 113,
    117, 321, 322, 390, 391
  Use of military force, **1930:** 38, 39, 94, 115, 119,
    133, 225, 240, 241, 341
  Veterans.
    See main heading, Veterans.
Armistice Day, **1929:** 275; **1930:** 356; **1931:** 404;
    1932–33: 393
Armour, Norman, **1929:** 81n.
Arms and Ammunition and Implements of War,
    Convention for the Supervision of the
    International Trade in, **1931:** 433; **1932–
    33:** 446
Arms and weapons.
  See also Disarmament.
  Embargo, **1929:** 2, 154, 295
  Exports, **1930:** 337; **1931:** 86
Armstrong, Frank C., **1931:** 202
Army, United States
  Bonus marchers, **1932–33:** 246, 248, 249, 250
  Chief of Staff, **1932–33:** 206, 246n.
  Office of the Chief of Engineers, **1932–33:** 251,
    353n., 423
Army Corps of Engineers, **1930:** 281n., 223, 261,
    262; **1931:** 88, 185, 260, 319, 416, 430, 440,
    453
Army Day, **1930:** 105; **1932–33:** 67
Army-Navy football game, **1929:** 231; **1932–33:**
    415
Army and Navy Legion of Valor, **1931:** 288
Army posts
  Committee to study the disposition of, **1931:** 181
  Committee on Abandoned, **1932–33:** 135
Army of the Republic, Grand, **1931:** 229n.
Army Reserve Corps, **1931:** 31, 32
Arnold, Wallace Greene, **1932–33:** 414.
Arosemena, Florencio H. (President of Panama),
    1929: 271; **1930:** 141, 353
Art, Metropolitan Museum of, **1932–33:** 153n.
Art, Museum of Modern, **1932–33:** 153
Art, Whitney Museum of American, **1931:** 415
Art Digest magazine, **1932–33:** 369n.
Artists Professional League, American, **1932–33:**
    369
Arts, Commission of Fine, **1932–33:** 423
Arts and Letters, American Academy of, **1930:**
    375n.
Ashurst, Sen. Henry F., **1931:** 238, 239
Associated Business Papers, Inc., **1932–33:** 41n.
Associated General Contractors, **1930:** 250; **1931:**
    314
Associated Press, **1929:** 43, 47; **1930:** 118, 123, 421;
    1931: 139
Association for Childhood Education, **1932–33:**
    145

Association of Community Chests and Councils, **1931:** 20, 290
Association of Grand Jurors, **1929:** 87
Association of Life Insurance Presidents, **1930:** 250; **1931:** 314; **1932–33:** 41n.
Association of Railway Executives, **1929:** 285n.
Athens, Ohio, **1932–33:** 357
Athletics.
  See Sports.
Atlanta Federal Prison, **1929:** 169, 170
Atlantic Deeper Waterways Association, **1929:** 211; **1931:** 346; **1932–33:** 352
Atterbury, William H., **1929:** 281n.
Atterbury, William W., **1930:** 428, 429
Attorney General (William D. Mitchell), **1929:** 60n., 92n., 169, 170
Attorneys, U.S.
  See U.S. Attorneys *under* Courts, United States.
Aurora, Ill., **1929:** 28
Australia, **1929:** 161, 317
  Wheat production, **1931:** 303
Austria, **1929:** 161
  Creditanstalt, collapse, **1931:** Supp. I
  Intergovernmental debts, **1932–33:** 431
  President Wilhelm Miklas, **1930:** 102, 366
  Radiotelegraphic service, **1931:** 143
  U.S. Ambassador to, **1930:** 102
  World War veterans, **1931:** 171
Autogiro, **1931:** 142, 218
Automobile Association, American, **1930:** 130
Automobile Chamber of Commerce, National, **1931:** 8
Automobiles
  Federal departments and agencies, appropriations, **1932–33:** 421
  New car sales, **1932–33:** 106, 107
Avery, Sewell L., **1932–33:** 264
Aviation.
  See also Aircraft; Airmail service.
  Aircraft carriers, **1930:** 112, 113, 117, 391
  Airmail, **1930:** 145, 273, 312, 407
  Armaments, **1931:** 37
  Army Air Corps, maneuvers, **1931:** 211, 212
  Autogiro, **1931:** 142, 218
  Budget message, **1930:** 391
  Budgetary impact, **1931:** 147, 148
  Collier Trophy
    Presented to Harold F. Pitcairn, **1931:** 142
    Presented to Packard Motor Car Co., **1932–33:** 105
  Construction, **1930:** 65, 347, 418, 423
  Distinguished Flying Cross, presentations, **1932–33:** 247, 252, 266
  Gordon Bennett International Balloon Races and Aerial Carnival, **1930:** 280
  Herbert Schiff Memorial Trophy
    Presented to Lt. Comdr. Richard P. White-head, **1931:** 435

Aviation — *continued*
  Herbert Shiff Memorial Trophy — *continued*
    Presented to Lt. Comdr. Samuel P. Ginder, **1930:** 398
  International air transport, **1931:** 162
  Lighter-than-air flight, **1930:** 317, 321, 323
  Medal of Honor, presented to Edward V. Rickenbacker, **1930:** 354
  National Advisory Committee for Aeronautics, 18th annual report, **1932–33:** 422
  National Air Races, **1930:** 275; **1931:** 306
  National Air Show, **1931:** 131
  National Geographic Society gold medal, presented to Amelia Earhart, **1932–33:** 203
  Rapidan conference, **1930:** 267n.
  Round-the-world-flight, **1931:** 247, 253
  Special Congressional Medal
    Presented to Charles A. Lindbergh, **1930:** 267
    Presented to Lincoln Ellsworth, **1931:** 23
  State of the Union message, **1930:** 390
  Stations, **1930:** 261
  Transatlantic flights, **1930:** 282, 283, 287; **1931:** 126, 279; **1932–33:** 173, 252, 266
  Wright Brothers National Memorial, **1932–33:** 403
Aviation, American Society for the Promotion of, **1929:** 187
Avigation Corporation, United, **1930:** 273n.
Awards and citations
  American Chemical Society's Priestley Medal to Francis P. Garvan, **1929:** 200
  American Hebrew Medal
    Presented to Archbishop Edward J. Hanna, **1931:** 417
    Presented to Dr. John H. Finley, **1932–33:** 406
  Baba, Eiichiro, **1932–33:** 327
  Collier Trophy
    Presented to Harold F. Pitcairn, **1931:** 142
    Presented to Packard Motor Car Co., **1932–33:** 105
  Congressional Medal of Honor
    Capt. Edward V. Rickenbacker, **1930:** 354
    Comdr. Claude A. Jones, **1932–33:** 270
  Distinguished Flying Cross, presentations
    Amelia Earhart, **1932–33:** 252
    John Polando and Russell Boardman, **1932–33:** 247
    Wiley Post and Harold Gatty, **1932–33:** 266
  Distinguished Service Cross, presented to Curtis Harrison, **1930:** 297
  Gottheil Medal, presented to Felix M. Warburg, **1930:** 155
  Herbert Schiff Memorial Trophy
    Lt. Comdr. Richard P. Whitehead, **1931:** 435
    Lt. Comdr. Samuel P. Ginder, **1930:** 398
  Hoover Gold Medal, presented to the President, **1930:** 108
  John Fritz Medal to the President, **1929:** 52

Awards and citations — *continued*
  Kane Gold Medal, presented to Rear Adm.
    Richard E. Byrd, **1930:** 220
  Kiwanis Club Medal for Distinguished Com-
    munity Service, presented to Emily P.
    Bissell, **1930:** 392
  Laetare Medal to Alfred E. Smith, **1929:** 65
  M. Carey Thomas Prize, presented to Jane
    Addams, **1931:** 165
  Medal of Honor, presented to Edward V.
    Rickenbacker, **1930:** 354
  Mining and Metallurgical Society of America,
    Gold Medal Award to Cornelius F.
    Kelley, **1929:** 252
  National Academy of Design Medal to Elihu
    Root, **1929:** 291
  National Geographic Society, Special Gold
    Medal
    Presented to Amelia Earhart, **1932–33:** 203
    Presented to Rear Adm. Richard E. Byrd,
      1930: 196
  Rotary Club Merit Award, presented to Julius
    Rosenwald, **1931:** 309
  Special Congressional Medal, presented to Lin-
    coln Ellsworth, **1931:** 23
  Star Pro Juventute, presented to the President by
    the Catholic Boys' Brigade of the United
    States, **1932–33:** 312
  Yale Bowl, presented to Eugene Meyer, **1931:**
    428
Ayora, Isidro (President of Ecuador), **1929:** 175

Bacharach, Repr. Isaac, **1931:** 238, 239
Bader, Jesse M., **1930:** 333n.
Baird, Sen. David, Jr., **1930:** 187
Baith Israel Anshei Emes Congregation, **1931:** 83
Baker, Bryant, **1930:** 129n.
Baker, George F., **1931:** 172
Baker, Joseph J., **1932–33:** 355n.
Baker, Newton D., **1931:** 27; **1932–33:** 294
Baldridge, Gov. H. Clarence, **1929:** 186
Baldwin, Stanley, **1929:** 116
Ball, J. Rodney, **1931:** 349
Ballantine, Arthur A., **1932–33:** 38, 39, 187
Baltimore, Md., **1932–33:** 363
Banham, W. J. L., **1930:** 110
Bank of Los Angeles, First National, **1930:** 271,
    272
Bankers Association, American, **1930:** 250, 311;
    1931: 66, 314; **1932–33:** 41n.
Bankers Association, Morris Plan, **1931:** 349
Bankers Association of America, Investment,
    1932–33: 41n.
Banking Co., Federal International, **1932–33:** 358
Banking and finance.
  See also Federal Reserve System; Moratorium
    on intergovernmental debts.

Banking and finance — *continued*
  American Bankers Association, address, **1930:**
    311
  Banking law, revision, **1931:** 436, 437
  Bankruptcy, investigation, **1930:** 244, 246
  British financial crisis.
    See United Kingdom.
  Capital, **1931:** 88, 226, 303, 320, 334, 347, 407,
    408, 430; **1932–33:** 1, 28, 76, 450
    Domestic, **1930:** 390, 402, 403
  Credit and interest, **1930:** 72, 76, 77, 144, 249,
    250, 265, 302, 311, 357, 390, 418; **1931:** 45,
    50, 121, 314, 333, 334, 343, 344, 350, 378,
    387, 389, 395, 407, 408, 425, 430, 436, 437,
    442, 446, 447; **1932–33:** 1, 27, 28, 36, 38,
    41, 48, 66, 73, 126, 157, 158, 159, 161, 169,
    170, 175, 187, 208, 209, 217, 221, 230, 233,
    251, 259, 264, 267, 272, 295, 322, 337, 347,
    371, 378, 380, 419, 470
  Currency.
    See main heading, Currency.
  Depositors, **1932–33:** 1, 346, 347, 358
  Farm mortgage relief conference, **1932–33:** 313
  Financial institutions, **1930:** 144, 249, 250, 311,
    390
    Agricultural credit corporations, **1931:** 43, 44,
      45, 50, 121, 181; **1932–33:** 347, 377, 380,
      419
    Clearinghouse associations, **1931:** 333, 334,
      343, 378
    Cotton credit pool, **1931:** 313, 358
    Federal farm loan bank system, **1931:** 226,
      334, 407, 408
    Federal Home Loan Bank Board.
      See main heading, Federal Home Loan Bank
        Board.
    Federal Reserve System.
      See main heading, Federal Reserve System.
    Home loan discount bank system, **1931:** 407,
      408, 411, 425, 430, 436, 437
    National credit association, **1931:** 333, 334,
      343, 350, 378, 395, 407, 408, 430, 436, 437;
      1932–33: 1, 259, 272, 347, 358, 371, 380
    Private institutions, **1931:** 66, 226, 293, 314,
      333, 334, 344, 349, 350, 387, 389, 395, 407,
      408, 430; **1932–33:** 76, 78, 82, 86, 92, 94,
      100, 126, 175, 187, 217, 221, 230, 238, 239,
      274, 313, 321, 322, 328, 337, 366
    Railway Credit Corporation, **1931:** 436, 442;
      1932–33: 76, 78, 87, 88
    Reconstruction Finance Corporation, **1931:**
      343, 430, 436, 437, 442, 446, 447
      See also main heading, Reconstruction
        Finance Corporation.
  Foreign loans, **1931:** 347; **1932–33:** 358
    Senate investigation, **1930:** 194
  German financial crisis.
    See Germany.

Banking and finance — *continued*
  Gold standard, **1931:** 320, 371, 387, 389, 420, 436; **1932–33:** 38, 41, 66, 322, 337, 347, 377, 378, 380, 387, 431, 457, 465
  Leaders, meeting with the President, **1932–33:** 36n.
  Life insurance, **1932–33:** 12, 358
  Recovery program, **1931:** 333, 334, 343, 350, 387, 389, 407, 436, 437, 442, 446, 447
  Reform, **1932–33:** 259, 347, 358, 419
  Silver interests, **1932–33:** 269, 343, 387, 388, 465
  State of the Union message, **1931:** 430; **1932–33:** 419
  Statement to bankers, **1931:** 333
  U.S. financial expansion abroad, **1930:** 119, 133, 314
Bankruptcy Act of 1898, amendments, **1932–33:** 63, 64, 69, 448, 451, 470
Bankruptcy law and practice, **1930:** 244, 246
Banks, Frank A., **1932–33:** 232
Banks, **1929:** 272, 280, 281, 295
Baptist Convention, Southern, **1931:** 191; **1932–33:** 162
Baptist Convention of America, National, **1930:** 290
Bar Association, American, **1929:** 25, 203; **1930:** 276, 277, 292; **1932–33:** 335
Bar Association, Federal, **1932–33:** 467
Baraboo, Wis., **1932–33:** 379
Barber, A. B., **1930:** 130n.
Barbour, Sen. W. Warren, **1932–33:** 221
Barnard, Dr. Harry E., **1929:** 140, 142; **1930:** 376
Barnes, James P., **1929:** 285n.; **1930:** 130n.
Barnes Julius, **1929:** 281n., 284n.; **1932–33:** 41n.
Barnum, Jerome D., **1929:** 208
Baron, Mrs. Richard F., **1930:** 212
Barstow, William S., **1929:** 57
Bartholomew, Harland, **1931:** 314
Bartlett, John H., **1929:** 84
Barton, Arthur James, **1932–33:** 162
Barton, Bruce, **1930:** 404
Barton, Clara, **1931:** 195, 310
Barton, William E., **1930:** 404
Baruch, Bernard, **1932–33:** 156n.
Baruch, Emanuel de Marnay, **1932–33:** 129
Baseball, **1931:** 327, 382
  Opening, **1932–33:** 111
Bassett, William H., **1930:** 57
Bastille Day, **1930:** 232; **1931:** 261; **1932–33:** 229
Batcheller, Arthur, **1929:** 12
Bates, Sanford, **1929:** 91, 169, 170; **1931:** 181ftn.
Battle of Manila Bay, anniversary, **1931:** 154
Battle of the Marne, **1932–33:** 280
Battle Monuments Commission, American, **1930:** 89n.
Battle y Ordóñez, José, **1929:** 251
Battle of Yorktown, **1932–33:** 301
  Address, **1931:** 364

Bausch, Edward, **1932–33:** 445
Baxter, William M., Jr., **1929:** 108
Belasco, David, **1931:** 188, 192
Belgium, **1929:** 161, 317
  Albert, King of the Belgians, **1930:** 171; **1931:** 125, 209; **1932–33:** 115, 185
  Intergovernmental debts, **1932–33:** 228n., 431
  U.S. Ambassador to, **1930:** 10n., 11n.; **1931:** 89; **1932–33:** 23, 25
  U.S. relations with, **1931:** 426
Bell, James F., **1931:** 299
Bellonte, Lt. Maurice, **1930:** 282, 283, 287
Beloit, Wis., **1932–33:** 379
Belvidere, Ill., **1932–33:** 379
Benevolent and Protective Order of Elks, **1930:** 224; **1932–33:** 41n.
Benjamin Franklin Society, International, **1932–33:** 18, 455
Bennett, H. W., **1930:** 37
Bennett, Richard B., **1931:** 39, 40
Berea College, **1931:** 207
Bergquist, C. W., **1931:** 356; **1932–33:** 320
Bernet, John J., **1929:** 281n.
Bernstein, Herman, **1929:** 39, 190n.
Best, William B., **1932–33:** 41n.
Bestor, Horace Paul, **1930:** 265n., 271, 272; **1932–33:** 41n., 187, 234, 251, 264, 267ftn.
Bethlehem Shipbuilding Corporation, **1929:** 193n.
Bethlehem Steel Corp., **1929:** 193n.; **1932–33:** 53n.
Better Business Bureau, **1930:** 363
Better Business Bureaus, Affiliated, **1932–33:** 281
Better Homes in America, **1929:** 22; **1930:** 250; **1931:** 314
Better Homes Week, **1931:** 151; **1932–33:** 134
Beverly, Gov. James R., **1932–33:** 33, 310
Bible, **1929:** 307
Bible Society, American, **1932–33:** 362
Bible Sunday, Universal, **1931:** 427; **1932–33:** 362
Biblical Seminary, **1932–33:** 176
Bicentennial of George Washington's birth, **1932–33:** 35, 54, 56, 57, 58, 122, 142, 174, 181, 194, 196, 262, 335
Bickel, Karl, **1930:** 124
Bicknell, Ernest P., **1929:** 108
Bingham, Sen. Hiram, **1930:** 275; **1931:** 238, 239; **1932–33:** 154n.
Biological Survey, **1929:** 50n.
  Bureau of, **1932–33:** 423
Bird, Mrs. Michael, **1932–33:** 211
Bishop, James W., **1932–33:** 278
Bissell, Emily P., **1930:** 392
Bituminous coal industry, **1930:** 315
Black, John D., **1929:** 46n.
Blacks
  Education, **1931:** 136, 272
  Emancipation proclamation, anniversary, **1932–33:** 438
  Equal employment opportunity, **1932–33:** 354

Blacks — *continued*
   Housing, **1931:** 149, 314
   Howard University, commencement address,
      1932–33: 191
   Interracial cooperation, **1930:** 106
   Job training, **1930:** 84
   Joint National Planning Committee to Get Out
      the Negro Vote, **1932–33:** 318
   Mississippi River flood control projects, charges
      of unfair labor practices, **1932–33:** 353
   National Association for the Advancement of
      Colored People, **1932–33:** 167
   Stowe, Harriet Beecher, Hall of Fame ceremo-
      nies, **1930:** 186
   Supreme Court nomination, opposition to, **1930:**
      92ftn.
Blandford, William, **1929:** 214
Bledisloe, Lord, **1930:** 229
Blind
   American Printing House for the, **1932–33:** 423
   Matilda Ziegler Magazine for the, **1932–33:** 70
   New York Association for the, **1932–33:** 4
Bliss, Collins P., **1931:** 314
Bliss, Robert Woods, **1930:** 111
Bliss, Tasker H., **1930:** 364
Block, Paul, **1931:** 332; **1932–33:** 104
Blythe, Samuel G., **1931:** 439
Boardman, Mabel T., **1931:** 195, 310
Boardman, Russell W., **1931:** 279; **1932–33:** 247
Bob, Charles V., **1929:** 110n.
Bodenhamer, Maj. Osee L., **1929:** 275n.
Bodfish, Morton, **1932–33:** 41n.
Bogley, Reuben A., **1932–33:** 41n.
Boissevain, Manitoba, Canada, **1932–33:** 227n.
Bok, Edward W., **1930:** 13
Bolívar, Simón, **1930:** 414
Bolivia, **1929:** 3n., 171, 295
   President Daniel Salamanca, **1931:** 282
   Revolution, **1930:** 390
   U.S. Ambassador to, **1930:** 34
Bolivia-Paraguay, Commission on Inquiry and
      Conciliation, **1931:** 433
Bolshevism, **1930:** 319
Bond, George H., **1929:** 67
Bond, Henry H., **1929:** 256
Bonfils, Frederick G., **1932–1933:** 460
Bonus, veterans, **1932–33:** 101, 102, 123, 126, 154,
      218, 225, 246, 248, 249, 250, 256, 275, 276,
      285, 293, 358
Bonus bill.
   See Emergency Adjusted Compensation Act,
      1931.
Bonus loans for veterans, **1931:** 147, 148, 214, 302,
      324, 325, 430, 432
Boole, Mrs. Ella A., **1929:** 210; **1930:** 370
Booth, Ballington, **1929:** 58
Booth, Evangeline, **1930:** 159
Booth, Ralph Harmon, **1931:** 237

Borah, Sen. William, **1929:** 161; **1931:** 238, 239;
      1932–33: 228
Borday, Henry, **1930:** 31
Borden, Albert G., **1932–33:** 12
Borden, Col. W. J., **1930:** 223
Border Patrol, **1930:** 135, 390
Borglum, Gutzon, **1931:** 249n.
Boris III, King of Bulgaria, **1931:** 331
Borland, James B., **1932–33:** 469
Borno, Louis, **1930:** 1, 85, 93
Boston Herald, **1931:** 312
Bostwick, Vice Adm. Lucius Allyn, **1930:** 146
Boulder Canyon Project, **1929:** 132, 133, 134
Boulder Canyon Project Act, **1929:** 134
Boulder City, Nev., **1932–33:** 394
Boulder Dam, **1929:** 295, 296; **1930:** 236, 237, 238,
      326, 328
Boundary Commission, United States and Mexico,
      International, **1931:** 433
Bowlby, H. L., **1931:** 429
Bowman, Celine MacDonald, **1932–33:** 71
Boy Scouts of America, **1929:** 173; **1930:** 81; **1931:**
      33; **1932–33:** 165, 244
Boys' Brigade of the United States, Catholic,
      1932–33: 312
Boys' Club, Kips Bay, **1931:** 105
Boys Club of America, **1932–33:** 178
Boys' Week, National, **1931:** 152
Boys Week Committee, National, **1930:** 134
Braddock, Pa., **1932–33:** 336
Bradford, Mrs. Hugh, **1931:** 246
Bradley, Frederick W., **1930:** 57
Braille Press, American, **1932–33:** 478
Brandeis, Justice Louis D., **1931:** 400
Brandjord, I., **1929:** 242
Bratton, Sen. Sam G., **1932–33:** 154n.
Brazil, **1929:** 89
   Airmail service, **1930:** 312, 407
   Ambassador to U.S., **1930:** 185
   Arms and munitions, exports, **1930:** 337; **1931:**
      86
   President Getulio Vargas, **1930:** 337n., 371, 407
   President Washington Luis Pereira de Souza,
      1930: 337n.
   President-elect Julio Prestes, **1930:** 157, 180, 185,
      199, 337n.
   Revolution, **1930:** 337n., 390
Breckenridge, Mrs. Henry, **1929:** 239
Bressler, D. M., **1929:** 83n.
Briand, Aristide, **1929:** 161; **1931:** 89; **1932–33:** 74
Bridgman, G. Temple, **1929:** 252
Britten, Fred E., **1929:** 248
Broadcasters, National Association of, **1931:** 376;
      1932–33: 412
Bronx House Committee, **1931:** 153
Brook, Lt. Col. Mark, **1930:** 223
Brookhart, Sen. Smith W., **1930:** 88n., 403n.

Brooklyn and Queens Young Men's Christian Association, **1932–33:** 68

Brossard, Edgar B., **1930:** 293, 294

Brotherhood of Locomotive Engineers, **1932–33:** 41n.

Brotherhood of Railroad Trainmen, **1930:** 383, 384; **1932–33:** 41n.

Broussard, L. O., **1932–33:** 86

Brown, David A., **1929:** 83

Brown, Elmer E., **1931:** 156

Brown, George William, **1931:** 427; **1932–33:** 362

Brown, Herbert D., **1931:** 41

Brown, Maj. Gen. Lytle, **1929:** 204; **1930:** 223

Brown, Walter F., **1929:** 104, 202n.; **1930:** 267, 299, 305, 316; **1931:** 200, 201; **1932–33:** 91n., 119n., 276

Brownell, E. E., **1929:** 31

Brucker, Gov. Wilbur M., **1932–33:** 347

Brundage, Avery, **1931:** 241

Brüning, Heinrich, **1931:** 259ftn., 266, 267, 327

Brush, Graham M., **1932–33:** 286

Bryn Mawr College, **1931:** 165

Buchanan, James, **1930:** 207

Buckner, Mortimer N., **1931:** 378

"Buddy Poppy" annual sale, **1929:** 40

 Campaign, **1931:** 145

Budget.

 See also Appropriations.

 County health units, funding, **1932–33:** 348

 Defense expenditures, **1930:** 65, 66, 67, 112, 113

 Deficits, **1930:** 103, 125, 200, 238, 274, 312, 369, 401, 402, 403; **1931:** 62, 63, 78, 147, 148, 214, 302, 318, 430; **1932–33:** 31, 92, 93, 126, 182, 183, 187, 217, 450, 452, 453, 459

 Departmental economy conferences, **1931:** 173, 200, 201, 211, 213, 219

 Efforts to balance, **1932–33:** 1, 9, 10, 31, 50, 76, 77, 92, 93, 101, 102, 106, 109, 126, 127, 137, 146, 147, 148, 154, 156, 158, 159, 169, 175, 182, 183, 186, 187, 207, 208, 209, 217, 221, 245, 259, 272, 287, 347, 380, 402, 419, 450, 451

 Fiscal year 1932, **1931:** 147, 148, 302, 397, 398, 430, 432

 Governmental reorganization, impact, **1931:** 430, 453, 454; **1932–33:** 59, 76, 77, 79, 198, 199

 Income tax revenues, statement, **1930:** 103

 Increases, **1930:** 65, 66, 67, 127, 132, 206, 236, 237, 418, 422

 Justice Department, supplemental appropriation, **1929:** 311

 Legislative action, impact, **1931:** 116, 117, 324, 327, 432

 Memorandum to Government departments and agencies, **1931:** 269

 Messages to Congress, **1929:** 296; **1930:** 391; **1931:** 432; **1932–33:** 146, 421

Budget — *continued*

 National economy program.

  See Economy program, national.

 Navy Department, controversy, **1931:** 327, 358, 359, 385, 387, 390, 392, 406, 432

 News conference remarks and statements, **1929:** 118, 132, 155, 156, 159, 218, 274, 294

 Public vs. private financing of relief efforts, **1931:** 43, 44

 Public debt, **1931:** 214, 302, 358, 359, 430; **1932–33:** 9, 10, 347, 402, 421

 Public debt, retirement, **1930:** 378, 379, 390, 391

 Public works expenditures, **1931:** 45, 63, 67, 101, 147, 148, 177, 184, 226, 248, 277, 278, 302, 307, 319, 430, 432, 436, 437

 State of the Union message, **1930:** 390; **1931:** 430

 Tax revenues, **1931:** 214, 302, 318, 430

 Veterans' agencies, consolidation of expenditures, **1930:** 226, 227

Budget, Bureau of the, **1929:** 97, 105, 128; **1930:** 55, 58, 65n., 72, 78, 86, 103, 125, 128, 140, 142, 193, 390, 395, 397, 401, 410

 Director, **1931:** 39, 41; **1932–33:** 26, 29, 83, 109, 119, 154n., 207, 218n., 225n., 287, 289, 290

 Executive branch reorganization, studies, **1932–33:** 289, 290, 423

 Federal spending, memorandum, **1932–33:** 287

Builder's Exchanges, National Association of, **1930:** 250; **1931:** 314

Building and Loan Association, United States League of, **1930:** 250

Building and Loan League, United States, **1931:** 293, 314; **1932–33:** 41n., 274

Building Trades Employers, National Association of, **1930:** 30n.

Building Trades Employers and Employees, conference, **1930:** 29, 30

Buildings and Public Parks of the National Capital, Office of Public, **1932–33:** 423

Bulgaria, **1929:** 161

 King Boris III, **1931:** 331

Bundy, Harvey H., **1931:** 189

Burgess, George K., **1931:** 314

Burke, Charles H., **1929:** 8

Burke, James Francis, **1932–33:** 258

Burlingham, Dr. Louis H., **1929:** 74

Burnet, David, **1930:** 266

Burnett, Lt. Col. Charles, **1930:** 11n.

Burns, Allen T., **1931:** 290

Burns, Mr. and Mrs. John A., **1930:** 251

Burroughs, Nannie H., **1930:** 314

Burtness, Repr. Olger B., **1929:** 270

Burton, Sen. Theodore, **1929:** 250, 262, 263; **1932–33:** 302

Bush, S. P., **1930:** 299

Business and industry

 Advertising, **1930:** 363

Business and industry — *continued*
  American Legion employment drive, **1932–33:**
    40n.
  Bankruptcy legislation, **1932–33:** 63, 69, 448, 451,
    470
  Child labor, **1930:** 376
  Christmas buying, **1929:** 310, 324
  Commerce Department surveys, **1930:** 3, 4, 76,
    76n., 77, 215, 315, 390
  Competition, **1932–33:** 346, 357
  Conditions, **1929:** 256, 257, 272, 280, 281, 284n.
  Conference on hoarding of currency, **1932–33:**
    36, 41
  Conference of industrialists and educators, **1930:**
    335
  Conference of Smaller Industries, **1931:** 287
  Conferences with business leaders, **1929:** 280,
    281, 297
  Construction programs, **1932–33:** 14, 157, 175,
    221, 337, 380
  Corporations, jurisdiction based on diversity of
    citizenship, **1932–33:** 69
  Credit availability, **1931:** 343
  Federal contractors, **1932–33:** 213, 353, 354
  Federal regulation, **1932–33:** 328, 335
  Federal Reserve District Banking and Industrial
    Committees, **1932–33:** 169, 187, 251, 260,
    264, 267, 272
  International Chamber of Commerce, address,
    1931: 168
  Labor relations, **1931:** 196, 226, 430
  Labor-management relations, **1930:** 260, 358, 390
  Patent system, **1932–33:** 122
  Regulation, **1929:** 1
  Retail, **1929:** 289
  Safety, **1932–33:** 320
  Small business, **1932–33:** 272
  State of the Union message, **1932–33:** 419
  Stock exchange, **1932–33:** 54, 155, 378
  Tariff protection, **1930:** 188
  Taxation, **1930:** 103, 390; **1932–33:** 137, 186, 419,
    421, 450
  Unemployment relief, **1930:** 3, 4, 55, 71n., 76, 77,
    133, 144, 215, 311, 315, 331, 332, 334, 336,
    338, 339, 363n., 390, 408
  Unemployment statistics, development, **1930:**
    244, 247
  Wage reduction agreements, **1932–33:** 337, 358,
    360, 380, 388
  Welfare and Relief Mobilization Conference,
    representatives, **1932–33:** 294
  Work hours, **1932–33:** 126, 132, 240, 251, 267,
    272, 294, 337, 358, 380, 404, 419
Business and Professional Women's Clubs, Inc.,
    National Federation of, **1932–33:** 41n., 71
Business Bureau, Better.
  See Better Business Bureau.
Business Bureaus, Affiliated Better.
  See Better Business Bureaus, Affiliated.

Business Papers, Inc., Associated, **1932–33:** 41n.
Business Survey Conference, National, **1930:** 3, 4n.,
    46n.
Business Women's Week, National, **1932–33:** 71
Buterly, George P., **1932–33:** 429
Butler, Nicholas M., **1929:** 241, 243
Butler, Maj. Gen. Smedley D., **1931:** 297
Buttenheim, Harold S., **1932–33:** 41n.
Butterworth, William, **1929:** 281n.; **1930:** 130n.
Byrd, Gov. Harry Flood, **1929:** 180n.; **1930:** 272
Byrd, Richard E., **1929:** 137, 244, 292, 293; **1930:**
    196, 211, 208, 220, 287
Byrnes, Sen. James F., **1931:** 238, 239; **1932–33:**
    154n.
Byrnes, Repr. Joseph W., **1931:** 238, 239; **1932–33:**
    59n., 79, 114n., 451

Cabinet, **1929:** 5, 32
  See also Appendix E—The President's Calendar;
    specific department.
  Committee on unemployment relief, **1930:** 331,
    332, 334, 390, 395
  Meetings with the President, **1932–33:** 402
    Mentions, **1931:** 147, 148
  Resignations, possibility of, **1931:** 120
  Salary reductions, **1932–33:** 119, 127, 231
Caffey, Francis G., **1929:** 37n.
Caldwell, John K., **1931:** 103
Caldwell, W. A., **1931:** 260, 440
California
  Child health and protection conference, **1932–**
    33: 5n.
  Lincoln's Birthday, message, **1932–33:** 45n.
  Mission Play, **1930:** 56
  Oil industry, tariffs, **1932–33:** 342
  Oil resources, **1931:** 100
  Olympic Games, **1931:** 241
  President's visit, **1932–33:** 390, 392, 394
  Roads program, **1931:** 248
  San Francisco Bay Bridge agreement, **1930:** 261,
    262
  10th Olympiad, **1932–33:** 253
California Bridge Commission, **1929:** 177, 178, 196,
    218
California Débris Commission, **1932–33:** 423
California Development Association, **1929:** 303
California representation at public lands confer-
    ence, **1929:** 185n.
California Society of Washington, D.C., **1932–33:**
    371
California State Narcotic Commission, **1931:** 103
California Water Commission, **1932–33:** 135
California water resource development, **1929:** 132,
    133, 134, 177, 178
Callan, Brig. Gen. Robert E., **1931:** 181ftn.
Calles, Leonor Llorente de, **1932–33:** 409

Calvert Associates, **1932–33:** 117
Camp Directors of America, **1932–33:** 414
Camp Marfa, Tex., **1929:** 302n.
Campaign addresses, 1928, **1929:** Supp. II
Campbell, Ira A., **1930:** 190
Campbell, Johnston B., **1930:** 3, 6
Campbell, Thomas E., **1931:** 403; **1932–33:** 212, 275, 276
Campbell, Col. William, **1930:** 319
Campisteguy, Juan (President of Uruguay), **1929:** 251; **1930:** 101, 239, 278
Canada, **1929:** 3n., 53, 54n., 125, 161, 317
    American Bar Association convention, guests, **1930:** 276, 277
    Great Lakes-St. Lawrence Deep Waterway, **1932–33:** 219, 226, 235, 322
    Immigration, **1930:** 288; **1931:** 113
    International Peace Garden, **1932–33:** 227
    Joint investigation of effects of dam construction, **1930:** 42
    Minister to U.S., **1932–33:** 235n., 273
    Natural resources, **1930:** 311
    Niagara Falls convention, **1930:** 109
    Prime Minister Richard B. Bennett, **1931:** 39, 40
    U.S. Minister to, **1930:** 158
    U.S. relations with, **1931:** 303, 383, 426
    Waterton-Glacier International Peace Park, **1932–33:** 201
    Wheat prices, **1930:** 390
Canal Association of Louisiana and Texas, Intracoastal, **1931:** 399
Canal Board, Interoceanic, **1931:** 185; **1932–33:** 135, 423
Cancer, **1931:** 42
Cannon, Repr. Joseph G. **1931:** 234
Canton, Miss., **1932–33:** 100
Capitol Park and Planning Commission, National, **1932–33:** 423
Capper, Sen. Arthur, **1929:** 46, 61; **1931:** 238, 239, 264
Cardozo, Benjamin N., **1932–33:** 16n.
Caribbean tour, President's
    Announcement, **1931:** 102
    News conference remarks, **1931:** 104, 106, 111
    Porto Rico, visit, **1931:** 108, 109
    Statement on conclusion, **1931:** 112
    Virgin Islands, visit, **1931:** 110
Carmody, Martin H., **1932–33:** 103
Carol II, King of Rumania, **1931:** 180
Carpenter, Niles, **1931:** 314
Carr, Claiborn M., Jr., **1932–33:** 330
Carr, Wilbur J., **1930:** 79, 221
Carran, Mollie Brown, **1932–33:** 314, 321
Carson, William E., **1929:** 172
Carter, Dr. George W., **1929:** 307
Carver, Eugene P., Jr., **1929:** 40
Case, Anna, **1932–33:** 128
Case, Everett, **1932–33:** 295n.

Case, J. H., **1930:** 348n.; **1931:** 20
Case, Gov. Norman S., **1931:** 421
Castle, William R., **1929:** 308; **1931:** 116, 189, 392; **1932–33:** 34
Cathcart, Arthur M., **1929:** 96
Catholic Boys' Brigade of the United States, **1932–33:** 312
Catholic Welfare Association, **1932–33:** 41n.
Catholic Women, National Council of, **1931:** 340
Caulfield, Gov. Henry S., **1930:** 265n.; **1931:** 329
Cavert, Samuel McCrea, **1932–33:** 41n.
Census, Bureau of the, **1930:** 244, 247, 396; **1932–33:** 423
Census, Fifteenth Decennial, **1930:** 98, 99, 373, 374, 396
Census and reapportionment bills, **1929:** 6
Central New York Conference of the Methodist Episcopal Church, **1931:** 336
Century of Progress Exposition, **1930:** 158, 417
Cermak, Anton, **1932–33:** 466
Chacon, Lazaro (President of Guatemala), **1929:** 326
Chamber of Commerce, **1929:** 284, 285, 292, 297, 304
Chamber of Commerce, Aeronautical, **1931:** 131
Chamber of Commerce, International, **1931:** 162, 168, 218, 226
Chamber of Commerce, National Automobile, **1930:** 130n.; **1931:** 8
Chamber of Commerce, United States Junior, **1932–33:** 96
Chamber of Commerce of Curwensville, Pa., **1932–33:** 82
Chamber of Commerce of Palo Alto, Calif., **1930:** 353
Chamber of Commerce of the United States, **1930:** 3, 4n., 110, 130n., 144, 244, 247, 250; **1931:** 160n., 314; **1932–33:** 36, 41n.
Chamberlin, Clarence D., **1929:** 110
Chandler, Harry, **1931:** 405
Chandor, Douglas, **1932–33:** 369n.
Chaney, Maj. James E., **1932–33:** 25n.
Chang Hsi Ying, **1930:** 9
Chapin, Roy D., **1932–33:** 257, 264, 267ftn., 449n.
Charleston, S.C., **1932–33:** 135
Charleston, W.Va., **1931:** 223; **1932–33:** 346
Charlotte Hungerford Memorial Hospital, **1930:** 411
Chase, Adm. J. V., **1930:** 145
Chase, Pearl, **1931:** 314
Chemical Industries, 12th exposition, **1929:** 66
Chemical Society, American, **1929:** 200
Chemistry, Institute of Paper, **1931:** 322
Chemistry and Soils, Bureau of, **1932–33:** 423
Chenango County, N.Y., Republican Women's Education League, **1932–33:** 333
Chesnut, Calvin, **1931:** 177
Chester, Pa., **1932–33:** 286, 363

Cheyenne Indians, **1931:** 65
Chiang Ah-erh, **1931:** 36
Chiang Kai-shek, **1929:** 232; **1930:** 2, 324, 399;
    1931: 296, 353
Chicago, University of, **1930:** 335n.
Chicago Daily News, **1929:** 146; **1931:** 179, 292
Chicago World's Fair Centennial Celebration,
    1930: 158, 417; **1932–33:** 135
Chickasaw Indians, **1931:** 65
Child Congress, Sixth Pan American, **1930:** 75
Child Feeding Committee, Porto Rico, **1932–33:**
    433
Child Health and Protection, Indiana Conference
    on, **1931:** 22
Child Health and Protection, New Jersey Confer-
    ence on, **1931:** 137
Child health and protection, State conferences,
    1932–33: 5n.
Child Health and Protection, White House Con-
    ference on, **1930:** 204n., 369, 379, 389;
    1931: 22, 137, 182, 206, 231, 246, 321;
    1932–33: 135, 171, 184, 259, 311, 312, 328,
    380, 383, 441
Child Health Association, American, **1929:** 14n.;
    1930: 204, 361
Child Health Bulletin, **1931:** 391n.
Child Health Day, 1929, **1929:** 14
Child Welfare League of America, **1929:** 22n.
Childhood Education, Association for, **1932–33:**
    145
Children, health and protection, **1929:** 140, 142
Children Fund, International Save the, **1932–33:**
    447
Children's Bureau, **1929:** 295; **1932–33:** 358
Children's Charter, **1931:** 124; **1932–33:** 311
Children's Hour, **1931:** 206
Chile, **1929:** 3n., 77, 89, 167, 207, 255, 295
    Communications development, **1930:** 100, 312
Chillicothe, Ohio, **1932–33:** 346, 357
Chillicothe News-Advertiser, **1931:** 410
China, **1929:** 3n., 8, 108, 161, 232, 295
    Claims against U.S., **1930:** 9, 138
    Disasters and disaster assistance, **1931:** 296, 297,
        299, 303, 304
    Foreign claim, **1931:** 36
    International Settlement at Shanghai, protection
        of U.S. citizens, **1932–33:** 34, 35
    President Chiang Kai-shek, **1930:** 2, 324, 399
        See also Chiang Kai-shek.
    President Lin Sen, **1932–33:** 334
    Radiotelegraphic service, **1930:** 399
    Territorial integrity, **1931:** 430, 433
    Tientsin siege, **1930:** 133
Chindblom, Repr. Carl R., **1931:** 238, 239
Chippewa Indians, **1931:** 75
Choate, Robert B., **1931:** 312
Choctaw Indians, **1931:** 65
Christ, Churches of, **1930:** 333

Christensen, Chris L., **1929:** 151
Christian Association, Young Men's, **1931:** 286;
    1932–33: 22, 41n., 68, 330
Christian Endeavor Society, **1929:** 143; **1930:** 257;
    1931: 38, 262
Christian Family Crusade, **1931:** 231
Christian and Jew, American Hebrew Medal for
    Better Understanding Between, **1931:** 417
Christian Science Monitor, **1929:** 184n.
Christian X, King of Denmark, **1930:** 306; **1932–
    33:** 308
Christmas
    Disabled veterans, message, **1929:** 320; **1931:**
        444; **1932–33:** 432
    Holiday for Federal employees, **1931:** 446, 448
    National tree lighting, **1929:** 323; **1930:** 426;
        1931: 451
Christmas Seals Campaign, **1930:** 382, 392n.; **1931:**
    424; **1932–33:** 408
Christmas Tree Association, Nation's, **1931:** 452;
    1932–33: 436
Christmas Tree Association of California, Nation's,
    1930: 427
Church, Col. Earl D., **1929:** 41
Church of the Good Shepherd, **1931:** 374
Churches, World Alliance for Friendship Through
    the, **1930:** 365
Churches of Christ, world convention, **1930:** 333
Churches of Christ in America, Federal Council of
    the, **1932–33:** 41n., 420
Cierva, Juan de la, **1931:** 142
Cincinnati, Ohio, **1932–33:** 357
Circleville, Ohio, **1932–33:** 346
Circuit Court of Appeals of the United States, 7th
    circuit, judge, **1932–33:** 15, 418
Circuit judges.
    See U.S. circuit judge *under* Courts, United
        States.
Citizens' military training camps, **1931:** 115
Citizens Reconstruction Organization, **1932–33:**
    38n., 41, 60, 73, 80, 81, 135
Citizenship, duties of, **1930:** 314, 319
City Planning, National Conference on, **1932–33:**
    41n.
Civic Association, American, **1930:** 250; **1931:** 314
Civic Service Club Executives, National Associa-
    tion of, **1932–33:** 41n.
Civil Engineers, American Society of, **1932–33:** 175
Civil Service Commission, United States.
    See United States Civil Service Commission.
Civil War Veterans' Act, **1930:** 182
Civitan, International, **1932–33:** 41n.
Claims by and against the United States
    American Indians, **1931:** 65, 75
    China, **1930:** 9, 138; **1931:** 36
    Cuba, **1930:** 28
    Denmark, **1930:** 139
    Egypt, **1931:** 35

Claims by and against the U.S. — *continued*
  France, **1930:** 12, 31
  Norway, **1930:** 83, 152
  Poland, **1930:** 136
  Sanchez, Mrs. Mercedes Martinez Viuda de,
      1930: 90
  United Kingdom, **1930:** 37
  Visas, refunds, **1930:** 22
Clark, Sen. Clarence D., **1929:** 53
Clark, Dr. Francis E., **1931:** 262
Clark, Grenville, **1932–33:** 245
Clark, J. Reuben, **1929:** 6, 113
Clark, J. Reuben, Jr., **1930:** 44n.; **1932–33:** 477
Clark, Paul F., **1929:** 217
Clark Sesquicentennial Commission, George
      Rogers, **1932–33:** 423
Clarksburg, W. Va., **1932–33:** 360
Classical League, American, **1930:** 375
Clearing House Association, New York City, **1931:**
      343
Clearinghouse associations, **1931:** 333, 334, 343,
      378
Clemenceau, Georges, **1929:** 288
Cleveland, Grover, **1931:** 43, 44
Cleveland, Ohio, **1932–33:** 337
Cloud, W. W., **1930:** 130n.
Coal industry, **1930:** 133, 260, 315; **1931:** 244
  Bituminous, **1932–33:** 346, 357
Coamo, **1932–33:** 433
Coast and Geodetic Survey, **1929:** 227; **1930:** 3,
      55n.; **1932–33:** 423
Coast Guard, United States, **1930:** 55n., 117, 139,
      152, 190, 391; **1932–33:** 423
Cobb, James A., **1932–33:** 353
Cobscook Bay, **1930:** 42
Cochran, Repr. John J., **1932–33:** 439, 440n.
Codification of International Law, International
      Conference for the, **1930:** 86
Coinage bill, veto, **1930:** 121
Cole, Vice Adm. William C., **1930:** 146
Coleman, Arch, **1930:** 316n.; **1931:** 200, 201
Colfax, Calif., **1932–33:** 390
Colgate, James C., **1932–33:** 61
Colindres, Vicente Mejía, **1932–33:** 299
Colleges and universities.
  See also Education.
  Berea College, 75th anniversary, **1931:** 207
  Bryn Mawr College, M. Carey Thomas Prize,
      1931: 165
  Colgate University, **1932–33:** 61
  Columbia University, **1930:** 228n.
  Commonwealth Conference, State University of
      Iowa, **1930:** 217
  Conference of educators and industrialists, **1930:**
      335
  Conference of Liberal Arts Colleges, **1930:** 91
  Cornell University, **1932–33:** 184n.
    War Memorial, **1931:** 199

Colleges and universities — *continued*
  Facsimile Text Society, Columbia University,
      1930: 228
  Howard University, **1932–33:** 191, 423
  Journalism banquet, University of Missouri,
      1930: 154
  Lafayette College, **1932–33:** 166
  Lawrence College, Institution of Paper Chem-
      istry, **1931:** 322
  Liberal Arts Colleges Association, **1931:** 409
  New York University
    Hall of Fame ceremonies, **1931:** 187
    100th anniversary, **1931:** 156
  Princeton University, **1932–33:** 151, 202
    School of Public and International Affairs,
      1930: 62
  Stanford University, **1932–33:** 392
  Students, poll on election, **1932–33:** 363
  Tuskegee Institute, address on 50th anniversary,
      1931: 136
  University of Wisconsin, **1932–33:** 379
Collier, Repr. James W., **1931:** 238, 239
Collier-Harrison bill, **1932–33:** 155
Collier Trophy, **1931:** 142; **1932–33:** 105
Colombia, **1929:** 3n., 158
  President Enrique Olaya, **1931:** 265
  Visit, **1930:** 124, 157
Colorado, **1929:** 134, 185n.
  Conference on Child Health and Protection,
      1932–33: 5
  President's visit, **1932–33:** 383
Colorado River, **1932–33:** 394, 396
Colorado River Basin Interstate Compact, **1929:**
      132, 133, 134; **1930:** 326, 328
Colored People, National Association for the Ad-
      vancement of, **1932–33:** 41n., 167, 353n.
Columbia (monoplane), **1929:** 110n.
Columbia Broadcasting Company, **1929:** 203n.
Columbia Institution for the Deaf, **1932–33:** 423
Columbus, Christopher, **1929:** 44, 230
Columbus, Ohio, **1931:** 229; **1932–33:** 346
Columbus Day, **1930:** 325n.; **1931:** 354; **1932–33:**
      331
Columbus Monument, Palos, Spain, **1929:** 44
Commemorative coins, **1930:** 121
Commodity markets, **1931:** 226, 256, 257, 320, 343
Commerce, Department of
  Administrative functions, **1931:** 430, 453, 454
  Aeronautics Branch, **1930:** 391
  Appropriations, **1930:** 395n.
  Assistant Secretary, **1929:** 10, 37, 41; **1932–33:**
      41n.
  Bankruptcy law, investigation, **1930:** 244, 246
  Bureau of the Census, **1930:** 244, 247, 396;
      1932–33: 423
  Bureau of Efficiency, **1930:** 55, 261; **1931:** 39, 41
  Bureau of Lighthouses, **1931:** 453; **1932–33:** 423
  Bureau of Mines, **1932–33:** 423

Commerce, Department of — *continued*
  Bureau of Navigation and Steamboat Inspection, **1932–33:** 423
  Bureau of Standards, **1930:** 158; **1932–33:** 423
  Business survey, **1931:** 8
  Coordinating public works with state and local governments, **1929:** 292, 304
  Employment, survey, **1932–33:** 240
  Export debenture plan, analysis, **1929:** 46n.
  Federal Employment Stabilization Board, **1931:** 54, 55
  Foreign trade, **1930:** 244, 293, 295
  Housing construction, survey, **1932–33:** 238, 239
  Imports, **1932–33:** 237, 349
  Laying cornerstone of building, **1929:** 115
  Patent Office, relocation, **1932–33:** 122
  Public works, surveys, **1930:** 3, 4, 76, 76n., 77, 215, 315, 390
  Railroad reconstruction, conferences, **1932–33:** 87
  Recovery efforts, **1932–33:** 123
  Reorganization, proposed, **1932–33:** 423
  Report on foreign investment, **1931:** 320
  Secretary of (Robert P. Lamont), **1929:** 61, 146n., 218, 286; **1930:** 76n., 130n., 166n., 247n., 249, 250, 331, 332, 334, 395, 417; **1931:** 55, 91, 244, 271n., 314, 324, 344n.; **1932–33:** 41n., 122, 251, 257, 264, 267ftn., 449n., 462
  Wage rates, comparative survey, **1932–33:** 337, 357, 364n.
Commerce Commission, Interstate.
  See Interstate Commerce Commission.
Commercial Conference, Fourth Pan American, **1931:** 347
Commercial Organization Secretaries, National Association of, **1932–33:** 41n.
Comiskey, Charles A., **1931:** 382
Commission to Attend Ceremonies in Iceland, **1929:** 270
Commission on Conservation and Administration of the Public Domain, **1929:** 241, 242, 295; **1932–33:** 135
Commission of Fine Arts, **1932–33:** 423
Commission on Inquiry and Conciliation, Bolivia and Paraguay, **1931:** 433
Commissions, fact finding, **1929:** 155
Committee on Abandoned Army Posts, **1932–33:** 135
Committee on the Conservation and Administration of the Public Domain, **1932–33:** 423
Committee on Coordination of Veterans Services, **1932–33:** 135
Committee of Twenty-five, **1929:** 303
Committees and commissions, use of, **1929:** 314; **1930:** 16, 38, 39, 144, 145, 177, 244, 247, 261, 262; **1931:** 26, 155, 181, 260, 392; **1932–33:** 135, 169

Commodities and commodity markets, **1932–33:** 186, 187, 208, 209, 221, 251, 259, 264, 267, 295, 322, 347, 377, 380, 449
  WCAU Radio Building, dedication, **1932–33:** 463
Communications development
  Airmail service, **1930:** 312, 407
  Morse, Samuel F. B., tribute, **1932–33:** 163
  National Association of Broadcasters, remarks, **1931:** 376
  National Radio Week, **1931:** 323
  Press wire, **1930:** 421
  Radio, **1930:** 341, 351, 358, 363, 389
  Radiotelegraphic service, **1930:** 141, 387, 399, 425; **1931:** 143
    with Hungary, **1932–33:** 254
  Radiotelephonic service, **1930:** 100, 101, 111
Communist demonstration, **1929:** 313
Communists, participation in bonus march, **1932–33:** 285
Community Chest, **1930:** 43, 406; **1931:** 387, 388
Community Chests, National Association of, **1932–33:** 338
Community Chests and Councils, Association of, **1930:** 348; **1931:** 20, 290
Community cooperation
  American Federation of Labor, address, **1930:** 315
  Anti-hoarding campaign, **1932–33:** 36, 38, 41, 71, 73, 80, 81
  Chamber of Commerce of the United States, address, **1930:** 144
  Child health, **1930:** 369, 376, 379, 389
  County health units, funding, **1932–33:** 348
  Drought.
    See Drought relief.
  Economic recovery program, **1931:** 333, 334, 343, 357, 358, 405, 407, 436, 437
  Foreign trade, **1930:** 160
  Indiana Republican Editorial Association, address, **1931:** 226
  Labor-management relations, **1930:** 358
  Lincoln's Birthday, address, **1931:** 58
  Methodist Ecumenical Congress, remarks, **1931:** 372
  Public vs. private financing of relief efforts, **1931:** 43, 44
  Relief efforts, **1932–33:** 85, 157, 186, 215, 337, 347, 351, 358, 366, 380, 383, 398, 419
  Recovery program, **1932–33:** 1, 86, 175, 259, 328, 347, 358
  State of the Union message, **1931:** 430
  Street and highway safety, **1930:** 130, 166
  Unemployment relief, **1930:** 3, 4, 55, 71n., 76, 77, 133, 144, 215, 311, 315, 331, 332, 334, 336, 338, 339, 363n., 390, 408; **1931:** 123, 155, 283, 284, 290, 294, 295, 329, 360, 418, 436, 437

Community cooperation — *continued*
  Unemployment statistics, development, **1930:**
    244, 247
  Welfare and relief mobilization, **1932–33:** 294,
    338
Comptroller of the Currency, **1932–33:** 238, 239,
  284
Comstock, Ada L., **1931:** 27
Conciliation treaties, **1931:** 433
Condon, Repr. Francis, **1931:** 271n.
Conference on the Crisis in Education, **1932–33:**
  442
Conference of Governors, **1932–33:** 137
Conference of Liberal Arts Colleges, **1930:** 91
Conference on the Limitation of the Manufacture
  of Narcotic Drugs, **1931:** 28, 87, 103
Conference of Major Industries, **1930:** 335
Conference of Railway Brotherhoods, **1931:** 442
Conference on Safety of Life at Sea, **1931:** 433
Conference of Smaller Industries, **1931:** 287;
  1932–33: 223
Conferences with business, industrial, agricultural,
  and labor leaders, **1929:** 280, 281, 282,
  284, 285, 289, 297
Congress.
  See also Congress, communications to.
  Accomplishments of the 71st Congress, **1930:**
    390
  Apportionment, **1930:** 373, 374, 390, 396
  Bicentennial of the birth of George Washington,
    address to Joint Session, **1932–33:** 56
  Committees and commissions, Federal, **1932–33:**
    135
  Democratic Congressional Policy Committee,
    1932–33: 9ftn., 10n.
  Democratic leadership, **1932–33:** 123
  Economy measures, **1932–33:** 76, 77, 109, 111,
    113, 114, 119, 123, 124, 125, 126, 127, 132,
    146, 147, 148, 154, 347, 440, 450, 453
  Expenditures in the Executive Departments,
    1932–33: 109, 439, 440n.
  House of Representatives
    Appropriations Committee, **1930:** 125, 127,
      406; **1931:** 226; **1932–33:** 76, 77, 109, 111,
      123, 126, 419, 450, 451, 456n., 459
    Committee on Indian Affairs, **1931:** 75
    Committee on Pensions, **1931:** 72
    Judiciary Committee, **1930:** 135
    Leaders, meeting with the President, **1930:** 55,
      65n.
    Majority leader, **1930:** 147
    Members, cancellation of reception, **1930:** 68
    Military Affairs Committee, **1931:** 73
    Minority leader, **1932–33:** 157
    Pensions, **1932–33:** 138n., 152n.
    Select Committee on Economy, **1932–33:** 59n.,
      76, 77, 79, 109, 114, 119, 123, 124, 125,
      126, 127, 146, 419

Congress — *continued*
  House of Representatives — *continued*
    Speaker, **1930:** 58, 69, 86, 128, 140, 142, 395,
      401, 410; **1931:** 6, 9, 21, 53, 60, 61, 87, 128,
      129, 130
    Ways and Means Committee, **1931:** 63n.;
      1932–33: 76, 77, 123n., 154, 186, 221n.,
      400, 407
  Intergovernmental debts, authority, **1932–33:**
    407
  Joint Committee to Investigate Pay and Allow-
    ances in the Army, Navy, Coast Guard,
    Coast and Geodetic Survey, and the Pub-
    lic Health Service, **1930:** 55
  Joint select committee to study prohibition en-
    forcement, proposed, **1930:** 15
  Leaders, meeting with the President, **1932–33:**
    216
  Leadership, **1930:** 55, 65n., 147, 200, 222, 402,
    403
  Legislative action, **1932–33:** 317, 322, 328, 337,
    346, 347, 358, 363, 366, 371, 378, 380, 387,
    388, 439, 440
  Meetings with the President.
    See also Appendix E—The President's Calendar.
    Conference with certain Members on econom-
      ic problems, **1931:** 337, 339, 341, 342, 343
    Leaders, **1931:** 446, 447
  Members, meetings with the President, **1932–33:**
    230, 400
  Moratorium on intergovernmental debts, **1931:**
    238, 239, 240, 251, 252, 433
  Relations with the President, **1929:** 35, 314
  Revocation of certain Executive orders, **1932–33:**
    453
  Salary reductions, **1932–33:** 119
  Senate
    Address by the President, **1932–33:** 186
    Appropriations Committee, **1930:** 125; **1932–**
      33: 109, 111, 126, 154, 186
    Commerce Committee, **1931:** 12n.
    Banking and Commerce Committee, **1932–33:**
      157n.
    Committee on Banking and Currency, **1931:**
      343
    Committee on Indian Affairs, **1931:** 65n.;
      1932–33: 136n.
    Committee on Postoffices and Post Roads,
      1930: 87, 88
    Cooperation on appropriations legislation,
      1930: 368
    District of Columbia Committee, **1930:** 135
    Economy Committee, **1932–33:** 154n., 199
    Expenditures in the Executive Departments,
      Committee on, **1932–33:** 234
    Federal Power Commission, appointments
      controversy, **1931:** 12, 13, 31n.

Congress — *continued*
 Senate — *continued*
  Finance Committee, **1930:** 127, 172, 200; **1931:** 63; **1932–33:** 186, 400, 407
  Foreign loans, investigation, **1930:** 194
  Foreign Relations Committee, **1930:** 225, 230; **1931:** 37ftn., 71n.; **1932–33:** 228
  Judiciary Committee, **1930:** 92ftn., 135
  Leaders, meeting with the President, **1930:** 65n.
  Majority leader, **1930:** 200, 222; **1931:** 226
  Military Affairs Committee, **1932–33:** 65n.
  Minority leader, **1931:** 50; **1932–33:** 156, 157
  President, **1932–33:** 207
  President pro tempore, **1930:** 72, 193, 219
  Public Lands and Surveys Committee, **1930:** 343n.
  Republican leadership, **1932–33:** 154ftn.
  Special session, **1930:** 161, 162, 218, 219, 221, 225, 234, 338, 339, 368, 383, 385, 408
  Speaker, **1932–33:** 26, 29, 32, 83, 183n., 217, 225, 293
  Special session, 1929, **1929:** 1, 4, 38, 97
  Possibility of, **1931:** 43, 44, 196, 197, 238, 251
Congress, communications to.
 See also Appendix B—Messages to the Congress; Appendix C—Presidential Reports to the 71st Congress, 1929; Appendix D—Presidential Reports to the 71st Congress, 1930; Appendix D—Presidential Reports to the 71st and 72nd Congresses, 1931; Appendix D—Presidential Reports to the 72nd Congress, During 1932–33; Veto messages.
 Agriculture Department, drought relief, appropriations, **1931:** 6
 Transmittal of supplemental appropriations, **1930:** 72
 American Samoan Commission, report transmittal, **1931:** 10
 Apportionment under the 15th Decennial Census, statement transmitting, **1930:** 396
 Bankruptcy legislation, message, **1932–33:** 448
 Bicentennial of the birth of George Washington, **1932–33:** 56
 Budget deficits, letter to Chairman of Senate Appropriations Committee, **1930:** 125
 Budget message, **1929:** 296; **1930:** 391; **1931:** 432; **1932–33:** 146, 421
 Chicago World's Fair Centennial Celebration committee, report transmittal, **1930:** 417
 Claim presented by Great Britain, transmittal of report recommending payment, **1929:** 312
  See also United Kingdom *under* Claims by and against the United States.
 Commission to investigate conditions in Haiti, transmittal of message requesting authorization, **1929:** 305

Congress, communications to — *continued*
 Conference on the Limitation of the Manufacture of Narcotic Drugs, appropriations, **1931:** 28, 87
 Coolidge, Calvin, message on death, **1932–33:** 443
 Congressional Medal, Special, **1930:** 267
 District of Columbia, appropriations, **1931:** 21
 Drought relief legislation, **1931:** 50
 Economic recovery program, messages, **1932–33:** 1, 470
 Emergency adjusted compensation bill, letter to Chairman of Senate Finance Committee, **1931:** 63
 Emergency construction fund, transmittal of request for supplemental appropriations, **1930:** 395
 Executive branch, transmittal of supplemental appropriations, **1930:** 410
 Executive branch reorganization, messages, **1932–33:** 50, 423
 Export debenture plan, letter to House Majority Leader, **1930:** 147
 Farm relief, tariff, and certain emergency legislation, message to special session, **1929:** 38
 Federal expenditures and revenues, message, **1932–33:** 450
 Federal Farm Board appropriations, letter to Speaker of the House of Representatives, **1929:** 123
 Transmittal of supplemental appropriations, **1930:** 78, 401
 Federal Farm Loan Board policies, letter to Chairman of Senate Committee on Expenditures in the Executive Departments, **1932–33:** 234
 Federal land banks, appropriations estimate, letter to Speaker of the House, **1932–33:** 29
 Federal Power Commission, refusal to return Senate resolutions of advice and consent to appointments, **1931:** 12
 Foreign loan flotations, report transmittal, **1930:** 194
 Foreign relations message, **1931:** 433
 General Disarmament Conference, appropriations for U.S. delegation, **1931:** 445
 Intergovernmental debts and international economic conditions, message, **1932–33:** 431
 International Conference for the Codification of International Law, transmittal of supplemental appropriations, **1930:** 86
 International Convention for the Suppression of International Trade in Arms and Ammunition and Implements of War, message, **1932–33:** 446

Congress, communications to — *continued*
  International Exposition at Seville, report transmittal, **1931:** 434
  International Fur Trade Exhibition and Congress, request for appropriations, **1930:** 18
  International Geological Congress, appropriations, **1931:** 25
  International Load Lines Convention, transmittal to Senate, **1931:** 57
  International Water Commission, United States and Mexico, appropriations, **1931:** 11
  Joint United States-Canada investigation of effects of dam construction, request for appropriations, **1930:** 42
  Judicial procedure, reform, message, **1932–33:** 69
  Labor Department
    United States Employment Service, **1931:** 61
  Labor Department, appropriations
    Bureau of Immigration, **1931:** 9, 53
    Bureau of Labor Statistics, **1931:** 60
  Lausanne agreements, letter to Chairman of the Senate Foreign Relations Committee, **1932–33:** 228
  Law enforcement
    Administrative reforms, special message, **1930:** 17
    Criminal law, special message, **1930:** 135
    Prohibition and narcotics, transmittal of appropriations, **1930:** 142, 193
  London Naval Treaty
    Diplomatic correspondence, message declining Senate request for, **1930:** 230
    Message to special session, **1930:** 225
    Transmittal to Senate, **1930:** 143
  Mexican claims arising from the occupation of Vera Cruz, transmittal of report recommending payment, **1929:** 300
  Mixed Claims Commission, United States and Germany, report transmittal, **1930:** 74
  Moratorium on intergovernmental debts, telegram to Members of Congress, **1931:** 240
  Muscle Shoals Commission, report transmittal, **1931:** 440
  National Advisory Committee for Aeronautics, report transmittal, **1929:** 298; **1930:** 394; **1932–33:** 422
  National Commission of Fine Arts, 11th report transmittal, **1929:** 301
  National Commission on Law Observance and Enforcement, report transmittal, **1931:** 27
  National Council of Intellectual Cooperation, appropriations, **1931:** 52
  National economy, **1932–33:** 186
    Letters to Chairman of House Select Committee on Economy, **1932–33:** 114, 125
    Message, **1932–33:** 109
  Nicaragua, U.S. relations, report transmittal, **1931:** 71

Congress, communications to — *continued*
  Nicaraguan claims, transmittal of report recommending settlement, **1929:** 299
  Panama Canal zone, message recommending boundary modification, **1930:** 419
  Permanent Court of International Justice, transmittal of protocols to Senate, **1930:** 405
  Permanent International Association of Road Congresses, request for appropriations, **1930:** 49
  Porto Rican Hurricane Relief Commission, report transmittal, **1930:** 20
  President's Emergency Committee for Employment, response to request for report, **1930:** 413
  President's Organization on Unemployment Relief, request for special appropriation, **1932–33:** 215
  Procurement of supplies for Federal departments and agencies, letter to Speaker of the House, **1932–33:** 32
  Prohibition enforcement, message, **1929:** 112
  Promotion of Safety of Life at Sea, transmittal of convention, **1929:** 317
  Public buildings projects, transmittal of supplemental appropriations, **1930:** 128
  Reconstruction Finance Corporation
    Appropriations, letter to Speaker of the House, **1932–33:** 26
    Board of Directors, membership, message, **1932–33:** 220
  Relief of the families of Emilio Cortez Rubio and Manuel Gomez, message recommending legislation, **1932–33:** 214
  River and harbor works, appropriations, letter to Speaker of the House, **1932–33:** 83
  Rivers and harbors, transmittal of supplemental appropriations, **1930:** 58
  Second Polar Year program, appropriations, **1931:** 56
  Sixth Pan American Child Congress, message recommending appropriations, **1930:** 75
  Special International Niagara Board, report transmittal, **1930:** 109
  Special session of the Senate, letter to President pro tempore of Senate, **1930:** 219
  State Department, message recommending appropriations, **1930:** 181
  State of the Union message, **1929:** 295; **1930:** 390; **1931:** 430; **1932–33:** 419
  Supplemental estimates of appropriations for the Department of Justice, fiscal year 1930, transmittal letter, **1929:** 311
  Tariff legislation, transmittal of report on foreign protests to Senate, **1930:** 172
  U.S. Minister to Liberia salary increase, message recommending, **1930:** 53

Congress, communications to — *continued*
  Veterans' Administration, appropriations, letters
    to the Speaker of the House, **1932–33:**
    218, 225
  Veterans' Bureau, transmittal of proposed
    changes in appropriations, **1930:** 140
  World economic conference, appropriations,
    letter to President of the Senate, **1932–33:**
    207
  World War Veterans' Act, 1924, Amendments,
    letters to Senate majority leader, **1930:**
    200, 222
  Yellowstone National Park Boundary Commis-
    sion, report transmittal, **1931:** 5
Congressional Medal, Special, **1931:** 23; **1930:** 267
Congressional Medal of Honor, **1930:** 354; **1932–
  33:** 270
Conley, Gov. William G., **1930:** 265n.; **1931:** 223,
  224
Connally, Sen. Tom, **1932–33:** 186
Connellsville, Pa., **1932–33:** 336, 375
Connersville, Ind., **1932–33:** 357
Conservation, **1930:** 65, 182, 388, 390; **1932–33:** 50,
  259
  See also Natural resources.
  Government agencies, consolidation, **1931:** 453,
    454
  Waterfowl, **1931:** 299
Conservation and Administration of the Public
    Domain, Commission on the, **1932–33:**
    135, 423
Conservation Board, Federal Oil, **1931:** 99, 100;
    1932–33: 423
Conservation Board, Timber, **1932–33:** 135
Conservation of natural resources, **1929:** 25, 186,
    241, 242, 295
Constantinople, U.S. Embassy, **1930:** 181
Constitution Day, **1930:** 292
Constitution Week, **1929:** 203
Constitutional separation of powers, **1931:** 12, 13
Construction
  Act of 1932, Emergency Relief and, **1932–33:**
    182, 183, 186, 208, 209, 216, 217, 220n.,
    221, 230, 233, 243n., 282, 283, 421
  American Institute of Steel, **1930:** 344, 345
  Domestic expansion, **1930:** 3, 4, 71n., 76, 76n.,
    77, 133, 137, 144, 145, 145n., 200, 215,
    249, 250, 311, 315, 345, 347, 357, 390, 391,
    397
  Fund, emergency, **1930:** 357, 369, 395, 397, 402,
    403, 406, 418, 423
  Industry, **1929:** 281, 284n., 285n.; **1932–33:** 14,
    187, 238, 239, 251
Consultive pact, **1930:** 94, 112, 113, 119, 183, 184,
    230
Contessa, Vita, **1929:** 230; **1930:** 325
Contracts.
  See specific types of contracts.

Contractors, Associated General, **1930:** 250
Convention for the Promotion of Safety of Life at
    Sea, **1929:** 17, 317
Convention for the Supervision of the International
    Trade in Arms and Ammunition and in
    the Implements of War, **1931:** 433
Cooke, Walter Platt, **1931:** 281
Cooksey, G. R., **1932–33:** 230n.
Coolidge, President Calvin, **1929:** 2, 14n., 25, 161;
    1930: 60n., 109n., 244, 247, 405; **1931:** 26,
    37ftn.; **1932–33:** 347, 443, 444
Cooper, Edwin H., **1931:** 288
Cooper, Repr. Henry Allen, **1931:** 84
Cooper, Gov. Myers T., **1930:** 265n.
Cooperative Marketing, Division of, **1929:** 219, 221
Copeland, Sen. Royal S., **1930:** 322n.
Copyright Convention, **1931:** 433
Cornell University.
  See Colleges and universities.
Corsi, Edward, **1931:** 245, 348n.
Cortelyou, George B., **1929:** 115; **1932–33:** 179, 228
Cortes Rubio, Emilio, **1931:** 221; **1932–33:** 214
Cortez Rubio, Salvatore, **1932–33:** 214n.
Corwin, Walter E., **1929:** 304n.
Costa, Philides, **1931:** 204; **1932–33:** 369n.
Costa Rica, **1929:** 3n.
  President Ricardo Jiménez, **1932–33:** 297
Costes, Capt. Dieudonne, **1930:** 282, 283, 287
Cotton, Joseph P., **1929:** 84; **1930:** 53n.; **1931:** 97
Cotton, **1931:** 303, 313, 359, 387, 389, 430
  Crop production loans, **1932–33:** 309n.
Cotton Textile Institute, **1932–33:** 341
Couch, Harvey, **1931:** 422; **1932–33:** 31n., 41n., 187
Coulter, John Lee, **1930:** 293, 294
Council on National Defense, **1931:** 324; **1932–33:**
    169, 192, 322
Council of Personnel Administration, **1932–33:**
    135, 212
Court of Claims, **1929:** 237
Court of International Justice, **1929:** 1, 12, 295,
    306; **1930:** 115, 119, 133, 365, 383, 385,
    390, 405; **1931:** 191n., 433
Courts, United States
  Appointments, preparation of, **1931:** 403
  Bankruptcy reform legislation, **1932–33:** 63, 64,
    69, 448, 451, 470
  Court of appeals, 7th circuit, judge, **1932–33:** 15,
    418
  Court of Claims, **1931:** 65, 75
  Grand jury, **1932–33:** 285
  Judicial procedure, reform, **1932–33:** 63, 64, 69,
    475
  Judicial reform, **1930:** 17, 135, 209, 210, 390
  Juvenile delinquents, transfer of jurisdiction
    from Federal courts, **1932–33:** 193
  Oregon lakes, title controversy, **1930:** 179n.

Courts, United States — *continued*
  Supreme Court of the District of Columbia,
    1931: 173, 174; **1932–33:** 250n.
  Supreme Court of the United States, **1930:** 40,
    41, 92; **1931:** 65, 75, 95, 400, 433
  U.S. attorney, New York, **1930:** 308
  U.S. attorneys, Oklahoma, **1931:** 211, 277
  U.S. circuit judge, 4th circuit, **1931:** 173
  U.S. Customs Court, **1930:** 299
  U.S. district judges
    Maryland, **1931:** 177
    Minnesota, **1931:** 46, 70
Cowie, Rear Adm. T. J., **1930:** 105
Cowles, Gardner, **1929:** 241, 242
Cowles, Gardner, Sr., **1932–33:** 208
Cox, Albert L., **1932–33:** 192
Cox, Channing H., **1930:** 233
Cox, James M., **1931:** 357
Cox, James R., **1932–33:** 7n.
Coxe, Alfred C., **1929:** 37n.
Crabtree, J. W., **1932–33:** 41n.
Cramer, Stuart W., **1931:** 314
Creamer, William C., **1931:** 159
Credit.
  See under Banking and finance.
Credit Association
  National, **1931:** 333, 334, 343, 350, 378, 395, 407,
    408, 430, 436, 437; **1932–33:** 1, 259, 272,
    347, 358, 371, 380
  National Retail, **1932–33:** 41n.
Credit Corporation, Railway, **1931:** 436, 442;
    1932–33: 76, 78, 87, 88
Credit corporations, agricultural, **1931:** 43, 44, 45,
    50, 121, 181; **1932–33:** 347, 377, 380, 419
Credit Men, National Association of, **1932–33:**
    41n.
Credit System, Intermediate, **1930:** 265
Crime, **1929:** 1, 169, 170, 324
  See also Law enforcement and crime.
Crisp, Repr. Charles R., **1931:** 238, 239
Cromwell, William Nelson, **1932–33:** 478
Crocker, Herbert S., **1932–33:** 175
Crosby, Herbert B., **1930:** 45; **1932–33:** 246n.
Crosscup Pishon Post, American Legion, **1932–33:**
    256
Crowell, Benedict, **1931:** 31, 32
Crowley, Patrick E., **1929:** 281n.; **1930:** 428, 429
Crowther, Repr. Frank, **1931:** 238, 239
Croxton, Fred C., **1931:** 295, 387
Cruiser construction suspension, **1929:** 162
Crumbine, Dr. S. J., **1930:** 204, 361
Cuba, **1929:** 3n., 161
  President Gerardo Machado y Morales, **1931:**
    194; **1932–33:** 172
  Sugar exports, tariff, **1932–33:** 387
  U.S. relations with, **1931:** 426
Cullen, Repr. Thomas H., **1931:** 238, 239
Culver, Harry H., **1929:** 131

Cumberland, Md., **1932–33:** 336
Cumming, Hugh S., **1931:** 144n., 297, 298; **1932–**
    33: 2n.
Cunningham, Edwin S., **1932–33:** 34
Curie, Madame Marie, **1929:** 266
Currency
  Comptroller of the, **1932–33:** 238, 239, 284
  Foreign, depreciation, **1932–33:** 349, 357, 360,
    363, 364, 371, 377, 379, 380, 386, 387, 431,
    457, 462, 465
  Gold standard, **1932–33:** 38, 41, 66, 322, 337,
    347, 377, 378, 380, 387, 431, 457, 465
  Hoarding, **1932–33:** 36, 38, 41, 48, 49, 60, 66, 71,
    73, 80, 81, 119, 126, 272, 322, 419
  Inflation, **1932–33:** 31, 217, 221, 238, 259, 293,
    322, 358, 363, 364, 366, 371, 378, 419
  Redemption of, **1929:** 128
  Silver, **1932–33:** 269, 343, 387, 388, 465
  Stabilization, **1932–33:** 186, 457, 465
Current Problems, Women's Conference on,
    1932–33: 311
Curtis, Vice President Charles, **1932–33:** 197n.,
    252n., 253n.
Curtis, Cyrus H. K., **1931:** 431
Curtis, James F., **1931:** 129
Curwensville, Pa., **1932–33:** 82
Custis, John T., **1929:** 95n.
Customs, Bureau of, **1930:** 391; **1932–33:** 237, 423
Customs, Collector of, Los Angeles, Calif., **1931:**
    218
Customs Court, United States, **1930:** 299
Customs taxes, **1932–33:** 450
Cutten, George B., **1932–33:** 41n.
Cutting, Sen. Bronson, **1932–33:** 366
Czechoslovakia, **1929:** 8ftn., p. 27, 161, 264
  Intergovernmental debts, **1932–33:** 431
  President Thomas G. Masaryk, **1931:** 384;
    1932–33: 359
  Radiotelegraphic service, **1930:** 387
  U.S. Minister to, **1932–33:** 210
  U.S. relations with, **1931:** 426

Daily News of St. Thomas, **1932–33:** 426
Daily Princetonian, **1932–33:** 202
Dale, J. Thomas, **1932–33:** 82
Dale, Sen. Porter H., **1930:** 59, 60
Dalton, Albert C., **1930:** 190
Daniel, Peter V., **1930:** 92
Danville, Ill., **1931:** 234
Darlington, Bishop James H., **1930:** 269
Darrow, Repr. George P., **1931:** 238, 239
Daughters of the American Revolution, **1930:** 115;
    1932–33: 301
Davenport, Iowa, **1932–33:** 321
Davis, Gov. Dwight F., **1929:** 77; **1932–33:** 11
Davis, H. P., **1930:** 351

Davis, James J., **1929:** 140, 142, 164, 281; **1930:** 76n., 233, 247n., 260, 331, 332, 384n., 386
Davis, Norman, **1931:** 453; **1932–33:** 3n., 25n., 111, 112, 454
Dawes, Gen. Charles G., **1929:** 116, 128; **1930:** 10n., 11n., 158, 231; **1931:** 211, 238, 239, 446, 449; **1932–33:** 3n., 23, 24, 25, 31n., 36, 41, 73n., 187, 189, 378
Dawes, William R., **1929:** 276
Day, Benjamin M., **1931:** 348
Days of observance
  Armistice Day, **1930:** 356; **1931:** 404; **1932–33:** 393
  Army Day, **1930:** 105; **1932–33:** 67
  Austrian Republic, anniversary, **1930:** 366
  Bastille Day, **1930:** 232; **1931:** 261; **1932–33:** 229
  Better Homes Week, **1931:** 151; **1932–33:** 134
  Bicentennial of George Washington's birth, **1932–33:** 56
  Birthday messages
    Albert, King of the Belgians, **1932–33:** 115
    Alexander I, King of Yugoslavia, **1932–33:** 430
    Fuad I, King of Egypt, **1932–33:** 97
    Haile Selassie I, Emperor of Ethiopia, **1932–33:** 241
    Hirohito, Emperor of Japan, **1932–33:** 139
    Holmes, Oliver Wendell, **1932–33:** 75
    Markham, Edwin, **1932–33:** 131
    Schwab, Charles M., **1932–33:** 53
    Sprague, Frank Julian, **1932–33:** 242
  Bolivian Republic, anniversary of founding, **1931:** 282
  Brazilian Republic, anniversary, **1930:** 371
  Christmas, **1930:** 420, 424, 427; **1931:** 446, 448, 451, 452
  Columbus Day, **1930:** 325; **1931:** 354; **1932–33:** 331
  Constitution Day, **1930:** 292
  Emancipation proclamation, anniversary, **1932–33:** 438
  Flag Day, **1932–33:** 196
  German Republic, anniversary of founding, **1931:** 289
  Independence days
    Argentina, **1931:** 203; **1932–33:** 177
    China, **1930:** 324; **1931:** 353; **1932–33:** 334
    Colombia, **1931:** 265
    Costa Rica, **1932–33:** 297
    Cuba, **1931:** 194; **1932–33:** 172
    Czechoslovakia, **1931:** 384; **1932–33:** 359
    Estonia, **1931:** 76
    Finland, **1932–33:** 417
    Greece, **1932–33:** 95
    Guatemala, **1932–33:** 300
    Haiti, **1930:** 1
    Honduras, **1932–33:** 299
    Mexico, **1930:** 298
    Nicaragua, **1932–33:** 298

Days of observance — *continued*
  Independence days — *continued*
    Norway, **1930:** 178
    Panama, **1930:** 353; **1931:** 393; **1932–33:** 373
    Poland, **1932–33:** 144
    Rumania, **1931:** 180
    Turkey, **1930:** 346; **1931:** 386; **1932–33:** 361
    Uruguay, **1931:** 300
  Life Insurance Day, **1932–33:** 12
  Lincoln's Birthday, **1932–33:** 45, 46
  Luther Day, **1932–33:** 262
  Memorial Day, **1930:** 170, 171; **1931:** 205, 206, 209; **1932–33:** 185
  National Boys' Week, **1931:** 152
  National Business Women's Week, **1932–33:** 71
  National Hospital Day, **1930:** 156; **1932–33:** 140
  National Pharmacy Week, **1930:** 329; **1931:** 352; **1932–33:** 329
  National Radio Week, **1931:** 323
  National Thrift Week, **1932–33:** 21
  National tribute to Thomas Alva Edison, **1931:** 366
  Naturalization Day, **1931:** 419
  Navy Day, **1931:** 380; **1932–33:** 356
  New Year's Day, **1930:** 2, 8; **1931:** 446, 448, 455
  Pan American Day, **1930:** 169; **1931:** 135
  Parents' Day, **1931:** 178; **1932–33:** 118
  Polish National Day, **1930:** 148; **1931:** 169
  Rosh Hashanah, **1930:** 256; **1931:** 308; **1932–33:** 303
  Thanksgiving Day, **1931:** 422
  Universal Bible Sunday, **1931:** 427; **1932–33:** 362
  Uruguayan national holidays, **1930:** 239, 278
  Weimar Constitution, anniversary, **1930:** 264
Dayton, George D., **1932–33:** 264
Deaf, Columbia Institution for the.
  See Columbia Institution for the Deaf.
Dean, 1st Lt. John P., **1929:** 125n.
Dearing, Fred Morris, **1930:** 34
Debenture plan, export, **1930:** 147
Decatur, Ill., **1931:** 235
De Coe, Darold D., **1932–33:** 41n.
Defense, Council on National.
  See Council on National Defense.
Defense, national.
  See National defense and security.
de Grasse, Adm. Comte, **1931:** 170
DeGroot, William A., **1929:** 56, 60
Delafield, John R., **1932–33:** 67
Delano, Frederic A., **1929:** 88; **1931:** 314, 438
de Laszlo, Philip, **1932–33:** 369n.
Delaware
  Child health and protection conference, **1932–33:** 5n.
  President's campaign, **1932–33:** 363
  Relief efforts, **1931:** 303
Delaware, Ohio, **1932–33:** 346
Demarest, W. H. S., **1930:** 330

Deming, William C., **1930:** 48
Democratic Party
  Legislative record, **1932–33:** 317, 322, 328, 337,
    347, 358, 363, 366, 371, 376, 377, 378, 380,
    387, 388, 452
  National committee, **1932–33:** 337, 358, 366, 378,
    380
  President-elect, **1932–33:** 391, 392, 395, 396, 399,
    405, 431, 434, 441, 451, 452, 454, 466, 480
  Presidential candidate, **1932–33:** 337, 346, 347,
    358, 363, 364, 366, 377, 378, 379, 380, 382,
    385, 387
  Vice-Presidential candidate, **1932–33:** 293, 322,
    337, 347, 358, 363, 366, 378, 380, 387
Deneen, Sen. Charles S., **1929:** 267n.
Denman, Cyrus B., **1929:** 136
Denmark, **1929:** 161, 317
  Claim against U.S., **1930:** 139
  King Christian X, **1930:** 306; **1932–33:** 308
  U.S. Minister to, **1931:** 237
Dennett, Carl P., **1932–33:** 264
Dennis, Alfred P., **1930:** 293, 294
Dental Society of the State of New York, **1931:** 182
Denver, Colo., **1932–33:** 383
Design, National Academy of, **1929:** 291
Des Moines, Iowa, **1932–33:** 322, 323, 324, 325
Detroit, Mich., **1929:** 245; **1930:** 331, 332; **1931:**
    318; **1932–33:** 5n., 347
Deutsch, Bernard S., **1930:** 400
Devaney, John P., **1931:** 70n.
Dewey, Adm. George, **1931:** 154
Dewey, Godfrey, **1931:** 98
Dice, Agnew T., **1929:** 281n.
Dickenson, Sen. L. J., **1932–33:** 154n.
Dickey, Walter S., **1931:** 34
Dickey, William Lawrence, **1931:** 34
Dingley tariff, **1930:** 188
Diphtheria Prevention Commission, **1932–33:** 8
Dirigibles
  Norge, **1931:** 23
  R–101, crash, **1930:** 317
Disabled persons.
  See Handicapped persons.
Disabled Veterans of America, **1929:** 268
Disarmament.
  See also London Naval Conference; London
    Naval Treaty.
  Armistice Day address, **1929:** 275
  Campaign remarks, **1932–33:** 259, 322, 328, 346,
    380, 387
  Economic impact, **1931:** 37, 168, 238, 239, 251,
    252, 347, 430, 433; **1932–33:** 259, 337, 347,
    380, 395, 431, 434
  Foreign relations, message to Congress, **1931:**
    433
  Franco-Italian agreement, **1931:** 89, 430
  General Disarmament Conference, **1931:** 37,
    168, 239, 371, 430, 433, 445, 446, 449, 453

Disarmament — *continued*
  General Disarmament Conf. — *continued*
    Geneva, **1932–33:** 3, 23, 25, 111, 112, 135, 204,
      205, 206, 304, 380, 395, 407, 419, 431, 434,
      441
  International Chamber of Commerce, address,
    1931: 168
  International Convention for the Suppression of
    International Trade in Arms and Am-
    munition and Implements of War, **1932–
    33:** 446
  Land, **1929:** 48n., 61
  MacDonald-Dawes discussions, **1929:** 181
  Naval, **1929:** 28, 34, 48n., 61, 67, 68, 75, 94, 162,
    166, 183, 202, 206, 224, 229, 241, 295
  Navy Day, **1932–33:** 356
  Propaganda against, **1929:** 192, 193, 195, 196,
    198
  Restrictions on arms trade, **1932–33:** 470
  Universal disarmament petition, presentation,
    1931: 351
Disarmament Conference, Preparatory Commis-
  sion for the, **1929:** 28, 34, 48n., 61, 68, 75
Disasters and disaster assistance
  China, famine and flood disasters, **1931:** 296,
    297, 299, 303, 304
  Dominican Republic, hurricane disaster, **1930:**
    286, 291, 299
  Drought, **1932–33:** 322, 358, 377
    See also Drought relief.
  Flood control projects, **1932–33:** 353
  France, flood disaster, **1930:** 82
  Italy, earthquake disaster, **1930:** 242
  Nicaragua, earthquake disaster, **1931:** 116, 118,
    433
  Porto Rico, hurricane disaster, **1930:** 20; **1932–
    33:** 310, 433
  United Kingdom, dirigible *R–101*, crash, **1930:**
    317
Dismissals, U.S. Attorney General for Eastern
  District of New York, **1929:** 56, 60
Distinguished Flying Cross, **1932–33:** 247, 252, 266
Distinguished Service Cross, **1930:** 297
District of Columbia
  Airport, **1929:** 28
  Appointments under U.S. Civil Service Commis-
    sion, **1930:** 373
  Appropriations, **1930:** 183, 218, 391; **1931:** 21
  Architecture, **1929:** 51
  Board of Public Welfare, **1932–33:** 423
  Bonus marchers, **1932–33:** 218, 225n., 246, 248,
    249, 250, 285n.
  Building program, **1929:** 144, 295
  Commissioners, **1930:** 45, 373; **1932–33:** 246,
    248, 423
  Community Chest, **1930:** 43
  Court system, **1932–33:** 69

District of Columbia — *continued*
　Law enforcement, **1930:** 17, 45, 135, 390; **1931:**
　　301
　Municipal center, **1931:** 21
　Pipeline, gas, **1931:** 1
　Postmaster, **1932–33:** 31
　Prohibition enforcement, **1929:** 214
　Prohibition law, **1932–33:** 69
　Public buildings projects, **1930:** 128, 158, 397;
　　1932–33: 421
　Public Utilities Commission, **1929:** 75, 181
　Railways, **1929:** 181
　Superintendent of Police, **1932–33:** 246n.
　Supreme Court of the District of Columbia,
　　1931: 173, 174; **1932–33:** 250n.
　Unemployment relief, **1931:** 387, 388
　War Memorial, dedication, **1931:** 404
District of Columbia Fiscal Relations, **1932–33:**
　135
District judges.
　See U.S. district judges *under* Courts, United
　　States.
Dixon, Joseph M., **1929:** 185; **1932–33:** 201n.
Doak, William N., **1930:** 383, 384; **1931:** 94n., 100,
　　244, 277n., 324; **1932–33:** 213, 264
Dollar.
　See Currency.
"Dollar diplomacy," **1929:** 35
Dominican Republic, **1929:** 3n., 128, 161
　Hurricane disaster, **1930:** 286, 291, 299
　President Horacio Vasquez, **1930:** 66ftn.
　President Rafael Leonidas Trujillo, **1930:** 268,
　　286, 425; **1931:** 81
　Radiotelegraphic service, **1930:** 425
　U.S. citizens, safety, **1930:** 66
Donovan, William J., **1932–33:** 345, 367
Doran, James M., **1930:** 165
Dougherty, Proctor L., **1929:** 214
Doumer, Paul, **1931:** 261; **1932–33:** 74, 149, 150
Doumergue, Gaston (President of France), **1929:**
　　24, 119, 288; **1930:** 82, 232, 283; **1931:** 4,
　　47n., 176
Downs, L. A. **1930:** 272
Drake, John W., **1929:** 179n.
Draper, Arthur S., **1930:** 198
Draper, Claude L., **1931:** 12, 13, 31n.
Draper, Walter A., **1929:** 285n.
Drought Committee, National, **1930:** 265, 271, 272;
　　1932–33: 135
Drought relief, **1930:** 253, 255, 258, 259, 261, 265,
　　266, 270, 271, 272, 276, 334, 357, 390, 391,
　　406, 418; **1931:** 6, 15, 16, 17, 20, 26, 29, 43,
　　44, 45, 50, 121, 133, 147, 148, 181, 275,
　　319, 430; **1932–33:** 322, 358, 377
Drought Relief, White House Conference on, **1930:**
　　258, 259, 261, 265, 270, 301, 390
Drugs, **1930:** 17, 61, 135, 193, 329; **1931:** 69, 352;
　　1932–33: 52

Drugs, Conference on the Limitation of the Man-
　ufacture of Narcotic, **1931:** 28, 87, 103
Dry Goods Association, National Retail, **1930:** 46;
　　1932–33: 428
Duffy, Francis P., **1932–33:** 211
Duncan, I. N., **1931:** 260
Duncan, James S., **1932–33:** 45
Dunseith, N. Dak., **1932–33:** 227n.

Earhart, Amelia, **1932–33:** 173, 203, 252
Earls, Robert, **1929:** 254
Earls, Mr. and Mrs. Strothers, **1929:** 254
Earthquake disasters
　In Italy, **1930:** 242
　In Nicaragua, **1931:** 116, 118, 433
East, Arthur M., **1932–33:** 41n.
Eastman, George, **1931:** 51; **1932–33:** 84
Eastman, Joseph B., **1929:** 315n.
Eastman, Lucius R., **1929:** 76
Eaton, J. M., **1930:** 130n.
Eau Claire, Wis., **1932–33:** 379
Echo, Utah, **1932–33:** 386
Eckener, Dr. Hugo, **1929:** 174, 188, 189
Ecker, Frederick H., **1931:** 314
Economic Changes, Committee on, **1930:** 244, 247
Economic Geologists, Society of, **1930:** 430
Economic Research, National Bureau of, **1930:**
　　244, 247; **1932–33:** 337, 378
Economy, international
　British financial crisis, **1931:** 299, 320, 387, 389,
　　420
　Currency.
　　See main heading, Currency.
　Domestic impact, **1931:** 155, 226, 264, 302, 303,
　　318, 320, 333, 334, 337, 343, 360, 404, 420,
　　430, 436, 437, Supp. I; **1932–33:** 73, 186,
　　259, 272, 322, 337, 347, 349, 357, 358, 360,
　　363, 364, 366, 371, 377, 378, 379, 380, 386,
　　387, 419, 431, 434, 457, 462, 465
　Flight of capital to U.S., **1931:** 303
　French Prime Minister Pierre Laval, discussions,
　　1931: 368, 369, 370, 371
　German financial crisis, **1931:** 236, 259, 264
　Gold standard, **1931:** 320, 371, 387, 389, 420, 436
　Intergovernmental debts, **1932–33:** 111, 112, 228,
　　259, 322, 337, 358, 377, 378, 395, 396, 400,
　　405, 407, 419, 431, 434, 452, 454, 465
　International Chamber of Commerce, **1931:** 162,
　　168, 218, 226
　International silver conference, possibility of,
　　1931: 215, 218
　Latin American debts, statement, **1931:** 243
　Lausanne agreement, **1932–33:** 228, 272
　Lincoln Day dinner, remarks, **1932–33:** 465
　London Conference of Ministers, **1931:** 263, 266,
　　267, 268

Economy, international — *continued*
 Military expenditures, impact, **1931:** 37, 168, 238, 239, 251, 252, 347, 430, 433
 Moratorium on intergovernmental debts, **1931:** 238, 239, 240, 251, 252, 255, 259, 264, 350, 433, 450, Supp. I
 Pan American Commercial Conference, address, **1931:** 347
 Special message to Congress, **1932–33:** 431
 State of the Union message, **1931:** 430; **1932–33:** 419
 U.S. fiscal policy, **1932–33:** 31
 World economic conference, **1932–33:** 207, 259, 269, 322, 337, 343, 347, 377, 380, 387, 388, 395, 407, 419, 431, 434, 441, 457, 465
 World trade conference, possibility of, **1931:** 313, 315; **1932–33:** 155
Economy, national, **1929:** 256, 257, 272, 282, 295, 297
 Address to the Senate, **1932–33:** 186
 American Bankers Association, address, **1930:** 311
 American Federation of Labor, address, **1930:** 315
 American Legion, remarks, **1931:** 318
 Balance of trade, **1930:** 293, 295
 Business surveys, **1930:** 3, 4, 76, 76n., 77, 110n., 215, 315, 390
 Campaign remarks, **1932–33:** 259, 322, 328, 336, 337, 346, 347, 357, 358, 360, 363, 364, 366, 377, 378, 382, 387, 388
 Chamber of Commerce of the United States, address, **1930:** 144
 Committee to study economic developments, proposed, **1930:** 144, 145
 Commodity markets, speculation, **1931:** 256, 257
 Conference of Governors, address, **1932–33:** 137
 Conference with certain Members of Congress on economic problems, **1931:** 337, 339, 341, 342, 343
 Congressional action, impact, **1931:** 196, 197, 324, 325, 432; **1932–33:** 3, 123, 146, 147, 148, 154, 156, 186, 287, 293, 317, 322, 328, 337, 346, 347, 358, 363, 366, 380, 387, 470
 Currency.
 See main heading, Currency.
 Economic indicators, **1932–33:** 357, 360, 364, 366, 380, 382, 387, 388, 419
 Effects of legislation, **1930:** 55
 Federal Reserve District Banking and Industrial Committees, **1932–33:** 169, 170, 187, 260, 264, 267, 272, 295, 313, 347
 Fiscal policy, **1932–33:** 31
 Foreign loans, **1931:** 347
 Gold accumulations, **1931:** 238, 239, 303
 Gold standard, **1932–33:** 38, 41, 66, 322, 337, 347, 377, 378, 380, 387, 431, 457, 465
 Governors' Conference, address, **1930:** 215

Economy, national — *continued*
 Gridiron Club, address, **1930:** 133, 408; **1931:** 155
 Indiana Republican Editorial Association, address, **1931:** 226
 National economy program.
 See Economy program, national.
 Production and consumption, **1930:** 119, 133, 144, 215, 311, 315, 363, 390; **1931:** 8, 226, 303
 Public confidence, **1932–33:** 36, 120, 126, 146, 147, 148, 157, 158, 159, 175, 337, 419, 450
 Railroads, recovery, **1931:** 1, 334, 430, 436, 437, 442; **1932–33:** 1, 76, 78, 87, 88, 92, 94, 175, 187, 251, 347, 360, 380, 419
 Rapidan Camp conference, **1932–33:** 187
 Recovery program, **1931:** 333, 334, 343, 350, 387, 389, 405, 407, 408, 430, 436, 437, 446, 447; **1932–33:** 1, 3, 27, 28, 36, 66, 78, 92, 93, 94, 106, 107, 146, 156, 157, 158, 159, 169, 170, 175, 186, 187, 204, 205, 206, 251, 259, 267, 272, 287, 322, 328, 347, 357, 358, 371, 377, 380, 388, 419
 Remarks after election, **1930:** 355
 Stability, **1930:** 46, 118, 119, 144, 215, 224, 250, 311, 390
 Standard of living, **1930:** 144, 188, 250, 302, 311, 315, 319, 363
 State of the Union message, **1930:** 390; **1931:** 430; **1932–33:** 419
 Tariff policy, effect, **1932–33:** 155, 237, 259, 322, 328, 336, 337, 342, 344, 346, 347, 349, 357, 358, 360, 363, 364, 366, 371, 376, 377, 378, 379, 380, 386, 387, 388, 390, 457, 462, 465
 War debts, **1930:** 74, 133, 200n., 273, 274, 378, 379, 390, 391, 402; **1931:** 162, 238, 239, 240, 243, 251, 252, 264, 343, 350, 371, 432, 433, 436, 450, Supp. I
Economy League, National, **1932–33:** 245
Economy program, national
 "Economy Act," **1932–33:** 9, 10, 50n., 76, 77, 109, 111, 113, 114, 119, 123, 124, 125, 126, 146, 147, 148, 154, 186, 198, 199, 212, 231, 289, 421
 Furlough plan for Federal employees, **1932–33:** 119, 126, 127, 132, 133, 137, 146, 175, 198, 199, 208, 212, 240, 307, 337, 419, 421
 Reorganization of executive branch, **1932–33:** 9, 10, 48, 50, 59, 76, 77, 79, 92, 93, 106, 109, 111, 113, 146, 198, 199, 212, 259, 289, 290, 347, 358, 396, 419, 423, 439, 440, 450, 452, 453, 462
Ecuador, **1929:** 3n., 175
 U.S. Minister to, **1930:** 25
Edge, Walter E., **1931:** 170n.
Edison, Thomas A., **1929:** 57, 157, 245, 246; **1931:** 361, 362, 366; **1932–33:** 278, 288
Edison Institute of Technology, **1929:** 57n., 246
Edison Pioneers, **1929:** 57, 157n.

Editorial Association, National, **1930:** 189

Education, **1929:** 1, 191; **1932–33:** 145, 311, 442
  See also Colleges and universities.
  Advisory Committee on, **1932–33:** 135
  American Indians, **1930:** 3, 5
  Appropriations, **1930:** 65
  Association for Childhood, **1932–33:** 145
  Blacks, **1931:** 136, 272
  Conference on the Crisis in, **1932–33:** 442
  Federal Board for Vocational, **1932–33:** 119, 423
  Government agencies, consolidation, **1931:** 453, 454
  Industry, cooperation with, **1930:** 335
  National Advisory Council on Radio in, **1931:** 198
  Office of, **1932–33:** 423
  Prisons, **1930:** 165
  Public and international affairs, **1930:** 62, 217
  Rapidan Community School, **1930:** 64
  Textile industry, **1930:** 182
  World Conference on Narcotic, **1930:** 61; **1931:** 69
  Youth, **1930:** 81, 134, 213, 376

Education Association, International Narcotic, **1930:** 61

Education Association, National, **1930:** 213; **1932–33:** 41n., 57, 62

Education in Haiti, United States Commission on, **1930:** 50, 51n.; **1932–33:** 135

Edwards, Edward C., **1932–33:** 256

Efficiency
  Bureau of, **1931:** 39, 41
  United States Bureau of, **1930:** 55, 261; **1932–33:** 423

Egypt, **1929:** 161
  Cotton production, **1931:** 303
  Foreign claim, **1931:** 35
  King Fuad I, **1930:** 96; **1931:** 114; **1932–33:** 97
  U.S. Minister to, **1930:** 25

18th Amendment.
  See Prohibition.

Einstein, Albert, **1929:** 39; **1931:** 90

Eisner, Monroe, **1931:** 326

El Salvador, **1929:** 3n., 326

Elections
  Addresses
    California Society of Washington, D.C., **1932–33:** 371
    Cleveland, Ohio, **1932–33:** 337
    Des Moines, Iowa, **1932–33:** 322
    Detroit, Mich., **1932–33:** 347
    Elko, Nev., **1932–33:** 389
    Indianapolis, Ind., **1932–33:** 358
    New York, N.Y., **1932–33:** 366
    Newark, N.J., **1932–33:** 364
    Republican Presidential nomination, acceptance, **1932–33:** 259
    St. Louis, Mo., **1932–33:** 378

Elections — *continued*
  Addresses — *continued*
    St. Paul, Minn., **1932–33:** 380
    Salt Lake City, Utah, **1932–33:** 387
    Springfield, Ill., **1932–33:** 377
    Women of America, **1932–33:** 328
  Democratic Party.
    See main heading, Democratic Party.
  Informal remarks
    California, **1932–33:** 390
    Delaware, **1932–33:** 363
    Illinois, **1932–33:** 321, 376, 379
    Indiana, **1932–33:** 326, 357, 376
    Iowa, **1932–33:** 321, 323, 324, 325
    Joint National Planning Committee to Get Out the Negro Vote, **1932–33:** 318
    Maryland, **1932–33:** 336, 363
    Michigan, **1932–33:** 346
    Nevada, **1932–33:** 388
    New Jersey, **1932–33:** 363
    New York, **1932–33:** 367
    Ohio, **1932–33:** 336, 346, 357
    Pennsylvania, **1932–33:** 336, 363, 375
    Utah, **1932–33:** 386, 388
    West Virginia, **1932–33:** 336, 346, 357, 360
    Wisconsin, **1932–33:** 379
    Wyoming, **1932–33:** 386
  Iowa Republican national committeeman, **1932–33:** 314n., 325
  Messages
    California Republican Party campaign chairman, **1932–33:** 342
    Carran, Mollie Brown, **1932–33:** 314
    Chenango County Republican Women's Educational League, **1932–33:** 333
    Hobart, Jennie, **1932–33:** 370
    Hoover-Curtis Committee, Wyoming State chairman, **1932–33:** 344
    Maine gubernatorial election, **1932–33:** 291
    Massachusetts State Convention, **1932–33:** 317
    Massachusetts State Republican Convention, **1932–33:** 317
    New Jersey Republican Campaign Committee, **1932–33:** 372
    New York First Voters' Donovan-for-Governor League, **1932–33:** 345
    Republican National Convention, acceptance of nomination, **1932–33:** 197
    Silver Bow County, Montana, Republican Committee, **1932–33:** 343
    Young Republican League, **1932–33:** 368
  Muscle Shoals legislation controversy, **1930:** 243
  New Jersey, Republican senatorial campaign, **1930:** 187, 191, 313
  News conference remarks, **1932–33:** 260, 382, 392
  Oil shale lands controversy, **1930:** 342, 343
  Remarks after election, **1930:** 355

Elections — *continued*
  Results
    President-elect Roosevelt, message of congratulations, **1932–33:** 391
    President's plans, **1932–33:** 392
  Statements
    Agricultural tariffs, **1932–33:** 384, 385
    Campaign plans, **1932–33:** 200
    Philippine independence, **1932–33:** 384
    United States Junior Chamber of Commerce "Get out the vote" drive, **1932–33:** 96
Electric lamp, **1929:** 245, 246
Electric Light Association, National, 145
Electric power, **1930:** 71n., 133, 145, 192, 315, 319, 390; **1931:** 1, 88, 366, 430; **1932–33:** 278, 288
Electric Railway Association, American, **1929:** 285n.
Electric Utilities Committee, **1930:** 145
Electrical Engineers, American Institute of, **1929:** 52n.
Electrical World, **1929:** 157n.
Elko, Nev., **1932–33:** 388, 389
Elks of the United States of America, Benevolent and Protective Order of, **1930:** 224; **1932–33:** 41n.
Elliott, Repr. Richard N., **1931:** 92
Ellsworth, Frank, **1931:** 70n.
Ellsworth, Lincoln, **1931:** 23
Elroy, Wis., **1932–33:** 379
Ely, Maj. Gen. Hanson E., **1931:** 115
Emancipation Proclamation, **1932–33:** 438
Emergency Adjusted Compensation Act, 1931, **1931:** 63, 67, 78, 79, 80
Emergency construction fund, **1930:** 357, 369, 395, 397, 402, 403, 406, 418, 423
Emergency Relief and Construction Act of 1932, **1932–33:** 182, 183, 186, 208, 209, 216, 217, 220n., 221, 230, 233, 243n., 282, 283, 421
Emergency Unemployment Relief Committee of New York City, **1932–33:** 85, 351
Emerson, Dr. Kendall, **1930:** 382
Emery, James A., **1932–33:** 41n.
Emmerson, Gov. Louis L., **1930:** 265n.; **1931:** 233
Empire State Building, **1931:** 163
Employees' Compensation Commission, United States, **1932–33:** 423
Employment, President's Emergency Committee for, **1930:** 347, 413; **1931:** 161, 295; **1932–33:** 135, 337ftn.
Employment Committee, New York City Emergency, **1930:** 336
Employment Service, United States, **1931:** 61, 94, 101, 277
Employment Stabilization Act of 1931, **1931:** 54, 55
Employment Statistics, President's Advisory Committee on, **1931:** 60n.

Employment and unemployment, **1929:** 282, 284n., 286, 295, 297
  Address to Nation, **1931:** 360
  American Legion, remarks, **1931:** 318
  American Legion employment drive, **1932–33:** 38, 40
  Cabinet committee on unemployment, **1930:** 331, 332, 334, 390, 395
  Cleveland, Ohio, address, **1932–33:** 337
  Commerce Department surveys, **1930:** 3, 4, 76, 76n., 77, 215, 315, 390
  Community cooperation, **1930:** 3, 4, 55, 71n., 76, 77, 133, 144, 215, 311, 315, 331, 332, 334, 336, 338, 339, 363n., 390, 408; **1931:** 123, 155, 283, 284, 290, 294, 295, 329, 360, 418, 436, 437
  District of Columbia, **1931:** 387, 388
  Drought areas, **1930:** 265, 418
  Emergency construction fund, **1930:** 357, 369, 395, 397, 402, 403, 406, 418, 423
  Emergency Unemployment Relief Committee of New York, **1932–33:** 85, 351
  Equal opportunity, **1932–33:** 354
  Exaggeration of conditions, **1931:** 311
  Federal expenditures for relief, **1930:** 55, 65, 66, 67, 137, 391, 402, 403, 408, 418, 422, 423; **1931:** 45, 63, 67, 101, 147, 148, 177, 184, 226, 248, 277, 278, 302, 307, 319, 358, 359, 430, 432, 436, 437
  Federal Reserve District Banking and Industrial Committees, conference, **1932–33:** 243, 267, 272
  Furlough plan for Federal employees, **1932–33:** 119, 126, 127, 132, 133, 137, 146, 175, 198, 199, 212, 240, 307, 337
  Girls' Service League of America, **1931:** 161
  Government employees, **1931:** 200, 201, 218, 283, 284, 302, 403, 413
  Immigration, **1930:** 288, 380, 390; **1931:** 113, 189, 226
  Indiana Republican Editorial Association, address, **1931:** 226
  Insurance, **1931:** 226
  International economy, impact, **1932–33:** 349, 457, 462, 465
  Job training, **1930:** 84
  Labor Department survey, **1930:** 25, 34, 76, 76n., 77, 334, 390; **1931:** 302
  Memorandum to Government departments and agencies, **1931:** 413
  Musicians Symphony Orchestra, **1932–33:** 429
  National employment system legislation, **1931:** 94
  Navy Department, personnel reductions, **1930:** 321, 322
  New England Conference on Reemployment, **1932–33:** 240

Employment and unemployment — *continued*
  Pennsylvania's unemployed, representatives,
    1932–33: 7
  Post Office Department, policy, **1930:** 316, 338
  President's Organization on Unemployment Re-
    lief.
    See main heading, President's Organization on
      Unemployment Relief.
  Private construction, **1930:** 71n., 215, 249, 250,
    331, 332, 334, 335n., 344, 345n.; **1931:**
    407, 408
  Public vs. private financing of relief efforts,
    1931: 43, 44
  Public works, **1930:** 3, 4, 55, 66, 67, 137, 215, 223,
    266, 331, 332, 334, 347, 357, 391, 418, 422,
    423; **1931:** 45, 54, 55, 67, 218, 297, 307,
    319, 360, 394, 421, 430, 431
    See also main heading, Public works.
  Railroad consolidation, **1930:** 428, 429
  State and local relief efforts, **1931:** 248, 283, 284,
    303, 329, 357, 421, 436, 437
  State of the Union message, **1930:** 390; **1931:** 430
  Statistical services, development, **1930:** 244, 247
  Statistics, **1932–33:** 337, 347, 363, 366, 376, 379,
    387, 388, 389, 390
    Accuracy, **1931:** 283
  Technological unemployment, **1930:** 144, 315;
    1932–33: 337
  Veterans, **1931:** 63, 78, 79, 80, 277n.
  Winter relief efforts, **1931:** 283, 284, 290, 294,
    295, 297, 302, 311, 318, 360, 387, 388, 430,
    436, 437, 446, 447
  Work hours, **1932–33:** 1, 126, 132, 240, 267, 272,
    294, 337, 358, 404, 419
Engelman, Morris, **1932–33:** 332
Engineering Co., American, **1932–33:** 41n.
Engineering Council, American, **1932–33:** 41n.
Engineers
  American Institute of Mining and Metallurgical,
    1930: 57
  American Society of, **1929:** 52n.
  American Society of Civil, **1932–33:** 175
  American Society of Mechanical, **1929:** 52n.
  Army Corps of, **1930:** 218n., 223, 261, 262; **1931:**
    88, 185, 260, 319, 416, 430, 440, 453
  Brotherhood of Locomotive, **1932–33:** 41n.
  Corps of, **1929:** 181, 204
  Office of the Chief of, **1932–33:** 251, 353n., 423
Equal opportunity, **1930:** 108, 115, 144, 319, 383;
    1931: 58, 88, 226; **1932–33:** 191, 259, 328,
    354, 366, 379, 380, 419, 424
Erickson, Gov. John E., **1930:** 265n.
Ericsson, Leif, statue, **1929:** 270n.
Erie Canal, **1930:** 132
Escobar, Gen. José G., **1929:** 2ftn., p. 13
Estep, Repr. Harry A., **1931:** 238, 239
Estes National Park, Colo., **1930:** 153

Estonia, **1929:** 161
  Independence day, **1931:** 76
  Intergovernmental debts, **1932–33:** 431
Ethiopia, **1929:** 161
  Emperor Haile Selassie I, **1930:** 120, 350; **1931:**
    93; **1932–33:** 241
Euler, W. D., **1932–33:** 371
Europe
  See also specific country.
  Allied Jewish Relief Campaign, **1930:** 80, 151n.
  British financial crisis, **1931:** 299, 320, 387, 389,
    420
  Consultive pact, **1930:** 94, 112, 113, 119, 183, 184,
    230
  Disarmament.
    See London Naval Conference.
  Foreign relations, message to Congress, **1931:**
    433
  Franco-Italian naval agreement, **1931:** 89, 430
  French Prime Minister Pierre Laval, visit, **1931:**
    367, 368, 369, 370, 371, 433
  German financial crisis, **1931:** 236, 259, 264
  Immigration, **1930:** 288; **1931:** 113
  Intergovernmental debts, **1932–33:** 111, 112, 228,
    259, 322, 337, 358, 377, 378, 395, 396, 400,
    405, 407, 419, 431, 434, 452, 454, 465
  International financial bloc, possibility of, **1930:**
    402
  Italian Foreign Minister Dino Grandi, visit,
    1931: 411, 433
  London Conference of Ministers, **1931:** 263, 266,
    267, 268
  Moratorium on intergovernmental debts, **1931:**
    238, 239, 240, 251, 252, 255, 264, 350, 430,
    433, 450, Supp. I
  Polish Corridor, **1931:** 373
  Radiotelegraphic service, **1930:** 387; **1931:** 143
  U.S. Army of Occupation, **1930:** 74
  U.S. fiscal policy, concern, **1932–33:** 31
  U.S. relations with, **1930:** 112, 113, 115, 119, 365,
    402, 405; **1931:** 302, 313, 318, 337, 341
  War debts, **1930:** 74, 133, 200n., 273, 274, 378,
    379, 390, 391, 402
European Broadcasting Conference, Prague, **1929:**
  8
European war relief work, memorial album, **1929:**
  81
Evangelical Church, German, **1931:** 363
Evans, Frank, **1931:** 283
Evanston, Wyo., **1932–33:** 386
Everson, Gen. Graham, **1929:** 209
Evison, Herbert, **1930:** 197n.
Ewald, Louis, **1929:** 102
Ewing, Dr. James, **1931:** 42
Excise taxes, **1932–33:** 186, 346, 419, 421, 450

Executive branch reorganization, **1932–33:** 9, 10, 48, 50, 59, 76, 77, 79, 92, 93, 106, 108, 109, 111, 113, 146, 198, 199, 212, 259, 289, 290, 347, 358, 396, 419, 423, 439, 440, 450, 452, 453, 462

Executive Office, appropriations, **1930:** 410

Executive orders.
  See also Appendix B—Messages to the Congress; Appendix C—Presidential Reports to the 71st Congress, 1929; Appendix D—Presidential Reports to the 71st Congress, 1930; Appendix D—Presidential Reports to the 71st and 72nd Congresses, 1931; Appendix D—Presidential Reports to the 72nd Congress, During 1932–33
  Cooperative Marketing Division, transfer to Federal Farm Board (EO 5200), **1929:** 221
  District of Columbia appointments (EO 5491), **1930:** 373
  Executive branch reorganization, **1932–33:** 289, 290, 440, 450, 453
  Longworth, Repr. Nicholas, death (EO 5595), **1931:** 130
  Post Office hiring (EO 5471), **1930:** 338
  Postmaster appointments, **1929:** 18n.
  Publication of internal revenue tax refund decisions (EO 5079), **1929:** 7
  Veterans' preference, amendment of Civil Service rules (EO 5610), **1931:** 150

Executive prerogatives, **1931:** 12, 13

Expenditures.
  See Budget.

Export debenture plan, **1929:** 46; **1930:** 147

Export duties.
  See Tariffs.

Exports.
  See also Trade.
  Agricultural, **1929:** 46
  Arms and munitions, **1930:** 337
  Helium, **1930:** 321, 323
  Revenues, **1930:** 293, 295

Exposition, Century of Progress, **1930:** 158, 417

Exposition, National Hotel, **1931:** 401

Exposition of Colonial and Overseas Countries, International, **1931:** 176

Exposition at Seville, International, **1930:** 201; **1931:** 434

Extradition treaty, **1931:** 433

Facsimile Text Society, **1930:** 228

Fagot, Emilio, **1931:** 108n.

Family Crusade, Christian, **1931:** 231

Far East.
  See also specific country.
  Foreign relations, message to Congress, **1931:** 433

Far East — *continued*
  Japanese Prince Takamatsu, visit, **1931:** 146, 217
  Manchurian crisis, **1931:** 430, 433
  Philippine independence, **1931:** 378, 379
  Siamese King Prajadhipok, visit, **1931:** 175, 273
  Sino-Japanese conflict, **1932–33:** 34, 35

Fariservis, Walter A., **1929:** 130

Farm Board, Federal, **1930:** 78, 253, 255, 258, 259, 265, 265n., 271, 272, 390, 391, 401, 423; **1931:** 92, 106, 147, 148, 210, 226, 242, 283, 297, 299, 303, 304, 358, 403

Farm Bureau Federation, American, **1930:** 250, 259n.; **1931:** 260, 314, 440; **1932–33:** 194

Farm economy, **1929:** 34, 38, 150, 285n., 295

Farm and Garden Association, Women's National, **1930:** 250; **1931:** 314

Farm Loan Act, amendments, Federal, **1932–33:** 28

Farm loan bank system, Federal, **1931:** 226, 334, 407, 408

Farm Loan Board, Federal, **1931:** 226, 303, 305

Farm Loan Bureau, Federal, **1930:** 258, 259, 265, 265n., 271, 272, 390

Farm Loan System, **1930:** 144

Farm marketing organizations, **1929:** 38

Farm relief, **1929:** 4, 12, 34, 38, 41, 42, 46, 98, 117, 121

Farmers' Educational and Cooperative Union, National, **1930:** 250, 259n.

Farmers Union, National, **1931:** 314

Farming.
  See Agriculture and agricultural programs.

Farnum, George, **1931:** 211

Farrell, James A., **1930:** 160n.; **1932–33:** 143

Farrington, Wallace R., **1929:** 48

Favrot, Leo M., **1930:** 51n.

Federal Bar Association, **1932–33:** 467

Federal Board for Vocational Education, **1932–33:** 119, 423

Federal Council of the Churches of Christ in America, **1932–33:** 41n., 420

Federal departments and agencies.
  See also Cabinet; *specific department or agency.*
  Appropriations, **1932–33:** 119, 421, 459, 482
  Committees and commissions, **1932–33:** 135
  Conferences
    Economy conferences with legislative branch, **1932–33:** 111, 113, 114, 119, 123, 124, 125, 127, 154
    Farm mortgage relief, **1932–33:** 313
    Federal Reserve District Banking and Industrial Committees, **1932–33:** 267, 272
  Currency hoarding, **1932–33:** 41
  Death of Calvin Coolidge, display of flags at half staff, **1932–33:** 444
  Federal contractors, equal employment opportunity directive, **1932–33:** 354
  Federal expenditures, memorandum, **1932–33:** 287

Federal departments and agencies — *continued*
  Job vacancies, **1932–33:** 421
  Procurement policy, **1932–33:** 31, 32
  Public building projects, **1932–33:** 282, 283, 307
  Regulatory reform, **1932–33:** 328, 335, 366, 439, 400
  Reorganization, proposed, **1932–33:** 9, 10, 48, 50, 59, 76, 77, 79, 92, 93, 106, 109, 111, 113, 146, 198, 199, 212, 259, 289, 290, 347, 358, 396, 419, 423, 439, 440, 450, 452, 453, 462
  Scientific research, **1932–33:** 435
Federal employees.
  See also Government employees.
  Blacks, **1932–33:** 354n.
  Furlough plan, **1932–33:** 119, 126, 127, 132, 133, 137, 146, 175, 198, 199, 208, 212, 240, 307, 337, 419, 421
  Political activities, civil service regulations, **1932–33:** 275, 276
Federal Employment Stabilization Board, **1931:** 54, 55
Federal Farm Board
  Agricultural relief efforts, **1931:** 226, 358; **1932–33:** 169, 186, 187, 251, 322, 366, 371, 377, 380
  Appointments, **1931:** 92, 106, 283, 403
  Appropriations, **1929:** 121, 123, 274; **1930:** 78, 391, 401, 423; **1931:** 147, 148
  Chairman, **1930:** 253, 255, 265n., 271, 272; **1931:** 92; **1932–33:** 264
  Conferences with industry, agriculture, and labor, **1929:** 281
  Cooperative Marketing Division, transfer, **1929:** 219, 221
  Drought relief, **1930:** 253, 255, 258, 259, 265, 271, 272, 390
  Establishment, **1932–33:** 135
  Export debenture plan, **1929:** 46
  First meeting, **1929:** 144, 150
  Members, **1931:** 106, 210, 242, 283
  Proposal, **1929:** 38, 117
  Selection and appointment of members, **1929:** 121, 128, 136, 140, 151
  State of the Union message, **1929:** 295
  Wheat sales to China, **1931:** 297, 299, 303, 304
Federal Farm Loan Act, amendments, **1932–33:** 28
Federal farm loan bank system, **1931:** 226, 334, 407, 408
Federal Farm Loan Board, **1929:** 59, 177; **1930:** 258, 259, 265, 265n., 271, 272, 390; **1931:** 226, 303, 305
  Economic recovery, role, **1932–33:** 169
  Farm Loan Commissioner, **1932–33:** 41n., 220, 234, 251, 264, 267ftn.
  Federal land and intermediate credit banks, **1932–33:** 1, 28, 29, 66, 226, 234, 251, 259, 272, 313, 322, 334, 343, 347, 366, 377, 380, 407, 408, 419, 430, 436, 437

Federal Forest Reserves, **1929:** 186
Federal Home Loan Bank Act, **1932–33:** 238, 239
Federal Home Loan Bank Board
  Campaign remarks, **1932–33:** 259, 311, 328, 337, 346, 357, 358, 366, 371, 380
  Chairman, **1932–33:** 264, 267ftn.
  Directors, **1932–33:** 251
  Establishment, **1932–33:** 1, 175, 187, 238, 239, 274
  Expansion, proposed, **1932–33:** 419, 470
  State of the Union message, **1932–33:** 419
Federal International Banking Co., **1932–33:** 358
Federal land banks, **1931:** 343, 407, 430, 436, 437
Federal lands and intermediate credit banks, **1932–33:** 1, 28, 29, 66, 226, 234, 251, 259, 272, 313, 322, 334, 343, 347, 366, 377, 380, 407, 408, 419, 430, 436, 437
Federal Oil Conservation Board, **1929:** 25; **1931:** 99, 100; **1932–33:** 423
Federal Power Commission, **1929:** 295; **1930:** 182, 192n., 195, 218, 236, 240, 390
  Appointments controversy, **1931:** 12, 13, 31
  Interstate power, **1932–33:** 358, 366
  Regulatory functions, **1931:** 430
Federal prison system
  Reform, **1929:** 169, 170
  Relief of overcrowding, **1929:** 181, 182, 183
  State of the Union message, **1929:** 295
Federal prisons.
  See Prisons.
Federal Radio Commission, **1929:** 12, 295; **1930:** 390; **1932–33:** 13
Federal Reserve Act, amendments, **1932–33:** 63, 66
Federal Reserve System, **1929:** 272, 280, 281, 295, 297
  Board of Governors, **1930:** 271, 272, 279, 284, 285, 289, 331, 332; **1931:** 173, 343; **1932–33:** 1, 23, 41n., 123, 220, 251, 264, 267n.
  British cabinet, pressure for change, **1931:** 299
  Campaign remarks, **1932–33:** 322, 347, 358, 366, 378, 380, 382
  Credit, availability, **1931:** 226, 333, 350; **1932–33:** 126, 175, 251, 259, 322, 347, 358, 366, 380, 419
  Credit and interest, **1930:** 76, 77, 144, 311
  Currency hoarding, **1932–33:** 60
  Discount facilities, **1931:** 436, 437; **1932–33:** 1
  District Banking and Industrial Committees, **1930:** 285; **1932–33:** 169, 170, 187, 251, 260, 264, 267, 272, 295, 313, 347
  Eligibility, extension, **1931:** 430
  Gold reserves, **1932–33:** 38, 66, 322
  Governor, New York bank, **1931:** 334
  New York Bank, Governor, **1930:** 402n.
  Staff, **1931:** 305
Federal Shipbuilding and Dry Dock Co., **1932–33:** 91
Federal spending.
  See Budget.

Federal-State relations, **1929:** 185, 186, 286, 292
Federal Trade Commission, **1931:** 100
Federal Triangle development, **1929:** 52n.
Federation for the Support of Jewish Philanthropic
    Societies, **1930:** 393; **1931:** 18n., 332;
    1932–33: 339
Feiker, Frederick M., **1931:** 314
Ferguson, Col. Harley B., **1930:** 223; **1931:** 260, 440
Ferguson, Mrs. John, **1932–33:** 447
Ferrera, Gen. Gregoria, **1931:** 140n.
Fess, Sen. Simeon D., **1931:** 238, 239
Fields, Lew, **1932–33:** 306
Fifteenth Decennial Census, **1930:** 98, 99, 373, 374,
    396
Fifth Avenue Association, **1932–33:** 316
Fifth International Oratorical Contest, **1930:** 340
Filipowicz, Tytus, **1929:** 233n.
Finance.
    See Banking and finance.
Finance Corporation, Reconstruction.
    See Reconstruction Finance Corporation.
Financial institutions.
    See under Banking and finance.
Fine Arts, Commission of, **1932–33:** 423
Finland, **1929:** 3n., 161, 317
    Intergovernmental debts, **1932–33:** 431
    President Pehr Evind Svinhufvud, **1932–33:** 417
Finley, John H., **1932–33:** 4, 176, 406
Fire in Executive office wing, **1929:** 324, 328; **1930:**
    3, 7n., 116
First Annual Patriotic Pilgrimage of the News-
    paper Boys of America, **1930:** 310
First National Bank of Los Angeles, **1930:** 271, 272
First Voters' Donovan-for-Governor League,
    1932–33: 345
Fish hatcheries, transfer to States, **1932–33:** 119
Fishing, **1929:** 35, 180
Fitts, W. S., **1930:** 265n.
Fitzpatrick, John C., **1931:** 59
Flag Association, United States, **1929:** 36
Flag Day, **1932–33:** 196
Fleming, Mrs. Vivian M., **1929:** 223
Fletcher, Sen. Duncan U., **1931:** 238, 239
Fletcher, Henry P., **1930:** 50, 51, 273, 293, 294;
    1931: 122, 270, 411, 412, 446, 449
Fljozdal, Frederick H., **1929:** 270
Flood control, **1930:** 237, 390; **1932–33:** 282, 283,
    353, 421
    See also Rivers, harbors, and waterways.
    Budget message, **1929:** 296
    Increased expenditures, 1931 budget, **1929:** 274
    Mississippi River, **1929:** 84, 85, 196, 197, 253
    State of the Union message, **1929:** 295
Flood Control Act, **1929:** 84, 85
Flood disasters
    China, **1931:** 296, 297
    France, **1930:** 82
Flores, Daniel, **1930:** 47n.

Florida, **1929:** 54, 155
    Roads program, **1931:** 248
Flying Cross, Distinguished, **1932–33:** 247, 252, 266
Foch, Marshal Ferdinand, **1929:** 11
Food ships, **1929:** 275
Forbes, W. Cameron, **1930:** 50, 51
Ford, Henry, **1929:** 57n., 246
Ford, James, **1931:** 314
Ford, Worthington C., **1931:** 59
Ford Museum, Dearborn, Mich., **1932–33:** 278n.
Fordney-McCumber tariff, **1930:** 188
Foreign claims.
    See Claims by and against the United States.
Foreign Consuls, Society of, **1930:** 356
Foreign Debt Commission, World War, **1932–33:**
    407
Foreign debts, **1929:** 163, 295, 296
Foreign policy, **1929:** 35, 161, 275, 295, 314
    Statement, **1932–33:** 434
Foreign relations, message to Congress, **1931:** 433
Foreign Service of the United States, **1929:** 295
Foreign trade.
    See Trade.
Foreign Trade Council, National, **1932–33:** 143
Forest protection, **1929:** 296
Forest Service, **1931:** 189, 190; **1932–33:** 423
Forests, national, **1931:** 189, 190
Fort, Repr. Franklin W., **1930:** 187; **1932–33:** 264,
    267ftn.
Fort Monroe, Va., **1931:** 360
Fort Russell, Wyo., **1929:** 302
Fort Wayne, Ind., **1932–33:** 326
Forum on House Construction, **1932–33:** 180
Foster, T. J., **1932–33:** 180
Fostoria, Ohio, **1932–33:** 346
Foulkes, Rev. William Hiram, **1930:** 248
Founders' Day, **1932–33:** 330
4-H Clubs, **1929:** 26; **1930:** 389
Fourth Pan American Commercial Conference,
    1931: 347
44-hour workweek for Government employees,
    1931: 62, 201
France, **1929:** 3n., 161, 163, 229n., 296, 317
    American Bar Association convention, guests,
    1930: 276, 277
    Bastille Day, **1930:** 232; **1931:** 261; **1932–33:** 229
    Claims against U.S., **1930:** 12, 31
    Counselor to U.S. Embassy, **1930:** 11n.
    DAR Pilgrimage to Paris, **1932–33:** 301
    Dirigible *R-101*, crash, **1930:** 317n.
    Disarmament, **1930:** 94n., 112, 113, 117, 143,
    221, 341; **1931:** 89, 430
    Financial bloc, possibility of, **1930:** 402
    Flood disaster, **1930:** 82
    Foreign Minister Aristide Briand, **1931:** 89
    Former Ambassador to U.S., **1932–33:** 236
    Former Foreign Minister, **1932–33:** 74
    Intergovernmental debts, **1932–33:** 228n., 395n.,
    431

France — *continued*
  International Exposition of Colonial and Overseas Countries, **1931:** 176
  Joint statement, **1931:** 371
  Moratorium proposal, acceptance, **1931:** 251, 252
  President Albert Lebrun, **1932–33:** 222, 229
  President Gaston Doumergue, **1930:** 82, 232, 283; **1931:** 4, 47n., 176
  President Paul Doumer, **1931:** 261; **1932–33:** 74, 149, 150
  Prime Minister Pierre Laval, **1931:** 266, 267, 343, 367, 368, 369, 370, 371, 377, 433
  Prime Minister André Tardieu, **1932–33:** 150
  Submarine *Prométhée*, sinking, **1932–33:** 222
  Transatlantic flights, **1930:** 282, 283, 287
  U.S. relations with, **1931:** 170, 364
France-America Committee, **1929:** 81n.
France-America Society, **1931:** 47; **1932–33:** 42
Francis, William T., **1929:** 152
Franklin Society, International Benjamin, **1932–33:** 18, 455
Free and Accepted Masons, District of Columbia, **1932–33:** 41n.
Freedman's Hospital, **1932–33:** 423
Freedom of the seas, **1929:** 275
Freeman-Thomas, Freeman, **1931:** 19
Freeport, Ill., **1932–33:** 379
Frelinghuysen, Joseph S., **1930:** 187
French, Daniel Chester, **1931:** 345
French Backgrounds of American Civilization, Lafayette College Conference on, **1932–33:** 166
French Company of Marine and Commerce, **1930:** 12
Frey, John B., **1930:** 247n.
Frohman, Daniel, **1932–33:** 474
Frost, Henry D., **1932–33:** 174
Fruit fly, Mediterranean, **1929:** 54, 155
Fuad I, King of Egypt, **1930:** 96; **1931:** 114; **1932–33:** 97
Fuller, Gov. Alvan T., **1930:** 233
Fuller, Gen. Ben H., **1930:** 253; **1931:** 219
Furlough plan for Federal employees, **1932–33:** 119, 126, 127, 132, 133, 137, 146, 175, 198, 199, 208, 212, 240, 307, 337, 419, 421

Gadsden, Philip H., **1929:** 284
Gadsden Purchase coinage bill, veto, **1930:** 121
Galston, Clarence G., **1929:** 37n.
Game Protective and Propagation Association, American, **1930:** 388
Games, III, Olympic Winter, **1931:** 98
Games of the Tenth Olympiad, **1931:** 241
Gannett, Frank E., **1930:** 122
Gardiner, William Howard, **1931:** 385, 390n., 392

Gardner, Archibald K., **1929:** 37n.
Garfield, Abram, **1931:** 314
Garfield, James R., **1929:** 241, 242; **1930:** 261; **1932–33:** 425
Garner, Repr. John N., **1932–33:** 32, 183n., 217, 378, 380, 387
Garner-Wagner bill.
  See Emergency Relief and Construction Act of 1932.
Garsaud, Marcel, **1931:** 12, 13, 31n.
Garvan, Francis P., **1929:** 200
Gary, Ind., **1932–33:** 376
Gas Association, American, **1929:** 285n.
Gas pipeline, **1931:** 1
Gasoline, Federal tax, **1932–33:** 421
Gassaway, Gerrish, **1932–33:** 41n.
Gatty, Harold, **1931:** 247, 253; **1932–33:** 266
General Accounting Office
  Assistant Comptroller General, **1931:** 92
  Comptroller General, **1932–33:** 423
General Disarmament Conference, Geneva, **1931:** 37, 168, 239, 371, 430, 433, 445, 446, 449, 453; **1932–33:** 3, 23, 25, 111, 112, 135, 204, 205, 206, 304, 380, 395, 407, 419, 431, 434, 441
General Federation of Women's Clubs, **1930:** 250; **1931:** 314; **1932–33:** 41n.
General Grant National Park, Calif., **1932–33:** 436n.
General Land Office, **1930:** 342, 343; **1932–33:** 423
General Motors Corp., **1932–33:** 404
General Pact for the Renunciation of War, **1929:** 1, 94, 161, 184, 229, 275, 295
General Supply Committee, **1932–33:** 423
General Treaty of Inter-American Arbitration, **1931:** 433
Genesee, Society of the, **1930:** 122; **1931:** 51; **1932–33:** 30, 445
Geneva Naval Conference, **1929:** 48n.; **1930:** 112, 113, 115
Geodetic Survey, Coast and, **1932–33:** 423
Geographic Society, National, **1932–33:** 203
Geological Congress, International, **1931:** 25
Geological Survey, **1929:** 227; **1930:** 3; **1932–33:** 423
George Rogers Clark Sesquicentennial Commission, **1932–33:** 423
George V, King (United Kingdom), **1929:** 107; **1930:** 8, 109, 175, 317; **1931:** 216
Geraud, Andre, **1930:** 119
German Evangelical Church, **1931:** 363
Germany, **1929:** 161, 176, 317
  Chancellor Heinrich Brüning, **1931:** 259ftn., 266, 267, 327
  Financial crisis, **1931:** 236, 259, 264
  General Disarmament Conference, participation, **1932–33:** 304
  International Fur Trade Exhibition and Congress, **1930:** 18

Germany — *continued*
Lausanne agreement, **1932–33:** 228n.
Mixed Claims Commission, United States and, **1930:** 74
Moratorium on intergovernmental debts, **1931:** 238, 239, 251, 252, 255, 259, 350, 430, 433, 450, Supp. I
Niobe, sinking, **1932–33:** 255
President Paul von Hindenburg.
See Hindenburg, Paul von (President of Germany).
Unemployment, **1930:** 315
U.S. Ambassador to, **1932–33:** 378
U.S. Army of Occupation, settlement of costs, **1930:** 74
War reparations, **1929:** 97, 99, 109, 125, 126, 295
Weimar Constitution, anniversary, **1930:** 264
World Power Conference, **1930:** 192
World War veterans, **1931:** 171
Gest, Morris, **1931:** 192
"Get out the vote" drive, **1932–33:** 96
Gettysburg Battlefield, address, **1930:** 170
Gibbons, James Cardinal, **1932–33:** 263
Gibson, Harvey D., **1932–33:** 85, 351n.
Gibson, Hugh, **1929:** 28, 34, 48, 61; **1930:** 10n., 11n.; **1931:** 89; **1932–33:** 23, 25
Giddings, Franklin Henry, **1931:** 222
Giddings, Joshua Reed, **1932–33:** 302
Gifford, Walter S., **1931:** 294, 295, 299, 303, 324, 360, 387, 388, 403, 436n.; **1932–33:** 215, 260, 261, 294, 337ftn.
Gilbert, Cass, **1929:** 291
Gilmore, Eugene A., **1929:** 84
Ginder, Lt. Comdr. Samuel P., **1930:** 398
Girls' Service League of America, **1931:** 161
Glacier National Park, **1930:** 153
Glacier Park, Montana, **1932–33:** 201
Glass, Sen. Carter, **1931:** 238, 239; **1932–33:** 239n.
Glass-Steagall Act.
See Federal Reserve Act, amendments.
Glassford, Gen. Pelham D., **1932–33:** 246n.
Glendale, Calif., **1932–33:** 394
Glenn, J. Lyles, **1929:** 37n.
Glenn, Sen. Otis F., **1931:** 234
Gloucester, Mass., **1929:** 132
Glover, Warren I., **1931:** 200, 201
Goethe Society of America, **1932–33:** 129
Gold accumulations, domestic, **1931:** 238, 239, 303
Gold standard, **1931:** 320, 371, 387, 389, 420, 436; **1932–33:** 38, 41, 66, 322, 337, 347, 377, 378, 380, 387, 431, 457, 465
"Golden Jubilee of Light," **1929:** 57n., 157, 245n., 246
Goldsborough bill, **1932–33:** 146ftn.
Goldstein, Israel, **1932–33:** 142
Gomez, Manuel, **1932–33:** 214
Gompers, Samuel, **1931:** 101; **1932–33:** 366
Good, James W., **1929:** 178, 196, 197, 283

Goodrich, James P., **1929:** 241, 242
Goodyear, A. Conger, **1932–33:** 153
Gordon, Charles, **1930:** 130n.
Gordon, George A., **1930:** 11n.
Gordon Bennett International Balloon Races and Aerial Carnival, **1930:** 280
Gorguloff, Paul, **1932–33:** 149n.
Gottheil Medal, **1930:** 155
Gould, Kenneth M., **1932–33:** 277
Gould, Olive J., **1932–33:** 333
Government departments and agencies.
See also Federal departments and agencies.
Aviation stations, **1930:** 261
Budget message, **1930:** 391; **1931:** 432
Consolidation and reorganization, **1931:** 430, 453, 454
Drought relief, **1930:** 253, 255, 261, 265, 271, 276
Economy conferences, **1931:** 173, 200, 201, 211, 213, 219
Government expenditures, reductions, **1930:** 236, 237, 273, 274
Law enforcement, administrative reforms, **1930:** 17
Memorandums
Fiscal year 1932, expenditures, **1931:** 269
Unemployment relief, **1931:** 413
Public buildings projects, **1930:** 3, 7, 127, 158n., 347, 357, 391, 397, 418; **1931:** 67, 177, 181, 184, 277, 278, 297, 303, 307, 319, 387, 388, 394, 432
Unemployment statistics, development, **1930:** 244, 247
Government employees, **1929:** 5, 295
See also Federal employees.
Administration employment policy, **1931:** 200, 201, 403, 413
Contract public works, **1930:** 347
District of Columbia, **1930:** 373
44-hour workweek, **1931:** 62, 201
Holiday weekends, **1931:** 446, 448
Memorial Day holiday, **1930:** 165
Merit employment system, **1931:** 88
Patronage investigation, **1930:** 87, 88
Pay increase, **1930:** 55, 65, 66, 67
Pensions, **1931:** 358, 359, 432
Public works, **1931:** 218, 283, 284, 297, 302
Retirement fund, **1930:** 59, 60, 65, 66, 67
U.S. Navy, reduction in force, **1930:** 321, 322
Wage equalization, **1930:** 391
Governors.
See under State and local government.
Governors' Conference, **1930:** 215; **1932–33:** 137
Governors' conference on drought relief, **1930:** 258, 259, 261, 265, 270, 301, 390
Grace, Eugene G., **1929:** 193n.
Grace Line, **1932–33:** 91
Graf-Zeppelin, **1929:** 174, 188, 189
Grafton, W. Va., **1932–33:** 360

Graham, Edwin C., **1932–33:** 264
Graham, Repr. George S., **1931:** 54, 55, 250
Grand Army of the Republic, **1931:** 229n.
Grand Jurors, Association of, **1929:** 87
Grand Street Boys' American Legion Post No.
    1025, **1932–33:** 51
Grandi, Dino, **1931:** 89, 266, 411, 433
Grange, National, **1930:** 250, 259n.; **1931:** 314
Grant, Ulysses S., **1931:** 166
Grant, Lt. Col. U.S., III, **1932–33:** 353
Grasshopper infestations, **1931:** 275
Graves, Maj. Ernest, **1929:** 125n.
Great Britain.
  See United Kingdom.
Great Lakes, **1930:** 190, 223, 225
Great Lakes-St. Lawrence River Deep Waterway,
    1929: 253; **1930:** 132, 223; **1931:** 383, 433;
    1932–33: 219, 226, 235, 259, 273, 322, 470
Great War, **1930:** 119, 133, 297, 314, 408
Greece, **1929:** 3n., 161
  Extradition treaty, **1931:** 433
  Intergovernmental debts, **1932–33:** 431
  President Alexander Zaimis, **1932–33:** 95
Greeley, A. H., **1932–33:** 68
Greeley, Col. William B., **1929:** 241, 242
Green, William, **1930:** 315, 383, 384; **1932–33:** 41n.
Greenfield Village, **1929:** 246n.
Greensburg, Ind., **1931:** 225
Greensfelder, A. P., **1931:** 314
Greenspan Brothers, warehouse, N.J., **1932–33:** 315
Gresham Junction, Ill., **1932–33:** 376
Greve, W. L., **1931:** 306
Gridiron Club, **1929:** 35, 314; **1930:** 133, 408; **1931:**
    155, 439; **1932–33:** 120, 424
Gries, John M., **1930:** 249, 250; **1931:** 314
Grimm, Peter, **1931:** 48
Grocers Association, National Retail, **1931:** 254
Grove, Col. Walter E., **1931:** 419
Grubb, William I., **1931:** 27
Guam, military value, **1931:** 219
Guatemala, **1929:** 161, 295, 326
  Boundary dispute, **1931:** 433
  President Jorge Ubico, **1932–33:** 300
Guggiari, José P., **1931:** 186
Gullion, Edmund, **1930:** 340n.
Gunther, Franklin Mott, **1930:** 25
Gurgél do Amaral, S., **1930:** 185
Gustaf V, King of Sweden, **1930:** 104; **1931:** 230
Gustavus Adolphus Tricentennial Festival, **1932–**
  33: 381
Guthrie, William D., **1931:** 47; **1932–33:** 42

H. J. Heinz International Radio Banquet, **1930:**
  358
Haakon VII, King (Norway), **1929:** 168; **1930:** 252
Haarlem House, **1931:** 245

Haas, Harry J., **1932–33:** 41n.
Haeberle, Daniel, **1930:** 63
Haig, Robert Murray, **1932–33:** 292
Haile Selassie I, Emperor of Ethiopia, **1930:** 120,
    350; **1931:** 93; **1932–33:** 241
Haiti, **1929:** 3n., 295, 304, 305
  American High Commissioner, **1930:** 38, 39, 93,
    349
  Committee for the Study of Education in, **1932–**
    33: 135
  Educational institutions, **1930:** 50, 51
  President Louis Borno, **1930:** 1, 85, 93
  President's Commission for the Study and Re-
    view of Conditions in the Republic of,
    1930: 38, 39, 50, 51, 85, 92, 93, 97, 261
  Temporary President Eugene Roy, **1930:** 85n.
  United States Commission on Education in,
    1930: 50, 51n.
  U.S. withdrawal, **1930:** 38, 39, 85, 92, 97, 390;
    1931: 433
Haitian Commission.
  See President's Commission for the Study and
    Review of Conditions in the Republic of
    Haiti.
Hale, Repr. Fletcher, **1931:** 375
Hall, A. V., **1930:** 130n.
Hall, L. C., **1930:** 189n.
Hall, William E., **1932–33:** 178
Hall of Fame, **1929:** 70; **1930:** 186; **1931:** 187
Hallanan, Walter S., **1931:** 224
Hamaguchi, Yuko, **1930:** 341
Hamden, Ohio, **1932–33:** 357
Hamilton, Ohio, **1932–33:** 357
Hammill, Gov. John, **1930:** 265n.
Hammond, John Hays, **1931:** 392
Hammond, Ogden, **1929:** 44n.; **1930:** 409n.
Handicapped persons
  American Braille Press, **1932–33:** 478
  Matilda Ziegler Magazine for the Blind, **1932–**
    33: 70
  New York Association for the Blind, **1932–33:** 4
  Veterans, **1932–33:** 51, 365, 432
Hanna, Archbishop Edward J., **1931:** 417
Hanna, John H., **1929:** 285n.
Hanna, Matthew E., **1931:** 116
Harbors.
  See Rivers, harbors, and waterways.
Harbord, James G., **1931:** 396
Hard, William, **1929:** 144
Harding, Warren G., **1930:** 244, 247, 405; **1931:**
    228; **1932–33:** 346
Harding Memorial, dedication, **1931:** 228
Harmon, Leonard J., **1931:** 166
Harney Lake, Oreg., **1930:** 179
Harrah, Charles J., **1930:** 28
Harris, George S., **1932–33:** 264
Harris, J. W., **1932–33:** 264
Harris, Sen. William J., **1931:** 238, 239

Harrison, Curtis, **1930:** 297
Harrison, Fairfax, **1929:** 281n.
Harrison, Floyd R., **1930:** 258; **1931:** 303, 305
Harrison, George L., **1930:** 402n.
Harrison, Harvey T., **1930:** 265n.
Harrison, Sen. Pat, **1931:** 238, 239
Harrison, Shelby M., **1929:** 318
Harrison, William Henry, **1931:** 65
Hart, Merwin K., **1929:** 303
Harvey, James A., **1931:** 123
Hastings, George A., **1932–33:** 171
Hatfield, Sen. Henry D., **1931:** 224; **1932–33:** 346
Hawaii, Governor of, **1929:** 48
Hawks, Mary G., **1931:** 340
Hawley, Repr. Willis C., **1929:** 267n.; **1931:** 238, 239; **1932–33:** 221
Hawley-Smoot tariff.
    See Tariff legislation.
Haycroft, Julius E., **1931:** 70
Haym Salomon Monument Committee, **1931:** 77
Hays, Warner S., **1932–33:** 41n., 296
Head, Walter H., **1930:** 134; **1931:** 313; **1932–33:** 165, 244
Health, Second Pan American Conference of Directors of, **1931:** 144
Health Association, American Public, **1932–33:** 348, 358
Health and medical care
    American Indians, **1930:** 3, 5
    American Public Health Association, **1932–33:** 348
    Cancer research, **1931:** 42
    Christmas seals, **1931:** 424; **1932–33:** 408
    Communicable diseases, **1930:** 390
    Conferences on child health and protection, **1932–33:** 5, 135, 171, 184, 259, 311, 312, 328, 380, 383, 441
    County health units, **1932–33:** 348
    Diphtheria Prevention Commission, **1932–33:** 8
    Drought areas, **1930:** 265, 266
    Economic depression, effects, **1931:** 297, 298, 430; **1932–33:** 2, 294, 337, 358, 380, 383, 419
    Government agencies, consolidation, **1931:** 453, 454
    Jewish Hospital of Brooklyn, N.Y., **1932–33:** 355
    Leisure time, **1931:** 134
    Narcotics and drugs, **1930:** 17, 61, 135, 193, 329
    National Hospital Day, **1930:** 156; **1932–33:** 140
    National Pharmacy Week, message, **1931:** 352
    Navy medical officers, selection, **1931:** 285
    Prisons, **1930:** 165
    Tubercle bacillus, 50th anniversary of detection, **1932–33:** 89
    Veterans, **1930:** 168, 173, 174, 200n., 202, 203, 206, 222; **1931:** 63, 72, 78
    Youth, **1930:** 81, 134. 213, 369, 376, 382, 389, 390; **1931:** 22, 137, 149, 182, 206, 231, 246, 321, 430

Health Association, American Child, **1930:** 204, 361
Health Nursing, National Organization for Public, **1931:** 391
Health and Protection
    Indiana Conference on Child, **1931:** 22
    New Jersey Conference on Child, **1931:** 137
    White House Conference on Child, **1930:** 204n., 369, 376, 389; **1931:** 22, 137, 182, 206, 231, 246, 321
Health Service, Bureau of Public, **1930:** 265; **1931:** 103, 297, 298
    See also Public Health Service, Bureau of the.
Hearst, William R., **1929:** 188n.; **1932–33:** 366, 378, 390
Heath, Ferry K., **1930:** 158
Hebblethwaite, R. C., **1931:** 336
Hebrew Medal, American, **1932–33:** 406
Hecht, George J., **1931:** 321
Heflin, Sen. J. Thomas, **1929:** 46; **1931:** 82n.
Heimann, Henry H., **1932–33:** 41n.
Heinz, Howard, **1930:** 358
Helium, exports, **1930:** 321, 323
Hellenic Republic.
    See Greece.
Henderson, Arthur, **1931:** 89
Henning, Arthur Sears, **1930:** 240
Hennrich, Killian J., **1932–33:** 312
Henry, Thomas P., **1930:** 130n.
Henry, Ill., **1932–33:** 376
Hepburn, Rear Adm. Arthur J., **1932–33:** 25n.
Herbert Schiff Memorial Trophy, **1930:** 398; **1931:** 435
Herrick, Myron T., **1929:** 20, 21, 24, 28, 29
Herrick, Parmely, **1929:** 20n.
Herridge, W. D., **1932–33:** 235n.
Hert, Mrs. Alvin T., **1932–33:** 328n.
Hibben, John Grier, **1930:** 62; **1932–33:** 151, 202
Highway Conference, Second Pan American, **1929:** 179
Highway construction programs, **1932–33:** 14, 175, 233, 421
Highway Education, Pan American Confederation for, **1929:** 179
Highway Safety, Third National Conference on Street and, **1930:** 130, 166
Highways, **1929:** 179, 285n., 295
    See also Streets and highways.
Hill, John Warren, **1930:** 220n.
Hill, Thomas L., **1929:** 187n.
Hilles, Charles D., **1930:** 163; **1931:** 348
Hindenburg, Paul von (President of Germany), **1929:** 176; **1930:** 235, 264; **1931:** 255, 289; **1932–33:** 255, 319, 378
Hines, Gen. Frank T., **1929:** 321; **1930:** 200, 202, 203, 206, 222, 226, 227, 331; **1931:** 63n., 79, 80, 147, 148, 453; **1932–33:** 225n.
Hirohito, Emperor (Japan), **1929:** 236, 331; **1931:** 146; **1932–33:** 139, 327

Hoarding of currency, **1932–33:** 36, 38, 41, 48, 49, 60, 66, 71, 73, 80, 81, 119, 126, 272, 322, 419

Hobart, Jennie, **1932–33:** 370

Hobbs, S. F., **1931:** 260, 440

Hodges, Gilbert T., **1931:** 227; **1932–33:** 41n.

Holden, Hale, **1929:** 281n.

Holderby, William Matthew, **1931:** 231

Holland, Rush L., **1932–33:** 41n.

Holloway, Gov. W. J., **1930:** 270

Holmes, Justice Oliver Wendell, **1931:** 95; **1932–33:** 15, 75

Holz, Julius, **1930:** 281

Home Building and Home Ownership, White House Conference on, **1930:** 249, 250, 302; **1931:** 149, 313, 314, 344, 395, 425; **1932–33:** 99, 135, 180, 184, 259, 311, 328, 358, 380

Home Economics Association, American, **1930:** 250; **1931:** 314

Home Loan Bank Board, Federal.
   See Federal Home Loan Bank Board.

Home loan discount bank system, **1931:** 407, 408, 411, 425, 430, 436, 437

Home Missions Council, **1929:** 62n.

Homes in America, Better.
   See Better Homes in America.

Homes Week, Better.
   See Better Homes Week.

Homma, Kiyoshi, **1932–33:** 327

Honduras, **1929:** 16, 295
   Boundary dispute, **1931:** 433
   President Vicente Mejía Colindres, **1932–33:** 299
   Revolt, **1931:** 140

Hoover, Herbert, Jr., **1930:** 273n.

Hoover, Lou Henry, **1929:** 252n.; **1930:** 195n., 267n., 277n.; **1931:** 366n.; **1932–33:** 43

Hoover Dam, Nev., **1932–33:** 394, 396

"Hoover Day in Madison," **1929:** 180

Hoover Gold Medal, **1930:** 108

Hope, Walter, **1929:** 256; **1931:** 67, 68

Horine, Homer N., **1931:** 49

Horthy, Nicholas von, **1932–33:** 254

Horton, Gov. Henry H., **1930:** 265n.

Hospital, Charlotte Hungerford Memorial, **1930:** 411

Hospital Congress, International, **1929:** 124

Hospital Day, National, **1930:** 156; **1932–33:** 140

Hotel Exposition, National, **1931:** 401

Houghton, Alanson B., **1930:** 35

House, Edward M., **1931:** 280; **1932–33:** 434

House Construction, Forum on, **1932–33:** 180

House of Representatives.
   See under Congress.

Housing
   Better Homes Week, **1932–33:** 134
   Homeownership, message, **1932–33:** 161

Housing — *continued*
   Mortgages, **1931:** 314, 344, 407, 408, 425, 436, 437; **1932–33:** 1, 161, 238, 239, 251, 264, 272, 328, 337, 346, 357, 358, 371, 380, 470
   Slum clearance program, **1932–33:** 251, 311
   Taxation, **1932–33:** 137, 292
   White House conference, **1931:** 149, 313, 314, 344, 395, 425
   White House Conference on Home Building and Home Ownership, **1932–33:** 99, 135, 180, 184, 259, 311, 328, 358, 380

Housing Association, National, **1931:** 314

Houston, George H., **1932–33:** 264

Hoving, Johannes, **1932–33:** 381

Howard, J. Gordon, **1929:** 78n.

Howard University, **1932–33:** 191, 423

Howell, Sen. Robert B., **1929:** 214

Hoyt, Paul D., **1932–33:** 401n.

Hubbard, O. S., **1930:** 427n.

Huber family, **1930:** 63

Hubert, Benjamin F., **1930:** 51n.

Hubert, Conrad, **1931:** 396

Hudson, Wis., **1932–33:** 379

Hudtloff, Paul, **1932–33:** 343

Huff, Clarence E., **1930:** 259

Hughes, Charles E., **1929:** 67; **1930:** 405; **1932–33:** 335n., 358

Hughes, Adm. Charles F., **1930:** 145, 146, 296

Hughes, Wilburn P., **1929:** 248

Huguenot Memorial Association, **1932–33:** 174

Hull, Sen. Cordell, **1931:** 238, 239

Humphrey, A. L., **1930:** 318

Hundred Year Club of New York, **1932–33:** 85

Hungary, **1929:** 161
   Intergovernmental debts, **1932–33:** 431
   Radiotelegraphic service, **1932–33:** 254
   U.S. Minister to, **1930:** 303

Hungerford, Charlotte, Memorial Hospital, **1930:** 411

Hunt, Edward Eyre, **1931:** 54, 55

Hunter, J. K. **1931:** 410

Huntington, W. Va., **1931:** 224; **1932–33:** 346

Hurley, E. N., **1930:** 190, 272

Hurley, Patrick J., **1929:** 6, 302, 304; **1930:** 129, 223, 253, 254, 331, 332, 395; **1931:** 73, 82n., 173, 211, 212, 324, 378, 379; **1932–33:** 34, 187n., 246n., 403, 449n.

Hurricane, Puerto Rico, **1932–33:** 310

Hurricane disasters
   Dominican Republic, **1930:** 286, 291, 299
   Porto Rico, **1930:** 20

Huston, Claudius, **1929:** 194

Hutcheson, John R. **1930:** 272

Hutchings, William J., **1931:** 207

Hyde, Arthur M., **1929:** 46n., 61, 128, 136, 155, 241, 281; **1930:** 253, 255, 258, 259, 259n., 265n., 271, 272, 276, 331, 332, 395; **1931:** 15, 45, 50, 120, 121, 181, 189, 190, 211, 213, 275, 324; **1932–33:** 76, 78, 264, 449n.

Hyde, Herbert K., **1931:** 211, 277
Hydraulic laboratory, **1930:** 158

Ibáñez del Campo, Carlos (President of Chile), **1929:** 167, 207, 255; **1930:** 100
Ibero-American Exposition, **1930:** 201
Iceland, **1929:** 161, 270
    1,000th Anniversary of the Althing, **1932–33:** 135
Idaho, **1929:** 185n.
    Lincoln's Birthday, message, **1932–33:** 45n.
Ihlder, John, **1931:** 314
Il Progresso Italo-Americano, **1930:** 360
Illinois
    Drought relief, **1930:** 258, 259, 271, 272
    Great Lakes-St. Lawrence Deep Waterway, **1932–33:** 235
    Governor, **1930:** 265n., 271, 272, 331, 332; **1931:** 233
    Pipeline, gas, **1931:** 1
    President's campaign, **1932–33:** 321, 376, 377, 379
    President's visit, **1931:** 232, 233, 234, 235
    Roads program, **1931:** 248
    Unemployment relief, **1930:** 331, 332
Illinois River, **1930:** 266
Illiteracy, Advisory Committee on, **1932–33:** 135
I'm Alone Commission, **1929:** 54
Immigration, **1929:** 12, 13, 295; **1930:** 22, 288, 311, 380, 390; **1931:** 113, 189, 226, 430
    Bureau of, **1931:** 9, 53, 348; **1932–33:** 423
    Restriction, **1932–33:** 259, 328, 337, 346, 347, 358, 376, 388
Imperial Order of the Dragon, **1932–33:** 47
Imports.
    See also Tariffs; Trade.
    Revenues, **1930:** 273, 274, 293, 295
    Tariffs, **1930:** 188
    Union of Soviet Socialist Republics, **1930:** 244, 380
Inaugural address, **1929:** 1
Income taxes, **1932–33:** 186, 450
India, **1929:** 161, 317
Indian Affairs, Bureau of, **1930:** 3, 5, 391; **1932–33:** 423
    Office of, **1929:** 8
Indiana
    Drought relief, **1930:** 258, 259, 265n., 272n.
    Great Lakes-St. Lawrence Deep Waterway, **1932–33:** 235
    Governor, **1931:** 22, 226
    Lincoln's Birthday, message, **1932–33:** 45n.
    President's campaign, **1932–33:** 326, 357, 358, 376
    President's visit, **1931:** 225, 226
Indiana Conference on Child Health and Protection, **1931:** 22

Indiana Republican Editorial Association, **1931:** 226
Indianapolis, Ind., **1932–33:** 358
Indians, American, **1929:** 296; **1930:** 3, 5, 65; **1931:** 65, 75; **1932–33:** 136, 458
Industrial Conference Board, National, **1932–33:** 41n.
Industries, Conference of Major, **1930:** 335
Industries, Conference of Smaller, **1931:** 287
Industry, **1929:** 280, 281, 284, 285, 297
    See also Business and industry.
Ingalls, David S., **1931:** 219n.; **1932–33:** 337
Inland Waterways Commission, **1929:** 250
Inland Waterways Corporation, **1932–33:** 423
Insley-Casper, Mrs. R., **1930:** 356
Institute of American Meat Packers, **1930:** 335n.
Institute of Architects, American, **1929:** 51
Institute of Electrical Engineers, American, **1929:** 52n.
Institute of Mining and Metallurgical Engineers, American, **1929:** 52n.
Institute of Pacific Relations, **1929:**261
Institute of Paper Chemistry, **1931:** 322
Institute of Steel Construction, American, **1929:** 278
Insurance, life, **1929:** 217; **1932–33:** 12, 358
Insurance companies, investments, **1930:** 76, 77, 249, 250
Insurance Presidents, Association of Life, **1930:** 250; **1931:** 314; **1932–33:** 41n.
Intellectual Cooperation, National Council of, **1931:** 52
Interdepartmental Committee on Marine Mail Contracts, **1929:** 104, 202n., 295
Interdepartmental Mail Contract Committee, **1932–33:** 135
Interest rates, fall of, **1929:** 272
Intergovernmental debts, **1932–33:** 111, 112, 228, 259, 322, 337, 358, 377, 378, 395, 396, 400, 405, 407, 419, 431, 434, 452, 454, 465
Interior, Department of the
    Appropriations, **1930:** 3, 395; **1932–33:** 133
    Assistant Secretary, **1932–33:** 201n.
    Bureau of Indian Affairs, **1930:** 3, 5, 391; **1932–33:** 423
    Bureau of Reclamation, **1931:** 453; **1932–33:** 423
    Employees, **1932–33:** 132
    General Land Office, **1930:** 342, 343
    National Park Service, **1930:** 153
    Oil shale lands controversy, **1930:** 342, 343
    Pensions Bureau, transfer to Veterans' Administration, **1930:** 226, 227
    Reorganization, **1931:** 430
    Reorganization, proposed, **1932–33:** 423
    Secretary of (Ray L. Wilbur), **1929:** 140, 142, 164, 241, 242; **1930:** 3, 5, 326, 327, 342, 343, 376; **1931:** 72, 75, 100, 120, 324; **1932–33:** 119n., 167n., 232n., 392, 394, 411n., 458

Interior, Department of the — *continued*
  Virgin Islands, administration, **1931:** 39, 41, 111,
    112
Intermediate credit banks.
  See Federal land and intermediate credit banks.
Intermediate Credit System, **1930:** 265
Internal Revenue, Bureau of, **1929:** 304n.; **1930:**
    266
Internal revenue tax.
  See Taxes.
International Advertising Association, **1929:** 103
International Association of Lions Clubs, **1932–33:**
    41n.
International Association of Chiefs of Police, **1931:**
    355
International Association of Road Congresses, Per-
    manent, **1930:** 49
International Benjamin Franklin Society, **1932–33:**
    18, 455
International Boundary Commission, United
    States and Mexico, **1931:** 433
International Chamber of Commerce, **1931:** 162,
    168, 218, 226
International Christian Endeavor, **1929:** 143; **1930:**
    257; **1931:** 38, 262
International Civitan, **1932–33:** 41n.
International Conference for the Codification of
    International Law, **1930:** 86
International Conference on Safety of Life at Sea,
    1929: 17
International conference on silver, possibility of,
    1931: 215, 218
International conference on trade, possibility of,
    1931: 313, 315
International Congress of Building Societies, **1931:**
    293
International cooperation.
  See also Economy, international; London Naval
    Conference; Treaties and other interna-
    tional agreements.
  American Society of Newspaper Editors,
    remarks, **1930:** 119
  Arbitration and conciliation treaties, **1930:** 365,
    390
  Canada-United States dam investigation, **1930:**
    42
  Consultive pact, possibility of, **1930:** 94, 112, 113,
    119, 183, 184, 230
  Daughters of the American Revolution, address,
    1930: 115
  Financial bloc, possibility of, **1930:** 402
  Gridiron Club, address, **1930:** 133
  International Chamber of Commerce, **1931:** 162,
    168, 218, 226
  Kellogg-Briand Pact, **1930:** 115, 119, 133, 314,
    365, 405; **1931:** 168, 371, 433
  League of Nations, **1930:** 365; **1931:** 103, 433
  Silver conference, possibility of, **1931:** 215, 218

International cooperation — *continued*
  State of the Union message, **1931:** 430
  World Court, **1930:** 115, 119, 133, 365, 383, 385,
    390, 405; **1931:** 191n., 433
  World trade conference, possibility of, **1931:** 313,
    315
International Exposition of Colonial and Overseas
    Countries, **1931:** 176
International Exposition at Seville, **1930:** 201;
    1931: 434
International Falls, Minn., **1929:** 129
International Fur Trade Exhibition and Congress,
    1930: 18
International Geological Congress, **1931:** 25
International Hospital Congress, **1929:** 124
International Joint Commission, United States and
    Canada, **1929:** 53, 84
International Justice
  American Conference of Institutions for the
    Establishment of, **1932–33:** 141
  Court of, **1929:** 1, 12, 295, 306
  Permanent Court of, **1929:** 1, 295, 306
International law, 275
International Livestock Show, **1930:** 389
International Load Lines Convention, **1931:** 57
International Longfellow Society, **1929:** 79
International Monetary and Economic Confer-
    ence.
  See World economic conference.
International Narcotic Education Association,
    1930: 61; **1932–33:** 52
International Niagara Board, Special, **1931:** 37
International Peace Garden, **1932–33:** 227
International Save the Children Fund, **1932–33:**
    447
International Settlement, Shanghai, China, **1932–
    33:** 34
International Telephone and Telegraph Corpora-
    tion, **1929:** 32
International Water Commission, United States
    and Mexico, **1931:** 11
Interoceanic Canal Board, **1929:** 125; **1931:** 185;
    1932–33: 135, 423
Interracial Cooperation, Commission on, **1930:** 106
Interstate Commerce Commission, **1929:** 80, 125,
    315; **1930:** 3, 6, 249, 428, 429; **1931:** 1,
    334n., 430, 436, 437, 442
  Building, cornerstone laying, **1932–33:** 427
  Railroad corporate reorganization, approval,
    1932–33: 448
  Railroad reconstruction, conferences, **1932–33:**
    87, 88
  Rates, **1932–33:** 76
  Transportation laws, reform, **1932–33:** 1, 358
Interstate Conference of Legislators, **1932–33:** 461
Intracoastal Canal Association of Louisiana and
    Texas, **1931:** 399
Investment Bankers Association of America,
    1932–33: 41n.

Iowa
    Agricultural relief, **1931:** 275, 378
    Child health and protection conference, **1932–33:** 5n.
    Drought relief, **1930:** 258, 259, 265n., 272n.
    Governor, **1932–33:** 313
    President's campaign, **1932–33:** 321, 322, 323, 324, 325
    Republican National Committeeman, **1932–33:** 325
    State University of, **1930:** 217
Ireland, Maj. Gen. Merritte W., **1931:** 181
Irigoyen, Hipolito (President of Argentina), **1929:** 86, 234, 322; **1930:** 111
Irish Free State, **1929:** 161, 317
Iron and Steel Institute, American, **1932–33:** 257n.
Ironton, Ohio, **1932–33:** 346
Ishita, Tomoyishi, **1932–33:** 327
Italian Benevolent Society, **1929:** 230; **1930:** 325; **1931:** 354
Italo-Americano, Il Progresso, **1930:** 360
Italy, **1929:** 3n., 161, 229n., 317
    Disarmament, **1930:** 112, 113, 117, 143, 221, 341; **1931:** 89, 430
    Earthquake disaster, **1930:** 242
    Foreign Minister Dino Grandi, **1931:** 89, 266, 411, 433
    Intergovernmental debts, **1932–33:** 228n., 431
    Prime Minister Benito Mussolini, **1931:** 297ftn.

Jackson, Arthur C., **1929:** 79
Jackson, Brig. Gen. Thomas H., **1930:** 223
Jacobson, O. P. B., **1929:** 270
Jacoby, H. Murray, **1930:** 350
Jadwin, Maj. Gen. Edgar, **1929:** 84ftn., p. 151, 125n., 204; **1930:** 218
Jahncke, Ernest L., **1929:** 6; **1931:** 219n., 285, 392
James, George F., **1931:** 115
James, Harlean, **1931:** 314
Janssen, August, **1931:** 96
Janssen, C. H., **1931:** 254
Japan, **1929:** 3n., 161, 229n., 236, 308, 317, 331
    Aviators, crash, **1932–33:** 327
    Disarmament, **1930:** 112, 113, 115, 117, 143, 183, 184, 221, 225, 341
    Emperor Hirohito, **1931:** 146; **1932–33:** 139, 327
    Invasion of Shanghai, China, **1932–33:** 34, 35
    Lausanne agreement, **1932–33:** 228n.
    Prince Takamatsu, **1931:** 146, 217
    Relations with China, **1931:** 430, 433
    Trade relations, **1932–33:** 357
Jarvis, J. Antonio, **1932–33:** 426
Jefferson, Ohio, **1932–33:** 302
Jefferson, Thomas, **1930:** 54, 114
Jenkins, Charles F., **1932–33:** 350n.
Jenkins, Perry, **1929:** 242n.

Jew, American Hebrew Medal for Better Understanding Between Christian and, **1931:** 417
Jewish Congress, American, **1931:** 167; **1932–33:** 72
Jewish Hospital of Brooklyn, N.Y., **1932–33:** 355
Jewish Joint Distribution Committee, **1929:** 83; **1931:** 107, 157; **1932–33:** 98
Jewish Ministers, New York Board of, **1932–33:** 142
Jewish National Fund of America, **1932–33:** 58
Jewish New Year, **1931:** 308
Jewish Philanthropic Societies, Federation for the Support of, **1930:** 393; **1931:** 18n., 332; **1932–33:** 339
Jewish Relief Campaign, Allied, **1929:** 45; **1930:** 80, 151n.
Jewish Tribune, **1930:** 416
Jewish Welfare Board, **1932–33:** 41n.
Jews
    American Hebrew Medal, **1932–33:** 406
    American Palestine Committee, **1932–33:** 19
    Maurice Schwartz, testimonial dinner, **1932–33:** 474
    National Conference on Palestine, **1932–33:** 20
    116th Street Synagogue, **1932–33:** 332
    Park Avenue Synagogue, **1932–33:** 116
    Rosh Hashanah, **1932–33:** 303
    Zionist Organization of America, **1932–33:** 374
Jiménez, Ricardo, **1932–33:** 297
Job training, **1930:** 84
Joffre, Joseph, **1931:** 4
John Fritz gold medal, **1929:** 52
Johns Hopkins Medical School, **1929:** 239
Johnson, Alba B., **1929:** 122
Johnson, Charles H., **1932–33:** 340
Johnson, Sen. Hiram, **1929:** 273
Johnson, Mordecai, **1930:** 51n.
Johnson, Robert U., **1929:** 70n.; **1931:** 187
Johnson, Sveinbjorn, **1929:** 270
Johnson, William H., **1929:** 191n.
Johnston, A., **1932–33:** 41n.
Joint Canada-United States dam investigation, **1930:** 42
Joint Committee to Attend Sesquicentennial Celebration of Battle of Kings Mountain, S.C., **1932–33:** 135
Joint Committee to Investigate Northern Pacific Land Grants, **1932–33:** 135
Joint Committee to Investigate Pay Readjustment of Army, Navy, Marine Corps, Coast Guard and Geodetic Survey, and Public Health Service, **1932–33:** 135
Joint statement, France, **1931:** 371
Joint statements, British Prime Minister MacDonald, **1929:** 226, 229
Joliet, Ill., **1932–33:** 376
Jones, Comdr. Claude A., **1932–33:** 270
Jones, Eugene Kinckle, **1930:** 84; **1932–33:** 353

Jones, Rear Adm. Hilary P., **1929:** 28, 195, 241;
    1930: 11n.
Jones, Jesse H., **1932–33:** 31n., 187
Jones, Melvin, **1932–33:** 41n.
Jones, Robert M., **1929:** 315n.; **1930:** 3, 6
Jones, Sen. Wesley L., **1930:** 125; **1932–33:** 154n.
Jordan, David Starr, **1930:** 24, 167; **1931:** 317
Joslin, Theodore G., **1931:** 116, 121, 275n., 297,
    420, 453; **1932–33:** 439
Joyce, M. M., **1931:** 70n.
Juárez, Mexico, **1929:** 5
Judd, Lawrence M., **1929:** 48
Judicial procedure, reform, **1932–33:** 63, 64, 69, 475
Judicial reform, **1930:** 17, 135, 209, 210, 390
Judicial system, **1929:** 1, 5
June, Harold I., **1930:** 208
Junior Chamber of Commerce, United States,
    1932–33: 96
Jusserand, Jean Jules, **1932–33:** 236
Justice, American Conference of Institutions for
    the Establishment of International,
    1932–33: 141
Justice, Department of, **1929:** 295, 296
  Acting Attorney General, **1931:** 301
  Appropriations, **1929:** 311; **1930:** 395n.
  Assistant Attorney General, **1930:** 36, 342, 343;
    1931: 211
  Assistant Attorney General, resignation, **1929:**
    90, 91, 270
  Attorney General (William D. Mitchell), **1929:**
    60n., 92n., 169, 170; **1930:** 17, 135, 165,
    179n., 220, 240, 244, 246, 342, 343, 381n.;
    1931: 13, 31, 46, 94, 120; **1932–33:** 69, 90,
    246, 285, 448, 456, 475
  Bankruptcy, investigation, **1932–33:** 69n.
  Bankruptcy law and practice, investigation,
    1930: 244, 246
  Bonus marchers, investigation, **1932–33:** 249,
    250, 285
  Building, cornerstone laying, **1932–33:** 472
  Committee to study the disposition of U.S. Army
    posts, **1931:** 181
  Construction program, **1930:** 391
  Oil shale lands, investigation, **1930:** 342, 343
  Parole Board, **1930:** 165
  Patronage investigation, **1930:** 87, 88
  Prohibition Bureau, **1931:** 27
  Transfer from Treasury Department, **1930:** 135,
    165, 390
  Reorganization, proposed, **1932–33:** 423
  Solicitor General, **1930:** 244, 246
Justo, Augustin P., **1932–33:** 177
Juvenile delinquency, **1932–33:** 69

Kane, Dr. Elisha Kent, **1930:** 220
Kane Gold Medal, **1930:** 220

Kansas
  Child health and protection conference, **1932–
    33:** 5n.
  Drought relief, **1930:** 258, 259, 265, 272n.
  Governor, **1931:** 91n.
  President's visit, **1932–33:** 397
Kearny, N.J., **1932–33:** 91n.
Kell, Frank, **1932–33:** 264
Kelley, Cornelius F., **1929:** 252
Kelley, Ralph S., **1930:** 342, 343
Kellogg, Frank B., **1929:** 6ftn., p. 23, 161; **1930:**
    115, 405
Kellogg, Vernon, **1929:** 144
Kellogg-Briand Pact, **1929:** 1, 94, 161, 184, 195,
    229, 275; **1930:** 115, 119, 133, 314, 365,
    405; **1931:** 168, 371, 433
Kemal, Mustapha (President of Turkey), **1929:**
    265; **1930:** 346; **1931:** 279, 386; **1932–33:**
    361
Kenmore, restoration of, **1929:** 223
Kenny, Edwin J., **1931:** 70
Kenova, W. Va., **1932–33:** 346
Kentucky
  Child health and protection conference, **1932–
    33:** 5n.
  Drought relief, **1930:** 258, 259, 265n., 272n.
  Roads program, **1931:** 248
Kenyon, William S., **1931:** 27
Kerney, James, **1929:** 260; **1930:** 50, 51
Kerr, Ben H., **1932–33:** 276
Kerr, Hugh T., **1931:** 208
Keyser, W. Va., **1932–33:** 360
Kiep, Dr. Otto C., **1929:** 189n.
Kimball, James H., **1931:** 126
Kincheloe, Repr. David H., **1930:** 299
King, Charles D. B. (President of Liberia), **1929:**
    152
King, Sen. William H., **1931:** 238, 239
King, William V., **1931:** 12n.
Kingdom of the Serbs, Croats, and Slovenes, **1929:**
    161
Kings Mountain, S.C., **1930:** 319
  Joint Committee to Attend Sesquicentennial Cel-
    ebration of the Battle of, **1932–33:** 135
Kingsbury, K. R., **1932–33:** 264
Kinkaid, Comdr. Thomas C., **1932–33:** 25n.
Kip, Isaac, **1929:** 27
Kips Bay Boys' Club, **1931:** 105
Kirchwey, George W., **1932–33:** 464
Kitty Hawk, N.C., **1932–33:** 403
Kiwanis Club, **1930:** 392
Kiwanis International, **1932–33:** 41n.
Kiwanis International Convention, **1930:** 216
Klein, Julius, **1929:** 41; **1932–33:** 41n.
Kneubuhl, Emily R., **1932–33:** 41n.
Knight, Harry C., **1931:** 418; **1932–33:** 41n.
Knights of Columbus, **1932–33:** 103
Knowles, Morris, **1931:** 314

Knox, Frank, **1931:** 292; **1932–33:** 38, 41, 60, 73, 80, 81
Koch, Dr. Robert, **1932–33:** 89
Kochler, A. W., **1930:** 130n.
Koechler, Rudolph, **1929:** 242
Kock, Alfred B., **1930:** 46
Krebs, John M., **1930:** 272
Krueger, J. W., **1932–33:** 433

Labor
    American Federation of Labor, address, **1930:** 315
    American Legion employment drive, **1932–33:** 40n.
    Child, **1930:** 376; **1932–33:** 311
    Circuit court of appeal, opposition to nomination of judge, **1932–33:** 5
    Community cooperation, **1930:** 55, 144, 244, 247, 311, 315
    Conference on hoarding of currency, **1932–33:** 36, 41n.
    Conferences, **1929:** 280, 281, 297
    Disputes, **1929:** 19; **1930:** 29, 30
    Equal opportunity, **1932–33:** 354
    Federal Reserve District Banking and Industrial Committees, conference, **1932–33:** 264, 267, 272
    Flood control projects, charges of unfair labor practices, **1932–33:** 353
    Immigration, **1930:** 288, 380, 390; **1931:** 113, 189
    Labor-management relations, **1930:** 260, 358, 390; **1931:** 196, 226, 430; **1932–33:** 380, 388
    National employment system legislation, **1931:** 94
    Norris-La Guardia Act, **1932–33:** 90
    Public buildings, laborers, **1932–33:** 213
    Railroad consolidation, **1930:** 428, 429
    Railway labor dispute, **1931:** 196
    Share-the-work movement, **1932–33:** 404
    Supreme Court nomination, opposition, **1930:** 92ftn.
    Tariff protection, **1930:** 188
    Technological unemployment, **1932–33:** 337
    Unemployment statistics, development, **1930:** 244, 247
    Wages, **1931:** 1, 43, 44, 226, 271, 430; **1932–33:** 213, 337, 346, 353, 357, 360, 363, 364, 379, 388
    Work hours, **1932–33:** 1, 126, 240, 251, 267, 272, 294, 311, 337, 358, 380, 419
Labor, American Federation of, **1930:** 29, 30n., 244, 247, 250, 315, 383, 384; **1931:** 101, 314; **1932–33:** 41n., 389, 390
Labor, Department of
    Acting Secretary, **1931:** 189

Labor, Department of — *continued*
    Appropriations, **1931:** 9, 53, 60, 61
    Building, cornerstone laying, **1932–33:** 427
    Bureau of Immigration, **1931:** 9, 53, 348
    Bureau of Labor Statistics, **1930:** 76n., 244, 247, 334; **1931:** 60
    Children's Bureau, **1932–33:** 358
    Employment statistics, **1932–33:** 337
    Employment surveys, **1930:** 25, 34, 76, 76n., 77, 334, 390; **1931:** 302
    Immigration report, **1931:** 189
    Labor disputes, report, **1930:** 315
    Reorganization, proposed, **1932–33:** 423
    Secretary of (James J. Davis), **1929:** 140, 142, 164, 281; **1930:** 76n., 233, 247n., 260, 331, 332, 383, 384, 386; **1931:** 101, 244, 277n., 324; **1932–33:** 213, 264
    United States Employment Service, **1931:** 61, 94, 101, 277
    Work hours, survey, **1932–33:** 240
Labor Statistics, Bureau of, **1930:** 76n., 244, 247, 334; **1931:** 60
Ladies' Home Journal, **1932–33:** 161
Laetare medal, **1929:** 65
Lafayette, Marquis de, **1932–33:** 280
Lafayette College, Conference on the French Backgrounds of American Civilization, **1932–33:** 166
Lafayette-Marne Day Committee, **1932–33:** 280
LaFollette, Sen. Robert M., Jr., **1930:** 413n.; **1932–33:** 366, 378
Lake Michigan, **1932–33:** 235
Lamont, Robert P., **1929:** 61, 146n., 281, 286; **1930:** 76n., 130n., 166n., 247n., 249, 250, 331, 332, 334, 395; **1931:** 55, 91, 244, 271n., 314, 324, 344n.; **1932–33:** 41n., 122, 257
Lamont, Thomas W., **1929:** 97, 99, 109; **1931:** 220; **1932–33:** 8
Lampson, E. C., **1932–33:** 302
Land banks, Federal, **1931:** 343, 407, 430, 436, 437
    See also Federal land and intermediate credit banks.
Land Grants, Joint Committee to Investigate Northern Pacific, **1932–33:** 135
Land Office, General, **1930:** 342, 343; **1932–33:** 423
Landman, Dr. Isaac, **1929:** 249; **1931:** 417; **1932–33:** 406
Landowsky, Paul, **1931:** 170n.
Lands, public, conservation of Western ranges, **1932–33:** 50
Larson, Gov. Morgan, **1931:** 137
LaSalle, Ill., **1932–33:** 376
LaSenay, Treffle R., **1932–33:** 436n.
Lathrop, Julia, **1932–33:** 128
Latin America.
    See also specific country.
    Airmail service, **1930:** 312, 407

Latin America — *continued*
  Communications development, **1930:** 100, 101,
      111, 141, 421, 425
  Debts, statement, **1931:** 243
  Foreign relations, message to Congress, **1931:**
      433
  Foreign Service appointments, **1930:** 25, 34, 303
  Fourth Pan American Commercial Conference,
      1931: 347
  Ibero-American Exposition, **1930:** 201
  Immigration, **1931:** 113
  Oil imports, **1931:** 100
  Pan American Day, **1930:** 169
  Pan American Union, **1930:** 414
      Address, **1931:** 135
  Second Pan American Conference of Directors
      of Health, **1931:** 144
  Sixth Pan American Child Congress, **1930:** 75
  Trade with U.S., **1932–33:** 91
  U.S. relations with, **1930:** 21, 124, 133
Latvia, **1929:** 161
  Intergovernmental debts, **1932–33:** 431
Lauer, Conrad N., **1930:** 108
Lausanne agreement, **1932–33:** 228, 272, 407
Laval, Josette, **1931:** 367n.
Laval, Pierre, **1931:** 266, 267, 343, 367, 368, 369,
      370, 371, 377, 433
Law, International Conference for the Codification
      of International, **1930:** 86
Law, Oratorical Contest on Loyalty and, **1930:** 248
Law Enforcement Commission.
  See National Commission on Law Observance
      and Enforcement.
Law enforcement and crime, **1929:** 1, 5, 10, 28,
      47, 295, 324
  American Bar Association, **1932–33:** 335
  Antitrust laws, **1931:** 430
  Appropriations, **1930:** 142, 193, 209, 210
  Bonus marchers, **1932–33:** 246, 248, 249, 250, 285
  Delinquent youth, **1930:** 376
  District of Columbia, **1930:** 17, 45, 135, 390;
      1931: 301
  International Association of Chiefs of Police,
      1931: 355
  Joint select committee to study prohibition en-
      forcement, proposed, **1930:** 15
  Judicial procedure, reform, **1932–33:** 63, 64, 69,
      475
  Juvenile delinquents, bill authorizing transfer of
      cases to local jurisdictions, **1932–33:** 193
  Leisure time, **1931:** 134
  Lindbergh kidnapping, **1932–33:** 160
  Messages to Congress, **1930:** 17, 135, 142, 193
  Methodist Ecumenical Congress, remarks, **1931:**
      372
  Narcotics, **1931:** 69

Law enforcement and crime — *continued*
  New York City police commissioner, **1932–33:**
      401, 468
  Newark, N.J., Chief of Police, **1932–33:** 413
  Patronage investigations, **1930:** 87, 88
  Prohibition, **1930:** 17, 19, 135, 193, 390; **1931:**
      27; **1932–33:** 69, 259, 268, 317, 372, 378
  Respect for, **1929:** 1, 47, 64, 92
  State law enforcement, **1930:** 19, 135, 380, 381
  State and local governments, responsibility,
      1932–33: 379
  State of the Union message, **1930:** 390
Law Observance and Enforcement, National Com-
      mission on, **1931:** 27; **1932–33:** 135
Lawrance, Charles L., **1931:** 131
Lawrence, Richard W., **1932–33:** 22
Lawrence College, **1929:** 258; **1931:** 322
League of Nations, **1929:** 12, 275; **1930:** 365; **1931:**
      103, 433; **1932–33:** 35, 269n.
Leather tanning industry, **1929:** 316n.
Leavenworth Federal Prison, **1929:** 169, 170, 224
Lebrun, Albert, **1932–33:** 222, 229
Lee, William E., **1930:** 6n.
Legge, Alexander, **1929:** 140; **1930:** 253, 255, 265n.,
      271, 272; **1931:** 92
Legislation.
  See also Appropriations; Congress, communi-
      cations to; Veto messages.
  Banking laws, revision, **1931:** 436, 437
  Bankruptcy Act of 1898, amendments, **1932–33:**
      63, 64, 69, 448, 451, 470
  Bonus
      Loans for veterans, **1932–33:** 101, 102, 123,
          126, 154, 293
      Marchers, appropriations for travel expenses,
          1932–33: 218, 225
  Budget message, **1932–33:** 421
  Budgetary impact, **1931:** 116, 117, 324, 325, 432
  Bureau of Narcotics, establishment, **1930:** 183n.
  Civil War Veterans' Act, **1930:** 182
  Common carriers, regulatory reform, **1932–33:**
      358
  Congressional action, impact, **1932–33:** 317, 322,
      328, 337, 347, 357, 358, 363, 366, 371, 376,
      377, 378, 380, 387, 388, 452
  Drought relief, **1931:** 45, 50
  Economic recovery program, **1932–33:** 1, 3, 92,
      93, 146, 156, 157, 158, 159, 347, 380,
      419, 470
  "Economy Act," **1932–33:** 9, 10, 50n., 76, 77,
      109, 111, 113, 114, 119, 123, 124, 125,
      126, 146, 147, 148, 154, 186, 198, 199,
      212, 231, 289, 421
  Emergency Adjusted Compensation Act, 1931,
      1931: 63, 67, 78, 79, 80
  Emergency construction fund, **1930:** 357, 369,
      395, 397, 402, 403, 406

Legislation — *continued*
  Emergency Relief and Construction Act of 1932,
      1932–33: 182, 183, 186, 208, 209, 216, 217,
      220n., 221, 230, 233, 243n., 282, 283, 421
  Employment Stabilization Act of 1931, **1931:** 54,
      55
  Executive branch reorganization legislation,
      1932–33: 48, 50, 59, 76, 77, 79, 92, 93, 109,
      111, 113, 146, 198, 199, 212, 289, 290, 396,
      419, 423, 439, 440, 450, 452, 453, 462
  Federal Farm Loan Act, amendments, **1932–33:**
      28
  Federal Home Loan Bank Act, **1932–33:** 238,
      239
  Federal Reserve Act, amendments, **1932–33:** 63,
      66
  44-hour workweek for Government employees,
      1931: 62, 201
  Hydraulic laboratory, **1930:** 158
  Judicial procedure, reform, **1932–33:** 63, 64, 69,
      475
  Juvenile delinquents, transfer to local jurisdic-
      tions, **1932–33:** 193
  Moratorium resolution, bill signing, **1931:** 450
  Muscle Shoals resolution, **1931:** 79, 82, 88
  Norris-La Guardia Act, **1932–33:** 90
  Perishable Agricultural Commodities Act, 1930,
      1930: 182
  Post Office site in New York City, legislation
      relating to purchase, **1932–33:** 224
  Prison reform, **1930:** 165, 409
  Prohibition Bureau, transfer, **1930:** 165
  Reconstruction Finance Corporation Act, **1932–
      33:** 27
  Relief of the families of Emilio Cortez Rubio
      and Manuel Gomez, **1932–33:** 214
  Retirement fund, Government employees, **1930:**
      59, 60
  Revenue Act of 1932, **1932–33:** 123, 126, 146,
      154, 186, 188
  River and Harbor Act, **1930:** 132, 223
  Spanish War veterans' pension bill, **1930:** 168,
      173, 174
  State of the Union message, **1930:** 390; **1931:**
      430; **1932–33:** 419
  Tariff Act of 1930, **1930:** 55, 147, 172, 188, 190,
      273, 274
  Textile Foundation Act, **1930:** 182
  Veterans' Administration, establishment, **1930:**
      226, 227
  World War Veterans' Act, 1924, Amendments,
      1930: 200, 202, 203, 206, 222
Legislators, Interstate Conference of, **1932–33:** 461
Leguía, Augusto B. (President of Peru), **1929:** 235,
      309
Lehlbach, Repr. Frederick R., **1930:** 59, 60
Leigh, Rear Adm. Richard H., **1930:** 146
Leisure time, **1931:** 134

Lemann, Monte M., **1931:** 27
Leon, Maurice, **1932–33:** 280
Leonard Wood Memorial for the Eradication of
      Leprosy, **1929:** 49
LeSenay, Treffle R., **1930:** 427
Leslie, Gov. Harry G., **1930:** 265n.; **1931:** 22, 226
Letters, messages, telegrams
  Airmail service betweeen United States and
      Argentina, message to President Irigoyen,
      1929: 234
  American Arbitration Association, message,
      1929: 76
  American Bar Association, message on Consti-
      tution Day activities, **1929:** 203
  American Hebrew, The, 50th anniversary, mes-
      sage, **1929:** 249
  American Institute of Steel Construction, mes-
      sage to annual convention, **1929:** 278
  American Newspaper Publishers and the Asso-
      ciated Press annual conventions, message,
      1929: 43
  American Red Cross, **1929:** 279
  Army and Navy aircraft programs, telegram to
      Thomas L. Hill, president, American So-
      ciety for the Promotion of Aviation, **1929:**
      187
  Assassination attempts on
    Ibáñez del Campo, President of Chile, mes-
        sage to, **1929:** 255
    Irigoyen, Hipolito, President of Argentina,
        message to, **1929:** 322
  Association of Grand Jurors, message, **1929:** 87
  Atlantic Deeper Waterways Association, mes-
      sage to the convention, **1929:** 211
  "Billy Opossum," return of mascot, letter to
      Robert M. Venemann, student Hyattsville
      High School, **1929:** 149
  Birthday messages
    Albert, King of the Belgians, **1929:** 30
    Booth, Ballington, 50th anniversary of min-
        istry, message to the Volunteers of Amer-
        ica, **1929:** 58
    King George V of Great Britain, **1929:** 107
    King Haakon of Norway, **1929:** 168
    Roosevelt, Theodore, tribute to, **1929:** 259
    Whitaker, Jane T., **1929:** 82
    Wiley, Louis, **1929:** 101
  Border shootings, letter to International Falls,
      Minn., City Council, **1929:** 129
  British-American track meet, **1929:** 153
  Brown, David A., message for the testimonial
      dinner for, **1929:** 83
  "Buddy Poppy" sale, message endorsing, **1929:**
      40
  Byrd, Comdr. Richard E.
    Antarctic expedition, message, **1929:** 244
    South Pole, flight over, message of congrat-
        ulations, **1929:** 293

Letters, messages, telegrams — *continued*
  Byrd, Comdr. Richard E. — *continued*
    Transatlantic flight, message on second anniversary, **1929:** 137
  Cathcart, Prof. A. M., message for banquet honoring, **1929:** 96
  Chemical Industries 12th exposition, message on opening, **1929:** 66
  Chicago Daily News, message on dedication of new building, **1929:** 146
  Christmas message to disabled veterans, **1929:** 320
  Columbus' discovery of America, message to the Italian Benevolent Society, **1929:** 230
  Columbus Monument, Palos, Spain, message for unveiling ceremony, **1929:** 44
  Condolence messages
    Battle y Ordoñez, José, to President Campisteguy of Uruguay, **1929:** 251
    Clemenceau, Georges, to President Doumergue of France, **1929:** 288
    Earls, Robert, to Mr. and Mrs. Strothers B. Earls, **1929:** 254
    Francis, William T., Minister to Liberia, to President King of Liberia, **1929:** 152
    Herrick, Myron T., to Parmely Herrick, **1929:** 20
    Matthews, Brander, to Florence Matthews, **1929:** 23
    Pallen, Condé B., to Mrs. Pallen, **1929:** 93
  DeGroot, William A., letter of removal from office, **1929:** 60
  Disabled American Veterans Forget-Me-Not Campaign, message endorsing, **1929:** 268
  District of Columbia Fire Department, letter to Fire Chief Watson, **1929:** 328
  Edison Pioneers, Sponsorship Committee of the, letter accepting honorary chairmanship, **1929:** 57
  Einstein, Albert, message in tribute on his 50th birthday, **1929:** 39
  Export debenture plan, letter to Sen. McNary, **1929:** 46
  Florida Republicans protest of appointment, letter to F. E. Britten, **1929:** 248
  Fort Russell, Wyo., renaming, letter to Acting Secretary of War Hurley, **1929:** 302
  Garvan, Francis P., American Chemical Society's Priestley medal, message, **1929:** 200
  German reparations discussions, message to American members of the Committee of Experts, **1929:** 109
  German Republic, anniversary of founding, message to President von Hindenburg, **1929:** 176
  Graf Zeppelin, round-the-world flight, messages to Dr. Hugo Eckener, **1929:** 174, 188
  Hall of Fame ceremonies, message, **1929:** 70

Letters, messages, telegrams — *continued*
  Herrick, Myron T., Ambassador to France, exchange of messages with President Doumergue, **1929:** 24
  Hirohito, Emperor of Japan, messages, **1929:** 236, 331
  Inauguration, messages acknowledging congratulations from foreign leaders, **1929:** 3
  Independence Day Americanization ceremonies, letter to Mayor Walker of New York City, **1929:** 120
  Independence Day messages
    Argentina, to President Irigoyen, **1929:** 86
    Bolivia, to President Siles, **1929:** 171
    Chile, to President Ibáñez del Campo, **1929:** 207
    China, to President Chiang Kai-shek, **1929:** 232
    Colombia, to President Méndez, **1929:** 158
    Czechoslovakia, to President Masaryk, **1929:** 264
    Ecuador, to President Ayora, **1929:** 175
    Mexico, to President Emilio Portes Gil, **1929:** 205
    Panama, to President Arosemena, **1929:** 271
    Rumania, to King Michael, **1929:** 72
    Turkey, to President Kemal, **1929:** 265
    Venezuela, to President Perez, **1929:** 145
  Industry and labor leaders, telegram inviting to White House conference, **1929:** 284
  Institute of Pacific Relations, message, **1929:** 261
  Institute of Paper Chemistry, Lawrence College, message on, **1929:** 258
  Interdepartmental Committee to Study Marine Mail Contracts, letter to Secretary of Commerce Lamont, **1929:** 104
  International Advertising Association, message to convention, **1929:** 103
  International Conference on Safety of Life at Sea, message to U.S. delegation, **1929:** 17
  International Hospital Congress, message, **1929:** 124
  International Joint Commission, United States and Canada, letter to Chairman Clark, **1929:** 53
  International Longfellow Society, letter accepting honorary presidency, **1929:** 79
  International Society of Christian Endeavor, message to convention, **1929:** 143
  Italian reception for American aviators, exchange of messages with King Vittorio Emmanuele, **1929:** 148
  Johnson, Sen. Hiram, letter of apology, **1929:** 273
  Jones, Adm. Hilary P., telegram to Repr. J. V. McClintic, **1929:** 195
  Journalism Week, University of Missouri, message, **1929:** 71

Letters, messages, telegrams — *continued*
  Kelley, Cornelius F., message for presentation ceremony of gold medal for mining achievement, **1929:** 252
  Kenmore, restoration as national shrine, letter to Mrs. Vivian Fleming, president of Kenmore Association, **1929:** 223
  Kip, Isaac, letter of appreciation, **1929:** 27
  Leguía, Augusto B., President of Peru, message on reinauguration, **1929:** 235
  Leonard Wood Memorial for the Eradication of Leprosy, message endorsing, **1929:** 49
  Lincoln University, 75th anniversary, message to President Johnson, **1929:** 191
  MacDonald, J. Ramsay, Prime Minister of Great Britain, messages, **1929:** 222, 240
  Memorial album on European war relief work, message of appreciation, **1929:** 81
  Memorial Day, message to Albert, King of the Belgians, **1929:** 100
  Mississippi Valley Association, message to 11th annual convention, **1929:** 276
  National Association of Real Estate Boards, message to convention, **1929:** 131
  National Committee on Boys' and Girls' 4-H Club Work, letter accepting honorary chairmanship, **1929:** 26
  National Conference of Retail Merchants, letter to Meyer Liberman, Arnold Constable & Co., on suggested conference, **1929:** 289
  National Congress of Parents and Teachers, message to 33d convention, **1929:** 64
  National Federation of Men's Bible Classes, message to the convention, **1929:** 63
  National Hospital Day, message, **1929:** 74
  National Life Insurance Conference, **1929:** 217
  National Music Week, message to National Music Week Committee, **1929:** 55
  National Recreation Congress, message, **1929:** 238
  National Saengerfest, message, **1929:** 102
  Naval parity with Great Britain, letter to Paul V. McNutt, National Commander of the American Legion, **1929:** 166
  New Year's messages
    Albert, King of the Belgians, **1929:** 329
    Vittorio Emmanuele III, King of Italy, **1929:** 330
  New York Bible Society, message, **1929:** 307
  New York and Its Environs, Regional Plan, message on completion of survey, **1929:** 88
  New York State-wide Economic Congress, letter endorsing proposed economic survey, **1929:** 303
  Orleans, France, message to mayor on the 500th anniversary of the raising of the siege by Jeanne d'Arc, **1929:** 69

Letters, messages, telegrams — *continued*
  ORT Jewish Relief campaign, message endorsing, **1929:** 45
  Pan American Highway Congress, message, **1929:** 179
  Permanent Court of International Justice, letter to Secretary of State Stimson, **1929:** 306
  Philadelphia Inquirer, message on 100th anniversary, **1929:** 95
  Prohibition enforcement incidents, letter to International Falls, Minn., City Council, **1929:** 129
  Public lands, message to Western Governors Conference, **1929:** 185
  Public works, telegrams to Governors urging State stimulation of, **1929:** 286
  Pulaski sesquicentennial celebration, exchange of messages with President Moscicki of Poland, **1929:** 233
  Radio service between United States and Peru, message to President Leguía, **1929:** 309
  Radiotelegraphic service with Spain, message to King Alfonso XIII, **1929:** 247
  Rail route between Guatemala and El Salvador, messages to Presidents Chacon and Romero Bosque, **1929:** 326
  Rapidan Camp, letter to W. E. Carson, chairman, Virginia State Conservation and Development Commission, **1929:** 172
  Resignations
    Clark, J. Reuben, Under Secretary of State, letter accepting, **1929:** 113
    Lord, Herbert M., Director of the Bureau of the Budget, letter accepting, **1929:** 105
    Meyer, Eugene, Federal Farm Loan Commissioner, letter accepting, **1929:** 59
    Willebrandt, Mabel W., Assistant Attorney General, letter accepting, **1929:** 91
    Work, Hubert, chairman, Republican National Committee, letter accepting, **1929:** 111
  Robert Burns Memorial Association, message, **1929:** 138
  Root, Elihu, National Academy of Design Medal, message for presentation ceremony, **1929:** 291
  Rosh Hashanah, message, **1929:** 201
  Rural Life Sunday, message to Home Missions Council, **1929:** 62
  St. John's Guild, New York City, message on work, **1929:** 106
  Smith, Alfred E., Laetare medal, letter to Dr. O'Donnell, president of the University of Notre Dame, **1929:** 65
  Smith, Fred B., message for testimonial dinner honoring, **1929:** 269
  Syracuse Post-Standard centennial, message, **1929:** 208

[References are to items except as otherwise indicated]

Letters, messages, telegrams — *continued*
  Tacna-Arica settlement
    Ibáñez del Campo, Carlos, President of Chile,
      exchange of messages on ratification of
      agreement, **1929:** 167
    Pereira de Souza, Washington L., President of
      Brazil, message acknowledging congratu-
      lations, **1929:** 89
  Tanners' Council, message, **1929:** 316
  Transatlantic flights
    Columbia, message on second anniversary of
      Chamberlin's flight, **1929:** 110
    Yellow Bird, message to President Doumergue
      of France, **1929:** 119
  Trenton, N.J., 250th anniversary, message, **1929:**
    260
  United Brethren in Christ, message to Young
    People's Superintendent, Lancaster, Pa.,
    1929: 78
  United States Flag Association, letter accepting
    appointment as Honorary Head, **1929:** 36
  Virginia Republican Convention, telegram of
    appreciation, **1929:** 135
  War Memorial, Orange, N.J., message for ded-
    ication, **1929:** 130
  Washington Cathedral, message, **1929:** 325
  White House industry and labor conferences,
    telegrams inviting leaders, **1929:** 284
  Wilmer Institute of Ophthalmology, Johns
    Hopkins University, message on dedica-
    tion, **1929:** 239
  Woman's Christian Temperance Union, message
    for national convention, **1929:** 210
  Work, Hubert, retirement, letter to Ralph E.
    Williams, chairman, Republican National
    Committee, **1929:** 194
  World Scout Jamboree, message, **1929:** 173
  YMCA, Philadelphia, Pa., message on dedica-
    tion of new building, **1929:** 122
  Zionist Organization of America, message, **1929:**
    139, 190
Letts, F. D., **1931:** 173
Levine, Charles A., **1929:** 110n.
Levine, Joseph M., **1931:** 153
Lewis, Edwin D., **1932–33:** 345
Lewis, Elizabeth Washington, **1929:** 223n.
Lewis, Col. Fielding, **1929:** 223n.
Lewis, John L., **1931:** 244
Lewis, William Mather, **1932–33:** 166
Lewis and Clark Expedition Celebration, **1932–33:**
  135
Lewis relief bill, **1932–33:** 146ftn.
Li Ying-ting, **1930:** 138
Liberal, Kans., **1932–33:** 397
Liberal Arts Colleges, Conference of, **1930:** 91
Liberal Arts Colleges Association, **1931:** 409
Liberia, **1929:** 152, 161
  U.S. Minister to, **1930:** 53

Liberman, Meyer, **1929:** 289
Life Insurance Conference, National, **1929:** 217
Life Insurance Day, **1932–33:** 12
Life Insurance Presidents, Association of, **1931:**
  314; **1932–33:** 41n.
Life Underwriters, National Association of, **1929:**
  217n.
Lighter-than-air flight, **1930:** 317, 321, 323
Lighthouses, Bureau of, **1931:** 453; **1932–33:** 423
"Light's Golden Jubilee," **1929:** 57n., 157, 245n.,
  246
Lin Sen, **1932–33:** 334
Lincoln, Abraham, **1930:** 52, 170, 367; **1931:** 58,
  232, 233; **1932–33:** 377
Lincoln Memorial, **1931:** 345
Lincoln's Birthday, **1932–33:** 45, 46, 465
Lincoln's Tomb, address, **1931:** 233
Lindbergh, Charles A., **1930:** 267, 287; **1931:** 397
Lindbergh, Charles Augustus, Jr., **1932–33:** 160
Lions Clubs, International Association of, **1932–**
  33: 41n.
Lipsky, Louis, **1930:** 400
Liquor Smuggling Treaty of 1924, **1929:** 54n.
Litchfield, P. W., **1930:** 247n.
Lithuania, **1929:** 161
  Intergovernmental debts, **1932–33:** 431
Little, Dr. Arthur D., **1929:** 66
Little America, **1929:** 137, 244
Littler, Robert M. C., **1929:** 96n.
Littleton, Benjamin H., **1929:** 237
Livestock, loans, **1932–33:** 295
Livestock Show, International, **1930:** 389
Lloyd, Horatio G., **1931:** 123
Loan Associations, United States League of Build-
  ing and, **1931:** 293, 314
Loan League, United States Building and, **1931:**
  293; **1932–33:** 41n., 274
Locomotive Engineers, Brotherhood of, **1932–33:**
  41n.
Loesch, Frank J., **1931:** 27
London Conference of Ministers, **1931:** 263, 266,
  267, 268
London Disarmament Conference, **1931:** 37
London economic conference.
  See World economic conference.
London Naval Conference, **1929:** 229, 241, 295;
  1932–33: 135
  American Society of Newspaper Editors,
    remarks, **1930:** 119
  Basis of agreement, remarks and statement,
    1930: 112, 113, 117
  Consultive pact, **1930:** 94, 112, 113, 119, 183, 184,
    230
  Daughters of the American Revolution, remarks,
    1930: 115
  Gridiron Club, remarks, **1930:** 133
  Press coverage, **1930:** 123
  U.S. delegation, **1930:** 10, 11, 11n., 85, 112, 113,
    117, 126, 261

London Naval Treaty
  Accomplishments, **1930:** 183, 184, 365
  Comparative tonnage, **1930:** 225
  Diplomatic correspondence, Senate request for, **1930:** 230, 231
  Instruments of ratification, **1930:** 341
  Messages to Senate, **1930:** 225, 230
  National defense, **1930:** 314, 390
  Partisanship, **1930:** 150
  Signing, remarks and statement, **1930:** 240, 241
  Special session of Senate, **1930:** 161, 162, 219, 221
  Transmittal to Senate, **1930:** 126, 143
  U.S. Navy, reduction in force of personnel, **1930:** 112, 113, 117, 321, 322, 390, 391
Long, Sen. Huey P., **1932–33:** 366
Long, John C., **1930:** 130n.
Longfellow, Henry Wadsworth, **1930:** 70
Longworth, Nicholas, **1929:** 250
Longworth, Repr. Nicholas, **1930:** 58, 69, 86, 128, 140, 142, 395, 401, 410; **1931:** 128, 129, 130
Lord, Gen. Herbert M., **1929:** 97, 105
Lord's Day Alliance of the United States, **1931:** 429
Loree, Leonor F., **1929:** 281n.
Lorimer, George H., **1929:** 241, 242
Loring, Charles, **1931:** 70
Louisiana
  Drought relief, **1931:** 121
  Roads program, **1931:** 248
Louisiana, Bank of Abbeville and Trust Co., **1932–33:** 86
Louisiana and Arkansas Railway Co., labor dispute, **1931:** 196
Louisiana and Texas, Intracoastal Canal Association of, **1931:** 399
Louvain, University of, Library, **1929:** 241, 243
Lowenstein, Solomon, **1930:** 393
Lowman, Seymour, **1930:** 165
Lucas, M. Grant, **1931:** 272
Lucas, Robert H., **1930:** 266
Lucknow, India, **1930:** 133
Luhring, Oscar R., **1932–33:** 250n.
Luther Day, **1932–33:** 262
Lynching, condemnation of, **1930:** 301

M. Carey Thomas Prize, **1931:** 165
MacArthur, Gen. Douglas, **1930:** 253, 254; **1931:** 185; **1932–33:** 34, 235, 246n.
MacCracken, William P., Jr., **1929:** 10, 37, 188n.
Macauley, Alvan, **1930:** 130n.; **1932–33:** 105n.
MacDonald, J. Ramsay (Prime Minister of the United Kingdom), **1929:** 116, 162, 209, 218, 222, 224, 226, 227, 228, 229, 240; **1930:** 115, 133, 341; **1931:** 266

Machado y Morales, Gerardo, **1931:** 194; **1932–33:** 172
Mackintosh, Kenneth, **1931:** 27
MacLean, James Nelson, **1932–33:** 41n.
MacNider, Hanford, **1930:** 158; **1932–33:** 273
Macomber, A. Kingsley, **1931:** 170n.
MacVay, Anna P., **1930:** 375
Madison, James B., **1931:** 303
Madison, Wis., **1932–33:** 379
Madison County, Va., **1929:** 10, 180
Magee, Wayland W., **1931:** 173
Magna, Mrs. Russell William, **1932–33:** 301
Maguth, John, **1932–33:** 47
Mahaffie, Charles D., **1930:** 249
Mahler, Ernst, **1931:** 322
Maier, William J., **1930:** 163
Mail Contract Committee, Interdepartmental, **1932–33:** 135
Maine
  Gubernatorial election, **1932–33:** 291
  Republican State Convention, **1930:** 95
Maine New England Council, **1930:** 70n.
Malheur Lake, Oreg., **1930:** 179
Mallery, Otto T., **1931:** 54, 55
Malone, George W., **1929:** 242
Mangan, Thomas, **1931:** 70
Manila Bay, anniversary of battle, **1931:** 154
Mann, A. R., **1931:** 314
Mann, Conrad, **1931:** 299
Manning, Bishop William T., **1931:** 183
Manufacturers, National Association of, **1932–33:** 41n.
Mapes, Repr. Carl E., **1931:** 238, 239
March, Charles H., **1931:** 70
Marine Corps, United States, **1930:** 38, 39, 55n., 92, 133, 236, 253; **1931:** 36, 71n., 138, 297; **1932–33:** 34
Marine mail, **1929:** 104, 202, 237, 295
Marine Mail Contracts, Interdepartmental Committee on, **1929:** 104, 202n., 295
Marion, Ohio, **1931:** 228; **1932–33:** 346
Maritime neutrality, treaty, **1931:** 433
Markham, Col. E. M., **1930:** 223
Markham, Edwin, **1932–33:** 131
Markham, Mr. and Mrs. Edwin, **1930:** 131
Marko, Joseph, **1931:** 73
Marland, E. W., **1930:** 129n.
Marlatt, Abby L., **1931:** 314
Marne, Battle of the, **1932–33:** 280
Marriner, J. Theodore, **1930:** 11n.; **1932–33:** 3n., 25n.
Marshall, Louis, **1929:** 199
Marston, Dr. Anson, **1929:** 125n.
Martinsburg, W. Va., **1932–33:** 336, 360
Marvel, Josiah, **1930:** 292
Maryland
  Calvert Associates, **1932–33:** 117

Maryland — *continued*
Drought relief, **1930:** 266
President's campaign, **1932–33:** 336, 363
U.S. district judge, **1931:** 177
Masaryk, Thomas G. (President of Czechoslova-
kia), **1929:** 264; **1930:** 387; **1931:** 384;
1932–33: 359
Masons, **1930:** 220
Masons, Free and Accepted, District of Columbia,
1932–33: 41n.
Massachusetts
Lincoln's Birthday, message, **1932–33:** 45n.
Republican State convention, **1932–33:** 317
Tercentenary commission, **1930:** 233
Massachusetts Bay Colony Tercentenary Commis-
sion, **1932–33:** 135
Massachusetts Commission on the Stabilization of
Unemployment, **1932–33:** 240n.
Matilda Ziegler Magazine for the Blind, **1932–33:**
70
Matson, Roderick N., **1932–33:** 344
Matthews, Brander, **1929:** 23
Matthews, Florence, **1929:** 23n.
Matthews, Mark A., **1930:** 248
Maury, Matthew Fontaine, **1931:** 187
Mayers, W. W., **1929:** 106
Mayes, Herbert R., **1931:** 352
Mayflower, The (yacht), **1929:** 12
McCarter, Thomas N., **1929:** 285n.
McCarthy, Wilson, **1932–33:** 31n., 41n., 187
McCartney, Rev. Albert Joseph, **1932–33:** 181
McClintic, Repr. James V., **1929:** 195
McClure, Mrs. Virgil, **1932–33:** 479
McCormick, Paul J., **1931:** 27
McCosker, Albert J., **1931:** 188; **1932–33:** 412, 473
McCullough, Crawford C., **1930:** 205n.
McDavid, Horace W., **1930:** 216n.
McDermott, George T., **1929:** 37n.
McDowell, Bishop William F., **1932–33:** 168, 420
McDuffie, Repr. John, **1932–33:** 114, 125
McFarland, W. F., **1931:** 260, 440
McGarrah, Gates W., **1930:** 402n.
McGlothlin, William J., **1931:** 191
McGovern, John T., **1929:** 153n.
McGrath, Myra, **1929:** 140, 155
McGroarty, John S., **1930:** 56
McKeesport, Pa., **1932–33:** 336
McKellar, Sen. Kenneth, **1930:** 88n., 403n.; **1932–
33:** 154n.
McKelvie, Samuel R., **1929:** 140ftn., p. 207, 165n.;
1931: 242
McKinley tariff, **1930:** 188
McKowne, F. E., **1931:** 401
McLaughlin, Repr. James C., **1931:** 238, 239
McLean, William R., **1931:** 274
McMeekin, Thomas, **1931:** 70n.
McMullen, Lt. Col. Joseph I., **1931:** 260, 440
McNab, John, **1929:** 219, 220

McNally, Carlton P., **1931:** 70
McNary, Sen. Charles L., **1929:** 46
McNeil Island Penitentiary, **1930:** 391
McNinch, Frank R., **1931:** 13
McNutt, Paul V., **1929:** 166
McRell, James A., **1932–33:** 413
Mead, Elwood, **1929:** 242
Meat Packers, Institute of American, **1930:** 335n.
Medals.
See Awards and citations.
Mediation Board, United States, **1931:** 196
Mediation efforts by the United States in inter-
national disputes
Bolivia-Paraguay dispute, **1929:** 295
Guatemala-Honduras dispute, **1929:** 295
Tacna-Arica dispute, **1929:** 77, 89, 167, 295
Medical Association, American, **1930:** 206
Medical care.
See Health and medical care.
Medical Care, National Conference on the Costs
of, **1932–33:** 411
Mediterranean fruit fly, **1929:** 54, 155
Meek, Burt C., **1929:** 178
Meetings with foreign leaders
Canadian Prime Minister Richard B. Bennett,
1931: 39, 40
French Prime Minister Pierre Laval, **1931:** 367,
368, 369, 370, 371, 433
Italian Foreign Minister Dino Grandi, **1931:** 411,
433
Mellon, Andrew W., **1929:** 7n., 10, 46, 281; **1930:**
200, 267, 273, 274, 331, 332, 395; **1931:**
120, 251, 263, 266, 268, 299, 333, 433;
1932–33: 37, 38, 39, 44
Mellon-Berenger Agreement, **1929:** 163
Meloney, Marie M., **1930:** 228
Meloney, Mrs. William B., **1929:** 266
Memorandum to Federal departments and agen-
cies on Federal expenditures, **1932–33:**
287
Memorandums to Federal departments and agen-
cies
Government expenditures for fiscal year 1932,
1931: 269
Unemployment relief, **1931:** 413
Memorial Bridge Commission, Arlington, **1932–33:**
423
Memorial Day, **1930:** 165, 170, 171; **1931:** 205, 206,
209; **1932–33:** 185
Memorial Day exercises, **1929:** 94
Mendenhall, D. A., **1930:** 353
Méndez, Miguel Abadía (President of Colombia),
1929: 158
Menlo Park Laboratory, **1929:** 57n.
Merchant Marines, U.S., **1929:** 104, 202, 237, 295;
1930: 112, 113, 133, 176, 177; **1931:** 62,
147, 148, 430, 453, 454; **1932–33:** 91, 106,
108
Act of 1928, **1929:** 202

Merriam, Charles E., **1929:** 318
Merrill, Henry F., **1930:** 70n.
Merrill, John L., **1930:** 21
Merrill, Oscar C., **1930:** 192n.
Merrill, Col. William E., **1929:** 250
Merrillan, Wis., **1932–33:** 379
Metcalfe, Ralph, **1932–33:** 318
Methodist Ecumenical Congress, **1931:** 372
Methodist Episcopal Church, Central New York
    Conference of the, **1931:** 336
Methodist Episcopal Church, Quadrennial General
    Conference, **1932–33:** 168
Metropolitan Museum of Art, **1932–33:** 153n.
Metzger, William E., **1930:** 130n.
Mexico
    Announcement of visit of President-elect, **1929:**
        310
    Claims against the United States, **1929:** 300
    Immigration, **1930:** 288, 390; **1931:** 113
    Inauguration congratulations, acknowledge-
        ment, **1929:** 3n.
    Independence Day message to President Portes
        Gil, **1929:** 205
    Legislation for the relief of the families of Emilio
        Cortez Rubio and Manuel Gomez, **1932–**
        33: 214
    Oil imports, **1931:** 100
    President Abelardo Rodríguez, **1932–33:** 279
    President Emilio Portes Gil, **1930:** 27
    President Pascual Ortiz Rubio, **1930:** 26, 27, 44,
        47, 133, 298, 421; **1931:** 221; **1932–33:**
        214n., 279
    Press association wire, **1930:** 421
    Revolution, **1929:** 2, 5, 8, 10, 25
    Shipment of arms to, **1929:** 2, 5, 154, 295
    Special Ambassador to inauguration, **1930:** 44n.
    U.S. Ambassador to, **1930:** 11n., 187n., 191, 313;
        1931: 433; **1932–33:** 477
    U.S. relations with, **1931:** 426
Mexico, International Boundary Commission,
    United States and, **1931:** 433
Mexico, International Water Commission, United
    States and, **1931:** 11
Meyer, Agnes E., **1929:** 238
Meyer, Eugene, **1929:** 59; **1930:** 157, 284, 285, 331,
    332; **1932–33:** 23, 24, 36, 41n., 187, 264,
    267ftn.
Meyersdale, Pa., **1932–33:** 336
Michael I, King (Rumania), **1929:** 72
Michel, Ernest, **1931:** 46
Michener, Repr. Earl C., **1931:** 238, 239
Michigan
    Governor, **1932–33:** 347
    Great Lakes–St. Lawrence Deep Waterway,
        1932–33: 235
    Lincoln's Birthday, message, **1932–33:** 45n.
    President's campaign, **1932–33:** 346, 347
    President's visit, **1931:** 318
    Roads Program, **1931:** 248

Migratory Bird Treaty regulations, **1929:** 50
Miklas, Wilhelm, **1930:** 102, 366; **1931:** 143
Miles, Brig. Gen. Perry L., **1932–33:** 246n.
Military.
    See Armed Forces.
Military expenditures, **1929:** 159, 160, 165, 295, 296
Military force, use of, **1930:** 38, 39, 94, 115, 119,
        133, 225, 240, 241, 314; **1931:** 138, 140,
        141, 433
Military Order of the World War, **1930:** 105;
        1932–33: 67
Military preparedness, **1929:** 275
Military Training Camp Association, **1931:** 115
Militia Bureau, **1929:** 136
Millbank, Jeremiah, **1929:** 281n.
Miller, Charles A., **1932–33:** 208n., 243n.
Miller, Roy, **1931:** 399
Millikan, Robert A., **1931:** 198
Mills, Ogden L., **1930:** 271, 272, 273, 274; **1932–33:**
    38, 39, 41, 73n., 119n., 154n., 156n., 264,
    267ftn., 283, 399, 454
Milwaukee Chamber of Commerce, protest on rail
    rates, **1929:** 61
Mine Workers, United, **1931:** 244
Mines, Bureau of, **1932–33:** 423
Mining industry, **1932–33:** 344, 346, 357
Mining and Metallurgical Engineers, American
    Institute of, **1929:** 52n.
Mining and Metallurgical Society of America,
    1929: 252
Minnesota
    Agricultural relief, **1931:** 275
    Great Lakes–St. Lawrence Deep Waterway,
        1932–33: 235
    Indian claims, **1931:** 75
    Pipeline, gas, **1931:** 1
    President's campaign, **1932–33:** 380
    Roads program, **1931:** 248
    U.S. district judge, **1931:** 46, 70
Mint, Bureau of the, **1930:** 121
Mission Play, **1930:** 56
Mississippi, Canton Exchange Bank, **1932–33:** 100
Mississippi, drought relief, **1931:** 121
Mississippi River, **1932–33:** 321, 421
Mississippi River Commission, **1932–33:** 353n., 423
Mississippi River Valley flood control program,
    1929: 84, 85, 196, 197, 253
Mississippi Valley Association, **1929:** 276
Mississippi waterways system, **1929:** 253
Missouri
    Drought relief, **1930:** 258, 259, 265n., 272n.
    President's campaign, **1932–33:** 378
    Unemployment relief, **1931:** 329
Missouri, University of, **1930:** 154
Mitchell, Wesley C., **1929:** 318; **1932–33:** 437
Mitchell, William D., **1929:** 60n., 92n., 169, 170;
    1930: 179n., 220, 240, 342, 343; **1931:** 13,
    31, 46, 94, 120; **1932–33:** 90, 285, 456,
    475n.

Mixed Claims Commission, United States and
    Germany, **1930:** 74
Modern Art, Museum of, **1932–33:** 153
Moffat, Jay P., **1929:** 306
Moffatt, Fraser M., **1929:** 316
Moffett, Adm. William, **1929:** 6
Moffett, William A., **1931:** 435n.
Moley, Raymond, **1932–33:** 454
Moncada, José María, **1931:** 118, 138; **1932–33:**
    298
Monetary and Economic Conference, Internation-
    al.
    See World economic conference.
Money rates, **1929:** 272
Monongahela Commission, United States Battle of
    the, **1932–33:** 135
Monopolies, **1930:** 133, 390
Monroe, James, **1931:** 187
Monroe, Mich., **1932–33:** 346
Montana, **1929:** 185n.
    Agricultural relief, **1931:** 275
    Drought relief, **1930:** 258, 259, 265n., 266
    Silver Bow County Republican Committee,
        chairman, **1932–33:** 343
Montclair Yale Club, **1931:** 428
Mooney, William M., **1932–33:** 31n.
Moore, Ernest C., **1930:** 52
Moore, J. Hampton, **1929:** 211; **1931:** 346; **1932–**
    33: 350, 352
Moore, R. L., **1931:** 440
Moran, J. Sterling, **1930:** 99
Moratorium on intergovernmental debts
    Announcement, **1931:** 238, 239
    Bill signing, **1931:** 450
    Congress, telegram to members, **1931:** 240
    Extension, possibility of, **1931:** 350
    Foreign relations, message to Congress, **1931:**
        433
    French acceptance, **1931:** 251, 252
    German President, message, **1931:** 255
    President's Diary of Developments, **1931:** Supp.
        I
    U.S. trade, impact, **1931:** 264
Morgan, Arthur, **1929:** 31
Morgan, John P., **1929:** 97, 99, 109
Morgan, Joy, **1930:** 213
Morgan, Junius S., **1931:** 314
Morgan, Russell V., **1932–33:** 110
Morgenthau, Henry, **1931:** 153
Morris, Ill., **1932–33:** 376
Morris Plan Bankers Association, **1931:** 349
Morrison, A. Cressy, **1931:** 127
Morrow, Dwight W., **1930:** 11n., 187n., 191, 313,
    409; **1931:** 238, 239, 335, 338; **1932–33:**
    364
Morse, Samuel F. B., **1932–33:** 163

Mortgages, **1930:** 76, 77, 144, 249, 250, 302; **1931:**
    314, 344, 407, 408, 425, 436, 437; **1932–33:**
    1, 161, 238, 239, 251, 264, 272, 313, 322,
    328, 337, 346, 357, 358, 371, 377, 380, 470
Moscicki, Ignacy (President of Poland), **1929:** 233;
    1930: 148; **1931:** 169; **1932–33:** 144
Moses, Sen. George H., **1930:** 219; **1931:** 238, 239
Mosessohn, Dr. David N., **1930:** 416
Moss, Col. James A., **1929:** 36
Motion Pictures, National Board of Review of,
    1932–33: 464
Moton, Robert R., **1930:** 50, 51, 106; **1931:** 136;
    1932–33: 353
Moton commission.
    See United States Commission on Education in
        Haiti.
Motor and Equipment Association, **1930:** 130n.
Mott, John R., **1931:** 286
Mount Rushmore National Memorial Commis-
    sion, **1932–33:** 423
Mount Vernon, Va., **1932–33:** 57
Mount Weather, Va., **1929:** 10
Mouser, Repr. Grant E., Jr., **1932–33:** 346
Moynihan, Charles J., **1929:** 242
Mullaney, B. J., **1929:** 285n.
Mulrooney, Edward P., **1932–33:** 401, 468
Mun, Thomas, **1930:** 228n.
Mundelein, George Cardinal, **1930:** 304n.
Munitions, exports, **1930:** 337; **1931:** 86
Murphy, Frank, **1931:** 70n.
Murphy, William J., **1929:** 268
Murray, William H., **1931:** 91n.
Muscle Shoals, **1929:** 295
    Commission, **1931:** 88, 260, 416, 430, 440
    Development, legislation, **1930:** 243, 390
    Legislation, **1931:** 79, 82, 88
Museum of Art, Metropolitan, **1932–33:** 153n.
Museum of Modern Art, **1932–33:** 153
Museum of Safety, American, **1932–33:** 179
Music Supervisors National Conference, **1932–33:**
    110
Music Week Committee, National, **1929:** 55n.
Musicians Symphony Orchestra, **1932–33:** 429
Mussolini, Benito, **1931:** 297ftn.
Myers, R. Holtby, **1931:** 293

NAACP.
    See National Association for the Advancement
        of Colored People.
Nappanee, Ind., **1932–33:** 376
Narcotic Commission, California State, **1931:** 103
Narcotic Defense Association, World, **1932–33:** 52
Narcotic Drugs, Conference on the Limitation of
    the Manufacture of, **1931:** 28, 87, 103
Narcotic Education, World Conference on, **1930:**
    61; **1931:** 69

Narcotic Education Association, International, **1930**: 61; **1932–33**: 52

Narcotics, Bureau of, **1930**: 183n., 299, 390; **1931**: 103

Narcotics and drugs, **1930**: 17, 61, 135, 193, 329; **1931**: 69, 352

Nash, I. H., **1929**: 242

National Academy of Design, **1929**: 291

National Advisory Committee on Aeronautics, **1930**: 391, 394; **1931**: 397; **1932–33**: 422, 423

Annual report, **1929**: 298

National Advisory Council on Radio in Education, **1931**: 198

National Aeronautic Association, **1930**: 275; **1931**: 142; **1932–33**: 105

National Air Races, **1930**: 275; **1931**: 306

National Air Show, **1931**: 131n.

National Archives Building, cornerstone laying, **1932–33**: 471

National Association for the Advancement of Colored People, **1930**: 92ftn., 301; **1932–33**: 41n., 167, 353n.

National Association of Broadcasters, **1931**: 376; **1932–33**: 412

National Association of Builder's Exchanges, **1930**: 250; **1931**: 314

National Association of Building Trades Employers, **1930**: 30n.

National Association of Civic Service Club Executives, **1932–33**: 41n.

National Association of Commercial Organization Secretaries, **1932–33**: 41n.

National Association of Community Chests, **1932–33**: 338

National Association of Credit Men, **1932–33**: 41n.

National Association of Life Underwriters, **1929**: 217

National Association of Manufacturers, **1930**: 247; **1932–33**: 41n.

National Association of Purchasing Agents, **1932–33**: 190

National Association of Real Estate Boards, **1929**: 131; **1930**: 250; **1931**: 314

National Association of Taxicab Owners, **1930**: 130n.

National Association of Teachers in Colored Schools, **1931**: 272

National Automobile Chamber of Commerce, **1930**: 130n.; **1931**: 8

National Baptist Convention of America, **1930**: 290

National Board of Review of Motion Pictures, **1932–33**: 464

National Boys' Week, **1931**: 152

Committee, **1930**: 134

National Bureau of Casualty and Surety Underwriters, **1930**: 130n.

National Bureau of Economic Research, **1930**: 244, 247; **1932–33**: 337, 378

National Business Survey Conference, **1930**: 3, 4n., 46n.

National Business Women's Week, **1932–33**: 71

National Capital Park and Planning Commission, **1929**: 52n.; **1932–33**: 423

National Capital Presbyterian Commission, **1932–33**: 181

National Citizens Committee for Welfare and Relief Mobilization, **1932–33**: 294n.

National Commission of Fine Arts, 11th report, **1929**: 301

National Commission on Law Enforcement and Observance, **1929**: 5, 54, 80, 92, 295, 324; **1930**: 15, 17, 19, 209, 210; **1931**: 27; **1932–33**: 135, 193

National Conference on City Planning, **1932–33**: 41n.

National Conference on the Costs of Medical Care, **1932–33**: 411

National Conference on Palestine, **1932–33**: 20

National Conference on Social Work, **1932–33**: 171

National Conference on State Parks, **1930**: 197

National Congress of Parents and Teachers, **1929**: 64; **1930**: 250; **1931**: 314

National Council of Catholic Women, **1931**: 340

National Council of Congregational Churches, **1929**: 269n.

National Council of Intellectual Cooperation, **1931**: 52

National Credit Association, **1931**: 333, 334, 343, 350, 378, 395, 407, 408, 430, 436, 437; **1932–33**: 1, 259, 272, 347, 358, 371, 380

National defense and security, **1929**: 295, 296

Appropriations, **1932–33**: 421

Aviation, **1932–33**: 422

Budget message, **1931**: 432

Council on, **1931**: 324; **1932–33**: 169, 192, 322

General Disarmament Conference, **1932–33**: 204, 205, 206, 259

International Convention for the Suppression of International Trade in Arms and Ammunition and Implements of War, **1932–33**: 446

Philippine independence, **1932–33**: 449

National Drought Relief Committee, **1930**: 265, 271, 272; **1932–33**: 135

National Economy League, **1932–33**: 245

National Editorial Association, **1930**: 189

National Education Association, **1930**: 213; **1932–33**: 41n., 57, 62

National Electric Light Association, **1929**: 285n.; **1930**: 145

National employment system legislation, **1931**: 94

National Eucharistic Congress, **1930**: 304

National Farmers' Educational and Cooperative Union, **1930**: 250, 259n.

National Farmers Union, **1931:** 314
National Federation of Business and Professional
    Women's Clubs, Inc., **1932–33:** 41n., 71
National Federation of Men's Bible Classes, **1929:**
    63
National Federation of Radio Associations, **1931:**
    323
National Foreign Trade Convention, **1930:** 160
National Foreign Trade Council, **1932–33:** 143
National forests, **1931:** 189, 190
National Geographic Society, **1930:** 196; **1932–33:**
    203
National Government of China.
    See China.
National Grange, **1930:** 250, 259n.; **1931:** 314
National Guard, **1929:** 209, 295
National Home for Disabled Volunteer Soldiers,
    1930: 226, 227, 391
National Hospital Day, **1929:** 74; **1930:** 156;
    1932–33: 140
National Hotel Exposition, **1931:** 401
National Housing Association, **1931:** 314
National Industrial Conference Board, **1932–33:**
    41n.
National Life Insurance Conference, **1929:** 217
National Loyalty Commission of the Presbyterian
    Church, **1930:** 248
National Memorial Commission, **1932–33:** 135
National Music Week Committee, **1929:** 55n.
National Organization for Public Health Nursing,
    1931: 391
National Park Service, **1930:** 153; **1932–33:** 423
National parks, **1931:** 5
National Pharmacy Week, **1930:** 329; **1931:** 352;
    1932–33: 329
National Prison Emergency Committee, **1930:**
    409n.
National Publishers' Association, **1932–33:** 41n.
National Radio Week, **1931:** 323
National Recreation Association, **1931:** 134, 291
National Recreation Congress, **1929:** 238
National Republican Club of New York City,
    1932–33: 46
National Retail Credit Association, **1932–33:** 41n.
National Retail Dry Goods Association, **1930:** 46;
    1932–33: 428
National Retail Grocers Association, **1931:** 254
National Safety Council, **1930:** 130n., 307; **1931:**
    356; **1932–33:** 320
National Screw Thread Commission, **1932–33:** 423
National Society of the Sons of the American
    Revolution, **1932–33:** 164
National Tax Association, **1932–33:** 292
National Thrift Committee, **1932–33:** 41n.
National Thrift Week, **1932–33:** 21
National Training School for Boys, **1932–33:** 423
National Tuberculosis Association, **1930:** 382, 392;
    1931: 424; **1932–33:** 408
National Urban League, **1930:** 84

National Woman's Christian Temperance Union,
    1929: 210
Nation's Christmas Tree Association of California,
    1930: 427; **1931:** 452; **1932–33:** 436
Natural resources
    Conservation, **1929:** 25, 186, 241, 242, 295;
        1930: 390
    Forests, **1931:** 189, 190
    Natural gas, **1930:** 315
    Overexpansion, **1930:** 311
    Petroleum, **1931:** 25, 91, 99, 100
    Water, **1930:** 158, 182; **1931:** 11, 13
Naturalization Day, **1931:** 419
Naval Advisory Committee, **1929:** 241
Naval Conferences
    Geneva, **1929:** 48n., 61, 68
    London, **1929:** 229, 241, 295; **1932–33:** 135
Naval disarmament.
    See Disarmament.
Naval Observatory, **1932–33:** 423
Navigation, Bureau of, **1930:** 145, 146; **1932–33:**
    423
Navigation and Steamboat Inspection, Bureau of,
    1932–33: 423
Navy, Department of the
    Appropriations, **1930:** 65, 66, 67, 238, 395n.;
        1932–33: 421
        Controversy, **1931:** 327, 358, 359, 385, 387,
            390, 392, 406, 432
    Assistant Secretary for Aeronautics, **1932–33:**
        337n.
    Assistant Secretaries, **1929:** 6; **1931:** 219n., 285,
        392
    Aviation, **1930:** 112, 113, 117, 261, 391, 398
    Bureau of Navigation, **1932–33:** 423
    Chief of Bureau of Navigation, **1930:** 145, 146
    Chief of Naval Operations, **1930:** 145, 146, 296
    Commander in Chief, U.S. fleet, **1930:** 145, 146
    Construction, **1930:** 145, 238, 347, 390, 391, 418,
        423
    Economy conference, **1931:** 219
    Foreign claim, **1931:** 36
    Land naval stations, closings, **1932–33:** 119
    Navy Selection Board, **1930:** 176
    Office of Naval Operations, Chief, **1932–33:** 34,
        206
    Panama transports, proposed abolition, **1932–33:**
        119
    Pay increase, **1930:** 55n., 65, 66, 67
    Procurement policy, **1932–33:** 32
    Reduction in personnel, **1930:** 112, 113, 117, 321,
        322, 390, 391
    Research achievements, **1931:** 127
    San Francisco Bay Bridge agreement, **1930:** 261,
        262
    Secretary (Charles F. Adams), **1929:** 104, 178;
        1930: 9, 11n., 145, 146, 267, 395; **1931:**
        218, 219n., 324, 327, 435n.; **1932–33:** 34,
        119, 206, 444

[References are to items except as otherwise indicated]

Navy, Department of the — *continued*
  Selection board for medical officers, **1931:** 285
  United States Marine Corps, **1930:** 38, 39, 55n.,
    92, 133, 236, 253; **1931:** 36, 71n., 138, 297;
    1932–33: 34
  Virgin Islands, administration, **1931:** 39, 41
Navy-Army football game.
  See Army-Navy football game.
Navy Day, **1931:** 380; **1932–33:** 356
Navy League, **1931:** 385, 387, 390, 392
Navy Legion of Valor, Army and, **1931:** 288
Nebraska
  Agricultural relief, **1931:** 275
  Drought relief, **1930:** 258, 259
  Governor, **1930:** 265n.
Negro Vote, Joint National Planning Committee to
    Get Out the, **1932–33:** 318
Needles, A. C. **1930:** 272
Negroes.
  See Blacks.
Neithercott, Harry A., **1931:** 154
Nelson, John E., **1930:** 95n.
Nelson, Sophie, **1931:** 391
Netherlands, **1929:** 161, 317
Neumann, Emanuel, **1932–33:** 19
Nevada, **1929:** 134, 185n.
  President's visit, **1932–33:** 388, 389, 394
Neville, Gen. Wendell C., **1930:** 253
New Brunswick, N.J., **1930:** 330
New England Conference on Reemployment,
    1932–33: 240
New England Council, **1929:** 303; **1930:** 377; **1931:**
    418; **1932–33:** 41n.
New Hampshire Unemployment Relief Commit-
    tee, **1932–33:** 240n.
New Jersey
  Governor, **1931:** 137
  President's campaign, **1932–33:** 363, 364
  Red Cross chapters, regional conference, **1931:**
    326
  Republican Campaign Committee, **1932–33:** 372
  Republican senatorial candidate, **1930:** 187, 191,
    313
New Jersey Conference on Child Health and
    Protection, **1931:** 137
New Mexico, **1929:** 134, 185n.
  Governor, **1931:** 91n.
  President's visit, **1932–33:** 397
New York
  Candidates for public office, **1932–33:** 345, 367
  Committee of Public Safety, **1930:** 381n.
  Erie Canal, **1930:** 132
  Federal Reserve Banking and Industrial Com-
    mittee, **1932–33:** 169, 170
  Federal Reserve District, **1930:** 284, 402n.
  Governor, **1932–33:** 219, 358
  Great Lakes-St. Lawrence Deep Waterway,
    1932–33: 219, 235

New York — *continued*
  Republican Party, **1930:** 163, 308n.
  Roads program, **1931:** 248
  State Department of Social Welfare, **1932–33:**
    340n.
  State Power Authority, **1931:** 383
  Unemployment relief, **1930:** 331, 332, 336
  U.S. attorney, **1930:** 308
New York, Dental Society of the State of, **1931:**
    182
New York, Hundred Year Club of, **1932–33:** 85
New York, N.Y.
  Jewish Hospital of Brooklyn, **1932–33:** 355
  Lincoln Day dinner, address, **1932–33:** 465
  Police Commissioner, **1932–33:** 401, 468
  Post office site, **1932–33:** 224
  President's campaign, **1932–33:** 365, 366, 367
  Union Square, centennial celebration, **1932–33:**
    130
New York, One Hundred Year Club of, **1931:** 30
New York, Real Estate Board of, **1931:** 48; **1932–
    33:** 17
New York Association for the Blind, **1932–33:** 4
New York Bible Society, **1929:** 307
New York Board of Jewish Ministers, **1932–33:** 142
New York Board of Trade, **1930:** 110
New York City, Young Men's Christian Associ-
    ation of, **1932–33:** 22
New York City Clearing House Association, **1931:**
    343
New York City Emergency Employment Commit-
    tee, 336
New York Conference of the Methodist Episcopal
    Church, Central, **1931:** 336
New York Federal Reserve Bank, Governor, **1930:**
    402n.
New York Harbor, Supervisor, **1932–33:** 423
New York Herald Tribune, **1929:** 314n.; **1932–33:**
    311n.
New York and Its Environs, Regional Plan, **1929:**
    88; **1931:** 438
New York State Barge Lines, **1929:** 61
New York Statewide Economic Congress, **1929:**
    303
New York Stock Exchange, **1932–33:** 54, 55
New York Times, **1929:** 137n., 293n., 314n.; **1931:**
    316
New York University, **1930:** 186n.; **1931:** 156, 187
New York World, **1930:** 343n.
New Yorker Herold, **1930:** 281
New Zealand, **1929:** 161
  Former Prime Minister Joseph Ward, **1930:** 229
Newark, Del., **1932–33:** 363
Newark, N.J., **1932–33:** 364, 413
Newark Star-Eagle, **1932–33:** 104
Newcastle, Pa., **1932–33:** 336
Newlin, Gurney E., **1929:** 203

Newman, Bernard J., **1931**: 314
Newport News Shipbuilding and Dry Dock Company, **1929**: 193n.
News conference procedures, **1929**: 2, 5, 6, 8, 202, 218
News conferences
  January 2 (No. 165), **1931**: 1
  January 3 (No. 79), **1930**: 3, (No. 263), **1932–33**: 439
  January 5 (No. 227), **1932–33**: 3
  January 6 (No. 166), **1931**: 7
  January 7 (No. 80), **1930**: 10
  January 8 (No. 228), **1932–33**: 9
  January 10 (No. 81), **1930**: 14
  January 12 (No. 229), **1932–33**: 15
  January 14 (No. 82), **1930**: 19
  January 17 (No. 83), **1930**: 23
  January 18 (No. 167), **1931**: 18; (No. 264), **1932–33**: 451
  January 19 (No. 230), **1932–33**: 23
  January 20 (No. 265), **1932–33**: 452
  January 21 (No. 84), **1930**: 25
  January 23 (No. 168), **1931**: 31
  January 24 (No. 85), **1930**: 32
  January 25 (No. 266), **1932–33**: 457
  January 26 (No. 231), **1932–33**: 31
  January 27 (No. 169), **1931**: 37
  January 28 (No. 86), **1930**: 34
  January 30 (No. 170), **1931**: 39
  January 31 (No. 87), **1930**: 36
  February 2 (No. 232), **1932–33**: 35
  February 3 (No. 171), **1931**: 43
  February 4 (No. 88), **1930**: 38
  February 5 (No. 172), **1931**: 45; (No. 233), **1932–33**: 38
  February 7 (No. 89), **1930**: 50
  February 8 (No. 267), **1932–33**: 462
  February 10 (No. 173), **1931**: 54
  February 16 (No. 234), **1932–33**: 48
  February 17 (No. 174), **1931**: 62
  February 18 (No. 90), **1930**: 55
  February 19 (No. 235), **1932–33**: 54
  February 20 (No. 175), **1931**: 67
  February 21 (No. 91), **1930**: 59
  February 24 (No. 176), **1931**: 74
  February 25 (No. 92), **1930**: 66
  February 26 (No. 236), **1932–33**: 63
  February 27 (No. 177), **1931**: 79
  February 28 (No. 93), **1930**: 71
  March 3 (No. 268), **1932–33**: 481
  March 4 (No. 94), **1930**: 73
  March 5 (No. 1), **1929**: 2
  March 6 (No. 178), **1931**: 92
  March 7 (No. 95), **1930**: 76
  March 8 (No. 2), **1929**: 5; (No. 237), **1932–33**: 76
  March 11 (No. 238), **1932–33**: 80
  March 12 (No. 3), **1929**: 6; (No. 179), **1931**: 99
  March 14 (No. 96), **1930**: 85

News conferences — *continued*
  March 15 (No. 4), **1929**: 8
  March 17 (No. 180), **1931**: 104
  March 18 (No. 97), **1930**: 87
  March 19 (No. 5), **1929**: 10
  March 20 (No. 181), **1931**: 106
  March 21 (No. 98), **1930**: 92
  March 22 (No. 6), **1929**: 12
  March 25 (No. 99), **1930**: 94; (No. 239), **1932–33**: 92
  March 26 (No. 7), **1929**: 15; (No. 182), **1931**: 111
  March 28 (No. 100), **1930**: 97
  March 29 (No. 8), **1929**: 18; (No. 240), **1932–33**: 101
  March 31 (No. 183), **1931**: 116
  April 1 (No. 101), **1930**: 98; (No. 241), **1932–33**: 106
  April 2 (No. 9), **1929**: 25
  April 3 (No. 184), **1931**: 120
  April 5 (No. 10), **1929**: 28; (No. 242), **1932–33**: 111
  April 7 (No. 185), **1931**: 121
  April 9 (No. 11), **1929**: 32
  April 11 (No. 102), **1930**: 112
  April 12 (No. 12), **1929**: 34; (No. 243), **1932–33**: 123
  April 15 (No. 103), **1930**: 116; (No. 244), **1932–33**: 126
  April 16 (No. 13), **1929**: 37
  April 17 (No. 186), **1931**: 138
  April 18 (No. 104), **1930**: 117
  April 19 (No. 14), **1929**: 41
  April 21 (No. 187), **1931**: 140
  April 22 (No. 105), **1930**: 126; (No. 245), **1932–33**: 132
  April 23 (No. 15), **1929**: 48
  April 24 (No. 188), **1931**: 147
  April 25 (No. 106), **1930**: 132
  April 26 (No. 16), **1929**: 54
  April 29 (No. 107), **1930**: 137
  April 30 (No. 17), **1929**: 56
  May 1 (No. 189), **1931**: 162
  May 2 (No. 108), **1930**: 145
  May 3 (No. 18), **1929**: 61
  May 5 (No. 190), **1931**: 173
  May 6 (No. 109), **1930**: 150; (No. 246), **1932–33**: 147
  May 7 (No. 19), **1929**: 67
  May 8 (No. 191), **1931**: 177
  May 9 (No. 110), **1930**: 153
  May 10 (No. 20), **1929**: 73; (No. 247), **1932–33**: 154
  May 12 (No. 192), **1931**: 181
  May 13 (No. 111), **1930**: 157; (No. 248), **1932–33**: 158
  May 14 (No. 21), **1929**: 75
  May 15 (No. 193), **1931**: 189
  May 16 (No. 112), **1930**: 158

News conferences — *continued*
  May 17 (No. 22), **1929:** 77
  May 20 (No. 249), **1932–33:** 169
  May 21 (No. 23), **1929:** 80
  May 22 (No. 194), **1931:** 196
  May 23 (No. 113), **1930:** 161
  May 24 (No. 24), **1929:** 84
  May 27 (No. 114), **1930:** 165; (No. 250), **1932–33:** 182
  May 28 (No. 25), **1929:** 90
  May 31 (No. 26), **1929:** 97
  June 2 (No. 195), **1931:** 211
  June 3 (No. 115), **1930:** 173
  June 4 (No. 27), **1929:** 108
  June 5 (No. 196), **1931:** 218
  June 6 (No. 116), **1930:** 176
  June 7 (No. 28), **1929:** 114
  June 10 (No. 117), **1930:** 182
  June 11 (No. 29), **1929:** 116
  June 13 (No. 118), **1930:** 183
  June 14 (No. 30), **1929:** 118
  June 17 (No. 119), **1930:** 190; (No. 251), **1932–33:** 198
  June 18 (No. 31), **1929:** 125
  June 20 (No. 120), **1930:** 195; (No. 197), **1931:** 238
  June 21 (No. 32), **1929:** 128
  June 22 (No. 252), **1932–33:** 204
  June 24 (No. 121), **1930:** 202; (No. 253), **1932–33:** 208
  June 25 (No. 33), **1929:** 132
  June 27 (No. 122), **1930:** 209
  June 28 (No. 34), **1929:** 136
  July 1 (No. 123), **1930:** 218
  July 2 (No. 35), **1929:** 140
  July 5 (No. 36), **1929:** 144
  July 6 (No. 198), **1931:** 251
  July 8 (No. 124), **1930:** 226
  July 9 (No. 37), **1929:** 147
  July 10 (No. 199), **1931:** 256
  July 11 (No. 125), **1930:** 231
  July 14 (No. 200), **1931:** 259
  July 15 (No. 126), **1930:** 233
  July 16 (No. 38), **1929:** 151
  July 18 (No. 127), **1930:** 236
  July 19 (No. 39), **1929:** 155
  July 22 (No. 128), **1930:** 240; (No. 254), **1932–33:** 238
  July 23 (No. 40), **1929:** 159
  July 29 (No. 129), **1930:** 244; (No. 255), **1932–33:** 249
  July 30 (No. 41), **1929:** 165
  August 1 (No. 130), **1930:** 249
  August 4 (No. 201), **1931:** 277
  August 5 (No. 131), **1930:** 253
  August 6 (No. 42), **1929:** 169
  August 7 (No. 202), **1931:** 283
  August 8 (No. 132), **1930:** 258

News conferences — *continued*
  August 12 (No. 133), **1930:** 261; (No. 256), **1932–33:** 260
  August 13 (No. 43), **1929:** 177
  August 15 (No. 134), **1930:** 266
  August 19 (No. 135), **1930:** 271
  August 20 (No. 44), **1929:** 181
  August 21 (No. 203), **1931:** 297
  August 22 (No. 136), **1930:** 273
  August 23 (No. 45), **1929:** 183; (No. 257), **1932–33:** 267
  August 25 (No. 204), **1931:** 299
  August 26 (No. 137), **1930:** 276
  August 27 (No. 46), **1929:** 186
  September 1 (No. 205), **1931:** 302
  September 4 (No. 206), **1931:** 303
  September 5 (No. 138), **1930:** 284
  September 6 (No. 47), **1929:** 192
  September 9 (No. 139), **1930:** 288; (No. 258), **1932–33:** 282
  September 10 (No. 48), **1929:** 196
  September 11 (No. 207), **1931:** 311
  September 12 (No. 140), **1930:** 291
  September 13 (No. 49), **1929:** 202; (No. 259), **1932–33:** 289
  September 15 (No. 208), **1931:** 313
  September 16 (No. 141), **1930:** 293
  September 17 (No. 50), **1929:** 204
  September 20 (No. 51), **1929:** 209
  September 22 (No. 209), **1931:** 320
  September 23 (No. 142), **1930:** 299
  September 24 (No. 52), **1929:** 215
  September 25 (No. 210), **1931:** 324
  September 27 (No. 53), **1929:** 218
  September 29 (No. 211), **1931:** 327
  September 30 (No. 143), **1930:** 309
  October 1 (No. 54), **1929:** 219
  October 3 (No. 144), **1930:** 312
  October 4 (No. 55), **1929:** 224
  October 6 (No. 212), **1931:** 341
  October 7 (No. 213), **1931:** 344
  October 8 (No. 56), **1929:** 227
  October 9 (No. 214), **1931:** 350
  October 10 (No. 145), **1930:** 321
  October 11 (No. 57), **1929:** 231
  October 14 (No. 146), **1930:** 326
  October 15 (No. 58), **1929:** 237
  October 16 (No. 215), **1931:** 358
  October 17 (No. 147), **1930:** 331
  October 18 (No. 59), **1929:** 241
  October 21 (No. 148), **1930:** 334
  October 24 (No. 149), **1930:** 338; (No. 216), **1931:** 369
  October 25 (No. 60), **1929:** 256
  October 27 (No. 217), **1931:** 378
  October 28 (No. 150), **1930:** 342
  October 29 (No. 61), **1929:** 262
  October 30 (No. 218), **1931:** 387

News conferences — *continued*
  October 31 (No. 151), **1930:** 347
  November 1 (No. 62), **1929:** 270
  November 5 (No. 63), **1929:** 272
  November 6 (No. 219), **1931:** 397; (No. 260),
    1932–33: 382
  November 7 (No. 152), **1930:** 355
  November 8 (No. 64), **1929:** 274
  November 9 (No. 261), **1932–33:** 392
  November 10 (No. 220), **1931:** 403
  November 12 (No. 65), **1929:** 277
  November 13 (No. 221), **1931:** 407; (No. 262),
    1932–33: 396
  November 14 (No. 153), **1930:** 369
  November 15 (No. 66), **1929:** 280
  November 17 (No. 222), **1931:** 411
  November 18 (No. 154), **1930:** 373
  November 19 (No. 67), **1929:** 282
  November 21 (No. 155), **1930:** 378
  November 22 (No. 68), **1929:** 285
  November 24 (No. 223), **1931:** 420
  November 25 (No. 156), **1930:** 380
  November 26 (No. 69), **1929:** 290
  November 28 (No. 157), **1930:** 383
  November 29 (No. 70), **1929:** 292
  December 3 (No. 71), **1929:** 294
  December 5 (No. 158), **1930:** 397
  December 6 (No. 72), **1929:** 304
  December 9 (No. 159), **1930:** 402
  December 10 (No. 73), **1929:** 308
  December 11 (No. 224), **1931:** 436
  December 12 (No. 160), **1930:** 406
  December 13 (No. 74), **1929:** 310
  December 16 (No. 161), **1930:** 412
  December 17 (No. 75), **1929:** 315
  December 19 (No. 162), **1930:** 418
  December 20 (No. 76), **1929:** 319
  December 22 (No. 225), **1931:** 446
  December 23 (No. 163), **1930:** 422
  December 27 (No. 77), **1929:** 324
  December 29 (No. 226), **1931:** 453
  December 30 (No. 164), **1930:** 428
  December 31 (No. 78), **1929:** 327
News conference on bonus marchers by Secretary
    of War Hurley and Army Chief of Staff
    MacArthur, **1932–33:** 246n.
News media.
  See Press.
News-Herald, Franklin, Pa., **1932–33:** 469
Newspaper Boys of America, First Annual Patri-
    otic Pilgrimage, **1930:** 310
Newspaper Editors, American Society of, **1931:**
    139
Newspaper Publishers Association, American,
    1930: 118; **1931:** 139, 405
Newton, Walter H., **1929:** 63n., 144; **1932–33:**
    154n.

Niagara Board, Special International, **1930:** 109;
    1931: 37
Nicaragua, **1929:** 159, 160, 161, 295, 299
  Bandit activities, **1931:** 71n., 138, 140, 141
  Earthquake disaster, **1931:** 116, 118, 433
  Interoceanic Canal Board, survey, **1931:** 185
  President José María Moncada, **1931:** 118; 138;
    1932–33: 298
  Presidential elections, **1931:** 433
  Relations with U.S., **1931:** 71, 430
  U.S. Minister to, **1931:** 116n.
  U.S. withdrawal, **1930:** 92
Nicaragua Canal, **1929:** 125
Nickelsburg, J. F. E., **1930:** 320; **1932–33:** 262
Nightingale, Florence, **1931:** 195
Niobe, **1932–33:** 255
Nobile, Umberto, 23n.
Norbeck, Sen. Peter, **1929:** 46, 270
Nordbye, Gunnar H., **1931:** 70
Nordisk Tidende, **1930:** 178
Norris, Sen. George W., **1931:** 82; **1932–33:** 366,
    378
Norris-La Guardia Act, **1932–33:** 90
North Carolina
  Republican State executive committee, **1932–33:**
    45
  Wright Brothers National Memorial, **1932–33:**
    403
North Dakota, agricultural relief, **1931:** 275
Norway, **1929:** 161, 168, 317
  Claims against U.S., **1930:** 83, 152
  King Haakon VII, **1930:** 252
Norwegian-Americans, **1930:** 178
Noyes, Frank B., **1930:** 123
Nulton, Adm. Louis McC., **1930:** 146
Nursing, National Organization for Public Health,
    1931: 391

Oakes, George Washington Ochs, **1931:** 381
Oakes, John B., **1932–33:** 202
Oakland, Calif., **1932–33:** 390
Obermayer, Leon J., **1932–33:** 41n.
O'Brien, Robert Lincoln, **1931:** 420; **1932–33:** 237,
    349
O'Connell, P. A., **1932–33:** 428
O'Connor, T. V., **1930:** 177
Ocean mail contracts, **1929:** 104, 202, 237, 295
Ochs, Adolph S., **1929:** 137n.; **1931:** 316, 381
O'Donnell, Charles L., **1929:** 65
Oddie, Sen. Tasker L., **1932–33:** 388
Odum, Howard W., **1929:** 318
O'Fallon Railway Company, **1929:** 80
Ogburn, William F., **1929:** 318
Ogden, Rollo, **1930:** 119
Ogden, Utah, **1932–33:** 388

Ohio
  Child health and protection conference, **1932–33:** 5n.
  Drought relief, **1930:** 258, 259, 265n.
  President's visit, **1931:** 228, 229
  Great Lakes rescue mission, **1930:** 190
  Great Lakes-St. Lawrence Deep Waterway, **1932–33:** 235
  Lincoln's Birthday, message, **1932–33:** 45n.
  Memorials to three prominent Republicans, **1932–33:** 302
  President's campaign, **1932–33:** 336, 337, 346, 357
  Relief efforts, **1931:** 357
  Unemployment relief, **1930:** 331, 332
Ohio River, **1929:** 250, 253
Ohio River Monument, Cincinnati, Ohio, **1929:** 250
Ohio State University, **1930:** 16
Ohio Valley Improvement Association, **1929:** 250
Oil, **1931:** 25, 91, 99, 100; **1932–33: 342, 346**
  Conservation, **1929:** 6, 8, 9, 25, 185
  Shale lands controversy, **1930:** 342, 343
Oil Conservation Board, Federal, **1929:** 25; **1931:** 99, 100; **1932–33:** 423
Oklahoma
  Governor, **1931:** 91n.
  Indian claims, **1931:** 65
  Lincoln's Birthday, message, **1932–33:** 45n.
  Oil resources, **1931:** 100
  Pipeline, gas, **1931:** 1
  Seminole Indians, land claims, **1932–33:** 458
  U.S. attorney, **1931:** 211, 277
Oklahoma, Governor, **1930:** 270
Olander, Victor A., **1930:** 272
Olav, Hans, **1930:** 178
Olaya, Enrique, **1930:** 124, 157; **1931:** 265
Olympiad, Games of the Tenth, **1931:** 241
Olympic Games, **1932–33:** 200, 253, 318
Olympic Winter Games, III, **1931:** 98
One Hundred, Committee of, Dayton, Ohio, **1931:** 357
One Hundred Year Club of New York, **1931:** 30
116th Street Synagogue, **1932–33:** 332
O'Neal, Edward A., **1931:** 260, 440
Opera Company, American, **1930:** 69
Orange (N.J.) Association for Permanent War Memorial, **1929:** 130
Oratorical Contest, Fifth International, **1930:** 340
Oratorical Contest on Loyalty and Law, **1930:** 248
Orbach, C. L., **1931:** 132
Ord, Maj. James B., **1932–33:** 25n.
Oregon, **1929:** 185n.
  California Society of Washington, D.C., radio address, **1932–33:** 371
  Child health and protection conference, **1932–33:** 5n.
  Lincoln's Birthday, message, **1932–33:** 45n.
  Roads program, **1931:** 248

Ortiz Rubio, Pasqual (President-elect of Mexico), **1929:** 310; **1930:** 26, 27, 44, 47, 133, 298, 421; **1931:** 221; **1932–33:** 214n., 279
Ottawa, Ill., **1932–33:** 376
Ottinger, Albert, **1931:** 157
Oulahan, Richard V., **1931:** 456
Owen, Russell, **1930:** 211
Owen, Repr. Ruth B., **1929:** 267n.
Owyhee Dam, Oreg., **1932–33:** 232
Oxford, Ohio, **1932–33:** 357

Pacific Foreign Trade Convention, **1932–33:** 143
Pacific Relations, Institute of, **1929:** 261
Packard Motor Car Co., **1932–33:** 105
Paderewski, Ignace, **1931:** 249n.
Page, Arthur Wilson, **1930:** 11n.
Page, Thomas Walker, **1930:** 276, 293, 294
Paitilla Point Military Reservation, Panama Canal Zone, **1930:** 419
Palestine, **1929:** 186, 190; **1930:** 151
  Campaign, American, **1931:** 90n.
  Committee, American, **1932–33:** 19
  National Conference on, **1932–33:** 20
Pallen, Condé B., death, **1929:** 93
Palm Sunday, **1930:** 54, 114
Palmer, Katherine, **1930:** 300
Palo Alto, Calif., **1932–33:** 390, 392
  Chamber of Commerce of, **1930:** 353
Pan American Child Congress, Sixth, **1930:** 75
Pan American Commercial Conference, Fourth, **1931:** 347
Pan American Confederation for Highway Education, **1929:** 179
Pan American Conference of Directors of Health, Second, **1931:** 144
Pan American Day, **1930:** 169; **1931:** 135
Pan American Highway Conference, Second, **1929:** 179
Pan American Society, **1930:** 21
Pan American Union, **1930:** 414; **1931:** 135
Panama, **1929:** 3n., 161, 271
Panama, President Ricardo J. Alfaro, **1931:** 393
Panama, President Harmodio Arias, **1932–33:** 373
Panama, Republic of
  President Florencio Arosemena, **1930:** 141, 353
  Radio telegraphic service, **1930:** 141
Panama Canal, **1930:** 100, 391, 419
  Appropriations, **1932–33:** 421
Paper Chemistry, Institute of, **1931:** 322
Paraguay, **1929:** 3n., 295
  Commission on Inquiry and Conciliation, Bolivia, **1931:** 433
  President José P. Guggiari, **1931:** 186
Parent-Teachers Association, **1931:** 246
Parents' Day, **1931:** 178; **1932–33:** 118
Parents' Magazine, **1931:** 321

[References are to items except as otherwise indicated]

Parents and Teachers, National Congress of, **1931:** 314

Park, Marion Edwards, **1931:** 165

Park, Waterton-Glacier International Peace, **1932–33:** 201

Park Avenue Synagogue, **1932–33:** 116

Park and Planning Commission, National Capital, **1932–33:** 423

Park Service, National, **1930:** 153; **1932–33:** 423

Parker, F. H., **1932–33:** 100

Parker, Fred C. W., **1932–33:** 41n.

Parker, John J., **1930:** 92

Parker, William Stanley, **1931:** 314

Parkersburg, W. Va., **1932–33:** 357

Parks, national, **1930:** 65, 153, 157, 234; **1931:** 5

Parks, National Conference on State, **1930:** 197

Parks of the National Capital, Office of Public Buildings and Public, **1932–33:** 423

Parkway Commission, Rock Creek and Potomac, **1932–33:** 423

Parmelee, Julius H., **1930:** 130n.

Parnell, Dr. C. G., **1930:** 156n.

Parnell, Gov. Harvey, **1930:** 265n.

Parole Board, **1930:** 165

Parsons, Charles L., **1929:** 200n.

Pasadena, Calif., **1932–33:** 394

Passamaquoddy Bay, **1930:** 42

Passover, **1930:** 54, 114

Pasts, Constantine, **1931:** 76

Patent Office, **1932–33:** 122

Patman, Repr. Wright, **1932–33:** 102n.

Patman bonus bill.

   See Bonus, veterans.

Patrick, Maj. Gen. Mason M., **1929:** 75

Patronage investigations, **1930:** 87, 88

Patterson, Frank Allen, **1930:** 228

Patterson, George S., **1931:** 204n.

Patterson, Maj. Gen. Robert U., **1931:** 181

Paulding, Charles C., **1931:** 30; **1932–33:** 85

Payne, Frederick Huff, **1930:** 126; **1932–33:** 265

Payne, John Barton, **1930:** 33, 265n., 271, 272, 362n.; **1931:** 15, 26, 29, 44, 195, 310

Payne-Aldrich tariff, **1930:** 188

Peace, **1929:** 1, 275, 295, 314

Peace Garden, International, **1932–33:** 227

Peace pact, Paris, **1929:** 1, 94, 161, 184, 229, 275, 295

Peace Park, Waterton-Glacier International, **1932–33:** 201

Peace Society, American, **1932–33:** 141

Pearson, A. C., **1932–33:** 41n.

Pearson, Paul M., **1931:** 39, 41; **1932–33:** 426

Pearson, T. Gilbert, **1929:** 31

Pease, Charles, **1930:** 190

Pedrick, William J., **1932–33:** 316

Peking, China, **1930:** 133

Pelley, John J., **1929:** 281n.

Penn, William, **1932–33:** 350, 363

Pennsylvania
  Curwensville, Chamber of Commerce, **1932–33:** 82
  Governor, **1932–33:** 305
  Lincoln's Birthday, message, **1932–33:** 45n.
  President's campaign, **1932–33:** 336, 363, 375
  Relief efforts, **1931:** 431
  Representatives of the unemployed, **1932–33:** 7
  Roads program, **1931:** 248
  Senator-elect, **1930:** 386n.

Pennsylvania Railroad Co., **1932–33:** 175

Pension bill, **1932–33:** 138

Pension Bureau, **1929:** 41

Pensions, **1931:** 150, 358, 359, 432
  Government employees, **1930:** 59, 60, 65, 66, 67
  Veterans, **1930:** 173, 174, 182, 202, 203, 206

Pensions, Bureau of, **1930:** 226, 227, 391

Peoria, Ill., **1932–33:** 376

Pereira de Souza, Washington L., (President of Brazil), **1929:** 89

Perez, Juan Bautista (President of Venezuela), **1929:** 145

Perishable Agricultural Commodities Act, 1930, **1930:** 182

Perkins, Thomas N., **1929:** 109

Permanent Court of International Justice, **1929:** 1, 12, 295, 306; **1930:** 115, 119, 133, 365, 383, 385, 390, 405; **1931:** 191n., 433

Permanent International Association of Road Congresses, **1930:** 49

Perry, Chester R., **1932–33:** 41n.

Perry, Commodore Oliver Hazard, **1931:** 276

Perry's Victory Memorial, **1931:** 276

Pershing, Gen. John J., **1930:** 89n.; **1931:** 364

Persia, **1929:** 3n., 161

Personnel Administration, Council of, **1932–33:** 135, 212

Personnel Administration, proposed, **1932–33:** 50

Peru, **1929:** 3n., 77, 89, 161, 167, 235, 295, 309
  Revolution, **1930:** 390
  Sixth Pan American Child Congress, **1930:** 75
  U.S. Ambassador to, **1930:** 34

Pétain, Marshal Henri, **1931:** 364

Peters, Herbert H., **1931:** 363

Peterson, Norman E., **1931:** 70

Peterson, William, **1929:** 242

Petrograd, U.S. Embassy, **1930:** 181

Petroleum, **1931:** 25, 91, 99, 100
  See also Oil.

Pettibone, C. E., **1930:** 130n., 307

Pharmacy Week, National, **1930:** 329; **1931:** 352; **1932–33:** 329

Phelan, James J., **1930:** 233

Philadelphia, Pa., **1929:** 286n.; **1931:** 204; **1932–33:** 363

Philip, John W., **1931:** 200, 201

Philippines
  Battle of Manila Bay, anniversary, **1931:** 154

Philippines — *continued*
  Governor General, **1929:** 77; **1932–33:** 11
  Independence, **1931:** 378, 379; **1932–33:** 384, 449
  Scouts, cost of support, **1932–33:** 119
  Sugar exports, **1932–33:** 384, 387
  Vice Governor, **1930:** 244, 245, 303
Phillips, Harry D., **1932–33:** 17
Phillips, Orie L., **1929:** 37n.
Phillips Exeter Academy, **1931:** 220
Piedmont, W. Va., **1932–33:** 360
Pierson, Stuart E., **1930:** 272
Pinchot, Gov. Gifford, **1932–33:** 305
Pioneer Woman statue, Ponca City, Okla., **1930:** 129
Pipelines, gas, **1931:** 1
Pitcairn, Harold F., **1931:** 142
Platt, Edmund, **1930:** 284, 285, 289
Platt, Warren C., **1932–33:** 41n.
Plumbers and Steamfitters, United States Association of, **1931:** 101
Plummer, Edward C., **1930:** 176; **1932–33:** 106, 108
Plyer, A. M., **1932–33:** 130
Poland, **1929:** 3n., 161, 233
  Claims against U.S., **1930:** 136
  Intergovernmental debts, **1932–33:** 431
  President Ignacy Moscicki, **1930:** 148; **1931:** 169; **1932–33:** 144
  Statue of Woodrow Wilson, unveiling, **1931:** 249
  Treaty of friendship, commerce, and consular rights, **1931:** 433
Polando, John, **1931:** 279; **1932–33:** 247
Polar expedition, **1930:** 196, 208, 211, 220
Polar Year program, Second, **1931:** 56
Pole, J. W., **1932–33:** 284
Police, International Association of Chiefs of, **1931:** 355
Poling, Daniel A., **1929:** 143; **1930:** 257; **1931:** 38; **1932–33:** 268
Polish Corridor, **1931:** 373
Polish National Day, **1930:** 148; **1931:** 169; **1932–33:** 144
Politics and political parties, **1929:** 15, 16, 33, 35, 135, 248
Polk, James K., **1930:** 207
Pollard, Gov. John Garland, **1930:** 265n.
Pomerene, Atlee, **1932–33:** 243, 264, 267ftn.
Pomona, Calif., **1932–33:** 394
Ponca City, Okla., **1930:** 129
Poole, John, **1932–33:** 41n.
Pope, Allan M., **1932–33:** 41n.
Porter, J. F., **1931:** 440; **1932–33:** 264
Porter, Repr. Stephen G., **1930:** 183n., 212
Portes Gil, Emilio (President of Mexico), **1929:** 205; **1930:** 27
Porto Rican Hurricane Relief Commission, report, **1930:** 20
Porto Rico
  Child Feeding Committee, **1932–33:** 433

Porto Rico — *continued*
  Governor, **1929:** 84; **1931:** 102, 106, 108, 109, 111; **1932–33:** 11, 33, 310
  Health conditions, **1930:** 204, 361
  Hurricane, **1932–33:** 310
    Relief, **1930:** 20
  President's visit, **1931:** 102, 106, 108, 109, 111, 112
Portugal, **1929:** 161
  U.S. Ambassador to, **1930:** 34
Pope, Generoso, **1930:** 360
Portraits, Presidential, **1932–33:** 369n.
Portsmouth, Ohio, **1932–33:** 346
Post, Wiley, **1931:** 247, 253; **1932–33:** 266
Post Office Department
  Acting Postmaster General, **1930:** 316n.
  Airmail, **1929:** 8, 234, 237, 295; **1930:** 145, 273, 312, 407
  Assistant Postmasters General, **1931:** 200, 201
  Building, cornerstone laying, **1932–33:** 307
  Deficit, **1929:** 147; **1930:** 236, 237, 238, 305; **1931:** 62, 147, 148, 214
  Economy conference, **1931:** 200, 201
  Employment policies, **1930:** 316, 338
  Federal expenditures, **1932–33:** 92, 93
  44-hour workweek, **1931:** 62
  Government employees, political activity, **1932–33:** 276
  Leases, **1930:** 299, 305, 390
  Patronage investigations, **1930:** 87, 88
  Post office construction, **1932–33:** 182, 183, 224
  Postal service contracts, **1929:** 104, 202, 237, 295
  Postmaster General (Walter F. Brown), **1929:** 104, 202n.; **1930:** 145, 267, 299, 305, 316; **1931:** 200, 201; **1932–33:** 76, 77, 91n., 106, 108, 119n., 276, 282
  Postmasters, appointment, **1929:** 18n.
  State of the Union message, **1929:** 295
  Third Assistant Postmaster General, **1929:** 108
Postell, Julius, **1930:** 272
Potomac Parkway Commission, Rock Creek and, **1932–33:** 423
Potter, Milton Chase, **1932–33:** 62
Power
  Federal regulation, **1932–33:** 259, 358, 366
  Great Lakes-St. Lawrence Deep Waterway, **1932–33:** 219, 235
  Hoover Dam, Nev., **1932–33:** 394, 396
Power Authority of the State of New York, **1931:** 383
Power Commission, Federal, **1930:** 182, 192n., 195, 218, 236, 240, 390; **1931:** 12, 13, 31, 430; **1932–33:** 358, 366
Power Conference, World, **1930:** 192
Prajadhipok, King of Siam, **1930:** 359; **1931:** 175, 273
Pratt, Henry C., **1929:** 214
Pratt, Joseph Hersey, **1931:** 314

Pratt, Repr. Ruth, **1932–33:** 367
Pratt, Adm. William V., **1929:** 241; **1930:** 11n., 145, 146; **1931:** 219; **1932–33:** 34
Preinaugural addresses
  Acceptance of nomination, **1929:** Supp I, p. 497
  Campaign, 1928, **1929:** Supp. II, p. 521
  Central and South American trip, **1929:** Supp. IV, p. 615
  Statement to the press after election, **1929:** Supp. III, p. 613
Prentice, Mrs. Bernon S., **1931:** 23
Preparatory Commission for the Disarmament Conference, **1929:** 28, 34, 48n., 61, 68, 75
Preparedness, military, **1929:** 275
Presbyterian Church, General Assembly, **1931:** 208
Presbyterian Church, National Loyalty Commission of the, **1930:** 248
Presbyterian Commission, National Capital, **1932–33:** 181
Presbyterian Magazine, **1929:** 191n.
Presidential receptions, **1932–33:** 43
President's Advisory Committee on Employment Statistics, **1931:** 60n.
President's Advisory Committee on Veteran Preference, **1931:** 150
President's calendar, **1931:** App. E
President's Commission for the Study and Review of Conditions in the Republic of Haiti, **1930:** 38, 39, 50, 51, 85, 92, 93, 97, 261; **1932–33:** 135
President's Conference on Home Building and Home Ownership.
  See White House Conference on Home Building and Home Ownership.
President's Diary of Developments of the Moratorium **1931:** Supp. I
President's Emergency Committee for Employment, **1930:** 347, 413; **1931:** 161, 295; **1932–33:** 135, 337ftn.
President's Organization on Unemployment Relief
  Advisory Committee, **1931:** 297, 299, 303
  Appropriations, **1932–33:** 215
  Community cooperation, **1931:** 360, 387, 388, 430, 436; **1932–33:** 135, 169, 260, 261, 294
  Director, **1931:** 294, 295, 299, 303, 324, 360, 387, 388, 403, 436n.; **1932–33:** 260, 261, 294, 337ftn.
President's post-election plans, **1932–33:** 392, 396, 462
President's Research Committee on Social Trends, **1932–33:** 437
President's salary, **1932–33:** 119, 231
President's staff.
  See White House staff.
President's travel.
  See also Appendix E—The President's Calendar.
  Akron, Ohio, **1932–33:** 336
  Athens, Ohio, **1932–33:** 357

President's travel — *continued*
  Baltimore, Md., **1932–33:** 363
  Baraboo, Wis., **1932–33:** 379
  Beloit, Wis., **1932–33:** 379
  Belvidere, Ill., **1932–33:** 379
  Boston, Mass., **1930:** 314, 315
  Boulder City, Nev., **1932–33:** 394
  Braddock, Pa., **1932–33:** 336
  Caribbean tour, **1931:** 102, 104, 106, 108, 109, 110, 111, 112
  Charleston, W. Va., **1931:** 223; **1932–33:** 346
  Chester, Pa., **1932–33:** 363
  Chillicothe, Ohio, **1932–33:** 346, 357
  Cincinnati, Ohio, **1932–33:** 357
  Circleville, Ohio, **1932–33:** 346
  Clarksburg, W. Va., **1932–33:** 360
  Cleveland, Ohio, **1930:** 311; **1932–33:** 337
  Colfax, Calif., **1932–33:** 390
  Columbus, Ohio, **1931:** 229; **1932–33:** 346
  Connellsville, Pa., **1932–33:** 336, 375
  Connersville, Ind., **1932–33:** 357
  Cumberland, Md., **1932–33:** 336
  Danville, Ill., **1931:** 234
  Davenport, Iowa, **1932–33:** 321
  Decatur, Ill., **1931:** 235
  Delaware, Ohio, **1932–33:** 346
  Denver, Colo., **1932–33:** 383
  Des Moines, Iowa, **1932–33:** 322, 323, 324, 325
  Detroit, Mich., **1931:** 318; **1932–33:** 347
  Eau Claire, Wis., **1932–33:** 379
  Echo, Utah, **1932–33:** 386
  Elko, Nev., **1932–33:** 388, 389
  Elroy, Wis., **1932–33:** 379
  Evanston, Wyo., **1932–33:** 386
  Fort Monroe, Va., **1931:** 360
  Fort Wayne, Ind., **1932–33:** 326
  Fostoria, Ohio, **1932–33:** 346
  Freeport, Ill., **1932–33:** 379
  Gary, Ind., **1932–33:** 376
  Gettysburg, Pa., **1930:** 170
  Glendale, Calif., **1932–33:** 394
  Grafton, W. Va., **1932–33:** 360
  Greensburg, Ind., **1931:** 225
  Gresham Junction, Ill., **1932–33:** 376
  Hamden, Ohio, **1932–33:** 357
  Hamilton, Ohio, **1932–33:** 357
  Henry, Ill., **1932–33:** 376
  Hudson, Wis., **1932–33:** 379
  Huntington, W. Va., **1931:** 224; **1932–33:** 346
  Indianapolis, Ind., **1932–33:** 358
  Ironton, Ohio, **1932–33:** 346
  Joliet, Ill., **1932–33:** 376
  Kenova, W. Va., **1932–33:** 346
  Keyser, W. Va., **1932–33:** 360
  Kings Mountain, S.C., **1930:** 319
  LaSalle, Ill., **1932–33:** 376
  Liberal, Kans., **1932–33:** 397
  Madison, Wis., **1932–33:** 379

President's travel — *continued*
    Marion, Ohio, **1931:** 228; **1932–33:** 346
    Martinsburg, W. Va., **1932–33:** 336, 360
    McKeesport, Pa., **1932–33:** 336
    Merrillan, Wis., **1932–33:** 379
    Meyersdale, Pa., **1932–33:** 336
    Monroe, Mich., **1932–33:** 346
    Morris, Ill., **1932–33:** 376
    Mount Vernon, Va., **1932–33:** 57
    Nappanee, Ind., **1932–33:** 376
    New York, N.Y., **1932–33:** 365, 366, 367, 465
    Newark, Del., **1932–33:** 363
    Newark, N.J., **1932–33:** 364
    Newcastle, Pa., **1932–33:** 336
    Oakland, Calif., **1932–33:** 390
    Ogden, Utah, **1932–33:** 388
    Ottawa, Ill., **1932–33:** 376
    Oxford, Ohio, **1932–33:** 357
    Palo Alto, Calif., **1932–33:** 390, 392
    Parkersburg, W. Va., **1932–33:** 357
    Pasadena, Calif., **1932–33:** 394
    Peoria, Ill., **1932–33:** 376
    Philadelphia, Pa., **1931:** 204; **1932–33:** 363
    Piedmont, W. Va., **1932–33:** 360
    Pomona, Calif., **1932–33:** 394
    Portsmouth, Ohio, **1932–33:** 346
    Richmond, Va., **1932–33:** 137
    Rock Island, Ill., **1932–33:** 321
    Rockford, Ill., **1932–33:** 379
    Rushville, Ind., **1932–33:** 357
    Sacramento, Calif., **1932–33:** 390
    Springfield, Ill., **1931:** 232, 233
    St. Louis, Mo., **1932–33:** 378
    St. Paul, Minn., **1932–33:** 380
    Salt Lake City, Utah, **1932–33:** 387
    San Bernardino, Calif., **1932–33:** 394
    San Francisco, **1932–33:** 390
    Springfield, Ill., **1932–33:** 377
    Toledo, Ohio, **1932–33:** 346
    Trenton, N.J., **1932–33:** 363
    Tucumcari, N. Mex., **1932–33:** 397
    Valley Forge, Pa., **1931:** 205
    Waverly, Ohio, **1932–33:** 346
    Wellsboro, Ind., **1932–33:** 376
    West Liberty, Iowa, **1932–33:** 321
    Wilmington, Del., **1932–33:** 363
    Woodville, Ind., **1932–33:** 376
    Yorktown, Va., **1931:** 364, 365
    Youngstown, Ohio, **1932–33:** 336
    Zelienople, Pa., **1932–33:** 336
President's vacation plans, **1930:** 153, 157, 234, 261, 263, 326
Press.
    See also News conferences.
    American Society of Newspaper Editors, remarks, **1930:** 119
    Anti-hoarding campaign, publicity, **1932–33:** 38, 81

Press — *continued*
    Associated Press, address to, **1929:** 47; **1931:** 139
    English press, welcome, **1929:** 227
    Farewell remarks, **1932–33:** 481
    Foreign language newspaper, **1930:** 218, 360; **1931:** 132
    French journalists, welcome, **1931:** 369, 370
    Gridiron Club addresses, **1929:** 35, 314; **1930:** 133, 408; **1931:** 155, 439; **1932–33:** 120, 424
    Indiana Republican Editorial Association, address, **1931:** 226
    Interview with the President, **1931:** Supp. II
    Iowa newspaper editors, remarks, **1932–33:** 325
    Messages to press conventions, **1929:** 43; **1930:** 118, 123, 124, 189; **1931:** 139, 179, 274, 292, 312, 316, 402, 405, 410, 456; **1932–33:** 104, 151, 426, 469, 478, 479
    New Year's greetings, **1929:** 327
    Oil shale lands controversy, press responsibility, **1930:** 342, 343
    Role in restoring public confidence in business situation, **1929:** 283, 292
    Scientific Monthly, introduction to series, **1932–33:** 435
    White House Correspondents' Association, dinner, **1932–33:** 76
    White House relations with, **1930:** 73, 310; **1931:** 311, 327, 341, 350
Prestes, Julio, **1930:** 157, 180, 185, 199, 337n.
Priestley medal, **1929:** 200
Princeton University, **1930:** 62; **1932–33:** 151, 202
Prison Emergency Committee, National, **1930:** 409n.
Prisons, **1930:** 17, 135, 165, 209, 210, 390, 391, 409
Private vs. public financing of relief efforts, remarks and statement, **1931:** 43, 44
Proclamations.
    See also Appendix B—Messages to the Congress; Appendix C—Presidential Reports to the 71st Congress, 1929; Appendix D—Presidential Reports to the 71st Congress, 1930; Appendix D—Presidential Reports to the 71st and 72nd Congresses, 1931; Appendix D—Presidential Reports to the 72nd Congress, During 1932–33.
    Amending the Migratory Bird Treaty regulations (Proc. 1876), **1929:** 50
    Calvin Coolidge, death (Proc. 2024), **1932–33:** 444
    Child Health Day, 1929 (Proc. 1873), **1929:** 14
    Colorado River Compact and the Boulder Canyon Project (Proc. 1882), **1929:** 134
    Creating a board to investigate a labor dispute between the Texas & Pacific Railway Company and its employees (Proc. 1874), **1929:** 19

Proclamations — *continued*
Exportation of arms and munitions to Brazil
(Proc. 1923), **1930:** 337; (Proc. 1939),
1931: 86
Exportation of arms and munitions of war to
Mexico (Proc. 1885), **1929:** 154
Extra session of Congress, April 1929 (Proc.
1870), **1929:** 4
George Washington, bicentennial of birth (Proc.
1986), **1932–33:** 35
Limiting aliens' immigration into the United
States on basis of national origin (Proc.
1872), **1929:** 13
Pan American Day (Proc. 1912), **1930:** 169
Special session of the Senate (Proc. 1915), **1930:**
221
Taft, William Howard, death (Proc. 1901), **1930:**
79
Waterfowl conservation (Proc. 1965), **1931:** 299
Proctor, Alexander M., **1932–33:** 65
Proctor, Redfield, **1930:** 377
Professional Women's Clubs, National Federation
of Business and, **1932–33:** 41n., 71
Progressive Conference, **1931:** 155
Prohibition, **1931:** 27; **1932–33:** 69, 259, 268, 317,
372, 378
Allied Forces for, **1932–33:** 268n.
Enforcement, **1930:** 15, 17, 19, 135, 193, 390
See also National Commission on Law En-
forcement and Observance.
Background discussions, **1929:** 10, 324
District of Columbia, **1929:** 214
Inaugural address, **1929:** 1
Incidents, **1929:** 28, 125, 127, 129
McNab study, **1929:** 219, 220
Message to Congress proposing study, **1929:**
112
State of the Union message, **1929:** 295
Prohibition Bureau, transfer to Justice Depart-
ment, **1929:** 34; **1930:** 135, 165, 390
Prométhée, **1932–33:** 222
Prosser, Seward, **1930:** 336
Protection of American citizens, **1929:** 5, 275
Protestant Reformation, message on anniversary,
1930: 320
Public buildings projects, **1930:** 3, 7, 127, 128, 158,
158n., 236, 237, 238, 305, 347, 357, 390,
391, 397, 418, 423; **1931:** 67, 177, 181, 184,
277, 278, 297, 303, 307, 319, 387, 388, 394,
432, 436, 437; **1932–33:** 213, 282, 283, 307,
357, 421
Public buildings
Budget, **1929:** 296
District of Columbia, **1929:** 51, 144, 295
Public Buildings and Public Parks of the National
Capital, Office of, **1932–33:** 423
Public debt, **1929:** 295; **1932–33:** 9, 10, 347, 402,
421

Public debt — *continued*
See also Economy, national.
Public Domain, Commission on Conservation and
Administration of the, **1929:** 241, 242,
295; **1932–33:** 135, 423
Public health, **1929:** 1, 295
Public Health Association, American, **1932–33:**
348, 358
Public Health Nursing, National Organization for,
1931: 391
Public Health Service, Bureau of, **1930:** 55n., 165,
265; **1931:** 43, 44, 103, 297, 298, 430
Health statistics, **1932–33:** 311, 337
Reorganization, proposed, **1932–33:** 423
Surgeon General, **1932–33:** 2, 294, 358, 419
Public Land Commission, **1929:** 218
Public lands, **1929:** 185, 186, 241, 242, 295
Public opinion, **1929:** 35
Public Roads, Bureau of, **1931:** 453; **1932–33:** 423
Public service, requirements for, **1929:** 248
Public utilities, **1930:** 3, 4, 71n., 76, 76n., 77, 144,
145, 215, 311, 315, 331, 332, 390
Public vs. private financing of relief efforts,
remarks and statements, **1931:** 43, 44
Public works
American Road Builders Association, **1932–33:**
14
American Society of Civil Engineers, **1932–33:**
175
Boulder Dam, **1930:** 236, 237, 238, 326, 328
Budget message, **1929:** 296; **1932–33:** 421
Budgetary impact, **1930:** 55, 58, 65, 66, 67, 137,
200, 236, 237, 238, 334, 347, 369, 408, 418,
423
Commerce Department surveys, **1930:** 3, 4, 76,
76n., 77, 215, 315, 390
Coordination of Federal works with state and
local governments, **1929:** 297, 304
Drought areas, **1931:** 43, 44
Emergency construction fund, **1930:** 357, 369,
395, 397, 402, 403, 406, 418, 423
Emergency Relief and Construction Act of 1932,
1932–33: 182, 183, 186, 208, 209, 216, 217,
221, 233, 282, 283, 421
Employment Stabilization Act of 1931, **1931:** 54,
55
Expansion by the states, **1929:** 286, 297
Federal expenditures, **1931:** 45, 63, 67, 101, 147,
148, 177, 184, 226, 248, 277, 278, 302, 307,
319, 430, 432, 436, 437; **1932–33:** 9, 10,
157, 182, 183, 186, 187, 208, 209, 217, 233,
251, 259, 282, 283, 287, 294, 322, 337, 347,
358, 366, 371, 378, 380, 419, 421
Federal employees, **1931:** 218, 283, 284, 297, 302
Federal nondiscrimination policy, **1932–33:** 354
Flood control, **1930:** 237, 390
Government agencies, consolidation, **1931:** 430,
453, 454

Public works — *continued*
  Government contracts, wage maintenance, **1930:**
    422
  Governors' Conference, remarks, **1930:** 215
  Public buildings projects, **1930:** 3, 7, 127, 128,
    158, 158n., 236, 237, 238, 305, 347, 357,
    390, 391, 397, 418, 423; **1931:** 67, 177, 181,
    184, 277, 278, 297, 303, 307, 319, 387, 388,
    394, 432, 436, 437; **1932–33:** 213, 282, 283,
    307, 357, 421
  Rivers, harbors, and waterways, **1930:** 55, 58, 65,
    132, 223, 236, 237, 238, 390, 391, 418,
    423; **1931:** 88, 346, 383, 430, 432, 433;
    1932–33: 282, 283, 321, 421, 470
  State of the Union message, **1929:** 295
    See State of the Union message.
  Streets and highways, **1930:** 166, 266, 390, 391,
    423; **1931:** 248, 319
  Surveys in the States, **1929:** 324
Public Works Administration, proposed, **1931:** 430,
    453, 454; **1932–33:** 50
Publishers' Association, National, **1932–33:** 41n.
Publishers Association, American Newspaper,
    1930: 118; **1931:** 139, 405
Puerto Rico.
  See Porto Rico.
Pulaski, Casimir, **1929:** 233
Pulitzer Prize, **1930:** 211n.
Peru, U.S. Ambassador to, **1930:** 34
Purchasing Agents, National Association of,
    1932–33: 190
Purnell, Repr. Fred S., **1931:** 226

Quartermaster Corps, **1931:** 72; **1932–33:** 152

R-101, dirigible crash, **1930:** 317
Radio, **1930:** 341, 351, 358, 363, 389
  See also Appendix F—Radio Addresses by the
    President.
  Industry, **1932–33:** 412
  Station WOR, 11th anniversary, **1932–33:** 473
  WCAU Building, dedication, **1932–33:** 463
Radio Banquet, H.J. Heinz International, **1930:**
    358
Radio Commission.
  See Federal Radio Commission.
Radio Corporation of America, **1929:** 32
Radio in Education, National Advisory Council
    on, **1931:** 198
Radio Week, National, **1931:** 323
Radiotelegraphic service
  Austria, **1931:** 143
  China, **1930:** 399
  Czechoslovakia, **1930:** 387

Radiotelegraphic service — *continued*
  Dominican Republic, **1930:** 425
  Hungary, **1932–33:** 254
  Panama, **1930:** 141
  Spain, **1929:** 247
Radiotelephonic service
  Argentina, **1930:** 111
  Chile, **1930:** 100
  Uruguay, **1930:** 101
Railroad Trainmen, Brotherhood of, **1930:** 383, 384
Railroads
  Bankruptcy legislation, **1932–33:** 448, 470
  Competition from waterways, **1932–33:** 352
  Conferences on economic conditions, **1929:**
    281n., 285n.
  Consolidation, **1929:** 12, 125; **1930:** 428, 429
  Construction programs, **1930:** 3, 4, 71n., 76, 76n.,
    77, 144, 311, 315, 331, 332, 390
  Drought relief, **1930:** 253, 255, 265, 271, 272, 276,
    334, 390, 418
  Economic recovery, **1931:** 1, 334, 430, 436, 437,
    442; **1932–33:** 1, 76, 78, 87, 88, 92, 94, 175,
    187, 251, 347, 360, 380, 419
  Expansion of, **1929:** 285n.
  Federal Reserve District Banking and Industrial
    Committees, **1932–33:** 264
  Labor dispute, committee, **1930:** 261
  Labor disputes, **1929:** 19
  Railway Emergency Board, **1931:** 196
  Rates, **1929:** 61, 80
  State of the Union message, **1929:** 295
  Transportation laws, revision, **1932–33:** 259, 358
Railway Association, American, **1929:** 285n.; **1930:**
    130n., 265, 271, 272
Railway Association, American Electric, **1930:**
    130n.
Railway Brotherhoods, Conference of, **1931:** 442
Railway Credit Corporation, **1931:** 436, 442;
    1932–33: 76, 78, 87, 88
Railway Executives, **1931:** 442
Railway Executives, Association of, **1929:** 285n.
Railway Employees Union, **1930:** 244, 247
Railway Presidents Association, **1932–33:** 87
Railway Trainmen, Brotherhood of, **1932–33:** 41n.
Rainey, Repr. Henry T., **1932–33:** 123n., 183n.
Rainey amendment, **1932–33:** 230, 233, 470
Raitt, Effie, **1931:** 314
Ramsdell, C. H., **1929:** 31
Ramseyer, Repr. C. William, **1931:** 63n., 238, 239
Rankin bill, **1932–33:** 146ftn.
Ransdell, Sen. Joseph E., **1929:** 46; **1930:** 158
Rapidan Camp, **1929:** 10, 34, 172, 180, 225, 226n.,
    229n.
  Visits.
    See Appendix E—The President's Calendar.
  Conference, **1932–33:** 187
Rapidan Community School, **1930:** 64
Ratshesky, Abraham C., **1932–33:** 210

Raw materials.
  See Natural resources.
Ray, E. Lansing, **1931:** 402
Reading, Sam H., **1930:** 301
Real Estate Board of New York, **1931:** 48; **1932–
    33:** 17
Real Estate Boards, National Association of, **1929:**
    131; **1930:** 250; **1931:** 314
Ready, Michael J., **1932–33:** 41n.
Reapportionment, **1930:** 373, 374, 390, 396
Receipts and expenditures, tables, **1929:** 296
"Recent Social Trends in the United States,"
    1932–33: 437
Reclamation, Bureau of, **1931:** 453; **1932–33:** 423
Reclamation Fund, **1929:** 185
Reclamation Service
  Proposed, **1932–33:** 50
  Reorganization, **1929:** 185, 186, 241, 242
Reconstruction Finance Corporation
  Appropriations, **1932–33:** 26
  Board of Directors, **1932–33:** 23, 24, 25, 31, 36,
      41n., 73n., 156n., 187, 189, 208, 220, 221,
      230, 251, 264, 267n., 378
  Emergency Relief Division, **1932–33:** 215n.
  Establishment, bill signing, **1932–33:** 27
  Loans
    Agriculture, **1932–33:** 76, 78, 92, 94, 175, 186,
        187, 208, 209, 221, 233, 238, 239, 251, 295,
        313, 322, 347, 377, 378, 380, 419
    Banking and financial institutions, 76, 78, 86,
        92, 94, 100, 126, 175, 187, 230, 233, 272,
        321, 328, 346, 347, 371, 378, 380, 419
    Public works, **1932–33:** 157, 175, 182, 183, 186,
        187, 208, 209, 217, 221, 233, 251, 311, 337,
        347, 357, 371, 378, 380, 394, 419
    Publicity amendment, **1932–33:** 230, 233, 470
    Railroads, **1932–33:** 76, 78, 87, 88, 92, 94, 175,
        187, 347, 380, 419
    Recovery efforts, **1932–33:** 1, 28n., 36, 123,
        158, 159, 169, 187, 259, 272
    Relief, **1932–33:** 157, 175, 186, 187, 208, 209,
        217, 221, 233, 294, 305, 337, 346, 347, 357,
        371, 380, 382, 387, 394, 419, 470
    Proposed, **1931:** 343, 430, 436, 437, 442, 446, 447
Reconstruction Organization, Citizens, **1932–33:**
    38n., 41, 60, 73, 80, 81, 135
Recreation, national program, **1929:** 238
Recreation Association, National, **1931:** 134, 291
Recreation Congress, National, **1929:** 238
Red Cross, American National, **1930:** 33n., 89, 149,
    214n., 265, 265n., 266, 271, 272, 362, 390,
    392, 406, 418; **1931:** 15, 16, 17, 20, 26, 29,
    43, 45, 116, 121, 133, 195, 275, 310, 326,
    396, 430; **1932–33:** 121, 249, 294, 398
Redfield, William C., **1932–33:** 195
Reece, Repr. B. Carroll, **1930:** 243; **1931:** 82n.
Reed, Gov. Clyde M., **1929:** 61; **1930:** 265

Reed, Sen. David A., **1930:** 11n., 380; **1931:** 238,
    239
Reed, Opie, **1930:** 372
Regional Plan of New York and Its Environs,
    1929: 88; **1931:** 438
Reichelderfer, Luther H., **1930:** 45n.; **1932–33:**
    246n., 248
Reid, Albert T., **1932–33:** 369
Reid, Elizabeth Mills, **1931:** 158
Relief
  Emergency Unemployment Relief Committee of
      New York City, **1932–33:** 351
  President's Emergency Committee on Employ-
      ment, **1932–33:** 337ftn.
  Reconstruction Finance Corporation loans,
      1932–33: 157, 175, 186, 187, 208, 209, 217,
      221, 233, 294, 305, 337, 346, 347, 357, 371,
      380, 382, 387, 394, 419, 470
  State and local programs, **1932–33:** 1, 157, 175,
      186, 187, 208, 209, 215, 217, 221, 233, 259,
      294, 305, 337, 347, 380, 419
  Voluntary efforts, **1932–33:** 1, 157, 175, 186, 259,
      358, 380, 383, 419
  Welfare and Relief Mobilization of 1932, **1932–
      33:** 338
  Welfare and Relief Mobilization Conference,
      1932–33: 294
Relief, President's Organization on Unemploy-
    ment.
  See President's Organization on Unemployment
    Relief.
Relief Administration, American, **1930:** 204n.
Relief and Construction Act of 1932, Emergency,
    1932–33: 182, 183, 186, 208, 209, 216, 217,
    220n., 221, 230, 233, 243n., 282, 283, 421
Religious freedom, **1930:** 54, 114, 319, 320
Renard, G. A., **1932–33:** 190
Renunciation of War, General Pact for the, **1929:**
    1, 94, 161, 184, 229, 275, 295
Reorganization of executive branch, **1932–33:** 9,
    10, 48, 59, 76, 77, 79, 92, 93, 106, 108, 109,
    111, 113, 146, 198, 199, 212, 259, 289, 290,
    347, 358, 396, 419, 423, 439, 440, 450, 452,
    453, 462
Reorganization of the executive departments, **1929:**
    295
Reparations.
  See Intergovernmental debts.
Reparations settlement, **1930:** 74n.
Reports to the President.
  See also Appendix A—Additional White House
    Releases.
  American Child Health Association, **1930:** 204n.
  Bureau of Indian Affairs, **1930:** 5
  Muscle Shoals Commission, **1931:** 416n.
  National Commission on Law Observance and
      Enforcement, **1930:** 17n.; **1931:** 27

Reports to the President — *continued*
President's Research Committee on Social Trends, **1932–33:** 437
Republican League, Young, **1932–33:** 366, 368
Republican National Committee
Chairman, **1932–33:** 200, 291, 476
Counsel, **1932–33:** 258n.
Women's Division, vice chairwoman, **1932–33:** 328n.
Young Republican League, **1932–33:** 368
Republican National Committee, retirement of chairman, **1929:** 111, 194
Republican National Convention, **1932–33:** 197, 198
Republican Party
Elections.
See main heading, Elections.
Florida, **1929:** 248
Gridiron Club, address, **1932–33:** 424
Indiana Republican Editorial Association, address, **1931:** 226
Lincoln Club, message, **1930:** 52
Lincoln's Birthday, **1932–33:** 45, 46, 465
Address, **1931:** 58
Maine, State convention, **1930:** 95
National committee, **1931:** 224, 348
National Republican Club of New York City, **1932–33:** 46
New York, appointments, **1930:** 163
New Jersey, senatorial candidate, **1930:** 187, 191
Ohio, memorials to three prominent Republicans, **1932–33:** 302
Political patronage, **1929:** 248
Post-election role, **1932–33:** 394, 476
South, **1929:** 15, 16
Virginia State convention, **1929:** 135
Requa, Mark, **1929:** 177, 178; **1930:** 262
Research, scientific and technological, **1929:** 246
Research Committee on Social Trends, President's, **1929:** 318; **1932–33:** 135
Resignations
Commerce Department, Secretary, **1932–33:** 257
Comptroller of the Currency, **1932–33:** 284
Federal Radio Commission, member, **1932–33:** 13
Philippines, Governor General, **1932–33:** 11
Porto Rico, Governor, **1932–33:** 11
President's Organization on Unemployment Relief, Director, **1932–33:** 261
Reconstruction Finance Corporation, Board of Directors, Director, **1932–33:** 189
Supreme Court of the United States, Associate Justice, **1932–33:** 15, 16
Treasury Department, Secretary, **1932–33:** 44
U.S. Ambassador to Mexico, **1932–33:** 477
U.S. Minister to Canada, **1932–33:** 273
U.S. Minister to Czechoslovakia, **1932–33:** 210

Resignations and retirements
Budget, Bureau of the, Director, **1929:** 97, 105
Commerce Department, Assistant Secretary, **1929:** 10
Corps of Engineers, Chief, **1929:** 204
Federal Farm Board, **1931:** 92, 210, 242
Federal Farm Loan Board, **1931:** 303, 305
Federal Farm Loan Board, Commissioner, **1929:** 59
Federal Reserve System, Board of Governors
Governor, **1930:** 279
Vice Governor, **1930:** 284, 285, 289
Haiti, American High Commissioner, **1930:** 349
Indian Affairs, Bureau of, Commissioner, **1929:** 8
Interstate Commerce Commissioners, **1930:** 3, 6, 249
Justice Department, Assistant Attorney General, **1929:** 90, 91; **1931:** 211
Labor Department, Bureau of Immigration, **1931:** 348
Secretary, **1930:** 386
Navy Department
Assistant Secretary, **1929:** 6
Chief of Naval Operations, **1930:** 296
Philippines, Vice Governor, **1930:** 303
Republican National Committee, chairman, **1929:** 111, 194
State Department, Under Secretary, **1929:** 6, 113
Supreme Court of the District of Columbia, **1931:** 174
Supreme Court of the United States, Chief Justice, **1930:** 40, 41
Treasury Department, Assistant Secretary, **1929:** 256; **1931:** 67, 68
United States Civil Service Commission, President, **1930:** 48
United States Marine Corps, **1931:** 297
United States Tariff Commission, **1931:** 270, 411, 412
U.S. Ambassador to Mexico, **1930:** 313
U.S. attorney, New York, **1930:** 308
War Department
Assistant Secretary, **1929:** 6
Chief of Cavalry, **1930:** 45
Chief of Staff, **1930:** 253, 254
White House staff
Administrative Assistant to the President, **1931:** 116
Secretary to the President, **1931:** 1, 2
Resnick, David, **1932–33:** 478
Retail business.
See Business.
Retail Credit Association, National, **1932–33:** 41n.
Retail Dry Goods Association, National, **1932–33:** 428
Retail Grocers Association, National, **1931:** 254
Retirement funds, **1932–33:** 421

Retirement legislation, Government employees,
    1930: 59, 60
Revenue Act of 1932, **1932–33:** 123, 126, 146, 154,
    186, 188
Reynolds, George, **1931:** 378
Reynolds, Mercer, **1931:** 260, 440
Rhoads, Charles J., **1929:** 37; **1930:** 3, 5
Rhode Island, unemployment relief efforts, **1931:**
    421
Richards, Bernard G., **1931:** 167; **1932–33:** 72
Richardson, Guy A., **1929:** 285n.
Richardson, Seth, **1930:** 342, 343
Richey, Lawrence, **1929:** 27n.; **1930:** 158
Richmond, Va., **1932–33:** 137
Rickard, Edgar, **1930:** 204
Rickenbacker, Edward V., **1930:** 287, 354
Ridder, Victor F., **1932–33:** 340
Riehl, Harry, **1932–33:** 281
Rinehart, Mary R., **1929:** 242n.
Ringland, Arthur, **1929:** 31
River and Harbor Act, **1930:** 132, 223
Rivers and harbors, budget, **1929:** 296
Rivers, harbors, and waterways
    Appropriations, **1932–33:** 83, 421
    Atlantic Deeper Waterways Association, **1931:**
        346; **1932–33:** 352
    Boulder Dam, **1930:** 236, 237, 238, 326, 328
    Budget message, **1931:** 432
    Federal expenditures, **1930:** 42, 58, 65, 236, 237,
        238, 391, 418, 423
    Flood control, **1931:** 88, 432; **1932–33:** 282, 283,
        353, 421
    Great Lakes-St. Lawrence Deep Waterway,
        1932–33: 219, 226, 235, 259, 273, 322, 470
    Hoover Dam, Nev., **1932–33:** 394, 396
    Inland waterways, **1931:** 399; **1932–33:** 321, 322
    International Water Commission, United States
        and Mexico, **1931:** 11
    Legislation, **1930:** 132, 223, 390
    Muscle Shoals development, **1931:** 79, 82, 88,
        260, 416, 430, 440
    Owyhee, Dam, Oreg., **1932–33:** 232
    Power production, Federal regulation, **1932–33:**
        259, 358, 366
    Public works projects, **1932–33:** 282, 283, 321,
        421, 470
    St. Lawrence waterway, **1930:** 132, 223; **1931:**
        383, 433
    State of the Union message, **1931:** 430
Road Builders Association, American, **1932–33:** 14
Road Congresses, Permanent International Asso-
    ciation of, **1930:** 49
Roads, Bureau of Public, **1931:** 453
Robb, Arthur R., **1930:** 118
Robbins, Charles B., **1929:** 6
Robert Burns Memorial Association, **1929:** 138
Roberts, Nicholas, **1931:** 428
Robertson, A. W., **1930:** 318

Robins, Lt. Col. T. M., **1930:** 223
Robinson, Sen. Arthur R., **1931:** 226
Robinson, Henry M., **1930:** 271, 272; **1932–33:**
    187n., 313
Robinson, Ira E., **1932–33:** 13
Robinson, Sen. Joseph T., **1929:** 196, 197; **1930:**
    11n., 265n.; **1931:** 50; **1932–33:** 73n.,
    123n., 156, 157, 208
Robinson, Theodore D., **1929:** 6
Robinson, William E., **1929:** 149n.
Rock Creek and Potomac Parkway Commission,
    1932–33: 423
Rock Island, Ill., **1932–33:** 321
Rockefeller Foundation, **1929:** 318
Rockford, Ill., **1932–33:** 379
Rockne, Knute, **1931:** 119
Rodgers, Capt. William B., **1929:** 250
Rodgríguez, Abelardo, **1932–33:** 279
Rodman, Adm. Hugh, **1931:** 392
Roeser, John, **1931:** 70n.
Rogers, James G., **1932–33:** 3n.
Romero Bosque, Pio (President of El Salvador),
    1929: 326
Roop, J. Clawson, **1930:** 65n., 78, 395; **1931:** 41;
    1932–33: 26, 154n., 218n.
Roop, Col. James C., **1929:** 128
Roosevelt, Edith Kermit Carow, **1932–33:** 366
Roosevelt, Franklin D., **1932–33:** 219, 337, 346,
    347, 358, 363, 364, 366, 377, 378, 379, 380,
    382, 385, 387, 391, 392, 395, 396, 399, 405,
    431, 434, 441, 451, 452, 454, 466, 480
Roosevelt, Nicholas, **1930:** 244, 245, 303
Roosevelt, Theodore, **1929:** 84; **1930:** 188, 247;
    1931: 134n.; **1932–33:** 425
Roosevelt, Theodore, Jr., **1930:** 204, 361; **1931:** 102,
    106, 108, 109, 111; **1932–33:** 11
Roosevelt, President Theodore, **1929:** 2n., 250, 259
Roosevelt Memorial Association, **1932–33:** 425
Root, Elihu, **1929:** 12, 275, 291
Rose, Flora, **1932–33:** 184
Rose, William G., **1930:** 280
Rosenberg, James N., **1930:** 151
Rosenwald, Julius, **1931:** 309; **1932–33:** 6, 98
Rosh Hashanah, **1929:** 201; **1930:** 256; **1931:** 308;
    1932–33: 303
Rotary Club of Chicago, **1931:** 309
Rotary International, **1930:** 134n., 205; **1932–33:**
    41n.
Rothenberg, Morris, **1932–33:** 19, 374
Rover, Leo A., **1929:** 214
Roy, Eugene, **1930:** 85n.
Rubinstein, Leon J., **1932–33:** 306
Rublee, George, **1930:** 11n.
Rugg, Charles B., **1930:** 36
Rumania, **1929:** 3n., 72, 161
    King Carol II, **1931:** 180
Rummel, Rev. Joseph F., **1930:** 304n.
Rumrunning, **1929:** 54

Rural Life Sunday, **1929:** 62
Rush-Bagot Agreement, **1930:** 225
Rushville, Ind., **1932–33:** 357
Russell, Charles A., **1931:** 12n.
Russell, Gen. David A., **1929:** 302n.
Russell, Brig. Gen. John H., **1930:** 38, 39, 93, 349
Russell Sage Foundation, **1930:** 250; **1931:** 314, 438
Russia.
    See Union of Soviet Socialist Republics.
Ruttenberg, Nelson, **1932–33:** 58
Rzeczyzany, Poland, **1930:** 136

Sackett, Frederic M., **1932–33:** 378
Sacramento, Calif., **1932–33:** 390
Sacramento River, **1932–33:** 421
Safety, American Museum of, **1932–33:** 179
Safety, streets and highways, **1930:** 130, 166, 307
Safety Council, National, **1930:** 307; **1931:** 356; **1932–33:** 320
Safety of Life at Sea, Conference on, **1931:** 433
Safety of Life at Sea, Convention for the Promotion of, **1929:** 17, 317
Safety of Life at Sea, International Conference on, **1929:** 17
St. Elizabeths Hospital, **1932–33:** 423
St. Lawrence River waterway.
    See Great Lakes-St. Lawrence Deep Waterway.
St. Lewis, Roy, **1931:** 211
St. Louis, Mo., **1932–33:** 378, 380, 382, 387
St. Louis Globe Democrat, **1931:** 402
St. Louis and O'Fallon Railway Company, **1929:** 80
St. Paul, Minn., **1929:** 286n.; **1932–33:** 380
Salamanca, Daniel, **1931:** 282
Salem, George J., **1931:** 35
Salisbury, Edith, **1932–33:** 41n.
Salomon, Haym, **1931:** 77
Salt Lake City, Utah, **1932–33:** 387
Saltzman, Gen. Charles M., **1929:** 12
Salvation Army, **1930:** 159; **1931:** 123
Samoan Commission, American, **1931:** 10
Sampson, Gov. Flem D., **1930:** 265n.
San Bernardino, Calif., **1932–33:** 394
San Francisco, Calif., **1932–33:** 390
San Francisco Bay Bridge, **1929:** 177, 178, 196, 218
San Francisco Bay Bridge Commission, **1930:** 261, 262; **1932–33:** 135
Sanchez, Mercedes Martinez Viuda de, **1930:** 90
Sand, Rene, **1929:** 124n.
Sanders, Everett, **1932–33:** 200, 291, 476
Sandino, Augusto Cesar, **1931:** 71n., 138, 140, 141
Sanford, Edward T., **1930:** 92
Santo Domingo.
    See Dominican Republic.
Sargent, Fred W., **1929:** 281n.; **1931:** 309
Sargent, Noel, **1930:** 247n.

Scattergood, J. Henry, **1930:** 3, 5
Schall, Sen. Thomas D., **1931:** 46, 70
Schiff, Mortimer, **1929:** 173
Schiff, William, **1930:** 398; **1931:** 435n.
Schiff Memorial Trophy, Herbert, **1931:** 435
Schilling, William F., **1929:** 140ftn., p. 207
Schofield, Adm. Frank H., **1930:** 146
Scholastic Magazine, **1932–33:** 277
Schools
    Conference on the Crisis in Education, **1932–33:** 442
    Organizations, representatives to conference on hoarding of currency, **1932–33:** 36
Schwab, Charles M., **1929:** 193n.; **1932–33:** 53
Science and technology, **1930:** 65, 107, 133, 144, 182, 196, 311, 315, 358, 389; **1931:** 42, 90, 126, 127
    Aviation, **1932–33:** 422
    50th anniversary of first commercial electric lighting and generating plant, **1932–33:** 278, 288
    Patent system, **1932–33:** 122
    President's Research Committee on Social Trends, report, **1932–33:** 437
    Scientific Monthly, introduction to a series of articles, **1932–33:** 435
    WCAU Radio Building, dedication, **1932–33:** 463
Scientific Monthly, **1932–33:** 435
Sconce, Harvey J., **1930:** 272
Scott, Frederick W., **1930:** 272
Scott, James Brown, **1932–33:** 141n.
Scouts of America, Boy, **1932–33:** 244
Scully, James J., **1930:** 29
Sea, Conference on Safety of Life at, **1931:** 433
Seager, Howard W., **1931:** 218n.
Seatrain Havana, **1932–33:** 286
Seatrain New York, **1932–33:** 286
Second Pan American Conference of Directors of Health, **1931:** 144
Second Polar Year program, **1931:** 56
Secretaries, National Association of Commercial Organization, **1932–33:** 41n.
Seligman, Arthur, **1931:** 91n.
Seminole Indians, **1932–33:** 458
Senate.
    See under Congress.
Senn, Fred W., **1931:** 70
Serbs, Croats and Slovenes, Kingdom of, **1929:** 161
Shambaugh, Benjamin F., **1930:** 217n.
Shanghai, China, **1932–33:** 34
Shanghai Electric Construction Co., **1931:** 36
Shankey, Anne, **1931:** 7
Shannahan, John N., **1929:** 285n.
Share-the-work organization, **1932–33:** 404
Shaw, Albert, **1931:** 314
Shearer, William B., **1929:** 193n., 195
Shearon, Lowe, **1932–33:** 347, 377, 378

Shelton, William C., **1930:** 310
Shenandoah National Park, Va., **1929:** 172; **1930:** 64, 153
Shenandoah Valley, **1930:** 276
Sheppard-Towner Act, **1929:** 295
Sherlock, Chesla C., **1932–33:** 161
Sherman Antitrust Act, **1930:** 390
Shipbuilding corporations' propaganda against naval reduction, **1929:** 192, 193, 195
Shipbuilding and Dry Dock Co., Federal, **1932–33:** 91
Shipping Board, United States, **1930:** 176, 177, 231, 347, 391; **1931:** 147, 148, 430, 432, 453; **1929:** 104, 224, 225, 295
   See also United States Shipping Board.
Shipping Board Sales, Advisory Committee on, **1930:** 176, 177, 190, 231
Shipping Committee, Advisory, **1932–33:** 135
Ships and shipping
   Appropriations, **1932–33:** 421
   Coamo, **1932–33:** 433
   Foreign claim, **1930:** 9, 12, 37, 138, 139, 152; **1931:** 36
   Freedom of the seas, **1930:** 365, 402
   Freighters *Seatrain New York* and *Seatrain Havana,* launchings, **1932–33:** 286
   Maritime neutrality, **1931:** 433
   Merchant marine, **1930:** 112, 113, 133, 176, 177; **1931:** 62, 147, 148, 430, 453, 454; **1932–33:** 91, 106, 108
   National economy program, impact, **1932–33:** 119
   Niobe, **1932–33:** 255
   Prométhée, **1932–33:** 222
   Rates, regulation, **1932–33:** 106, 108
   SS *Santa Rosa,* **1932–33:** 91
Shipstead, Sen. Henrik, **1930:** 403n.
Shoup, Paul, **1929:** 285n.
Schwartz, Maurice, **1932–33:** 474
Siam, **1929:** 161
Siam, King Prajadhipok, **1930:** 359; **1931:** 175, 273
Sigall, Joseph, **1932–33:** 369n.
Siles, Hernando (President of Bolivia), **1929:** 171
Silver, Rabbi Abba Hillel, **1930:** 164
Silver, **1932–33:** 269, 343, 387, 388, 465
Silver, international conference, possibility of, **1931:** 215, 218
Simmons, Edward Alfred, **1931:** 330
Simonds, Brig. Gen. George S., **1932–33:** 25n.
Sinclair, Harry F., **1929:** 213
Sinking fund, public debt retirement, **1930:** 378, 379, 390
Sippel, Mrs. John F., **1932–33:** 41n.
Sixth Pan American Child Congress, **1930:** 75
Skipper, Glenn B., **1929:** 248
Slemp, C. Bascom, **1930:** 273
Sloan, Alfred P., **1932–33:** 404
Sloan, George, **1932–33:** 341

Sloane, Matthew, **1929:** 285n.; **1930:** 71n., 145
Slomovitz, Philip, **1929:** 139
Slovak Amerike, **1931:** 132
Slum clearance, **1932–33:** 251, 311
Smaller Industries, Conference of, **1932–33:** 223
Smith, Alfred E., **1929:** 65; **1931:** 163n.; **1932–33:** 378
Smith, Cortland, **1931:** 193
Smith, Earl C., **1930:** 272
Smith, Dr. Fred B., **1929:** 269
Smith, George, **1931:** 70n.
Smith, George Otis, **1931:** 12, 13, 31n.
Smith, Herbert Knox, **1931:** 443
Smith, John R. W., **1929:** 138
Smith, Leslie C., **1931:** 160
Smith, Will Howard, **1931:** 440
Smith, William R., **1932–33:** 14
Smoot, Sen. Reed, **1931:** 63, 215, 218; **1932–33:** 269, 387
Smoot-Hawley tariff.
   See Tariff legislation.
Snell, Repr. Bertrand H., **1931:** 238, 239; **1932–33:** 197n.
Snyder, Frederic S., **1930:** 335
Social conditions, **1929:** 318
Social Science Research Council, **1929:** 318; **1932–33:** 411n.
Social service programs, **1929:** 295
Social Trends, President's Research Committee on, **1932–33:** 137, 437
Social Work, National Conference on, **1932–33:** 171
Society of Economic Geologists, **1930:** 430
Society of Foreign Consuls, **1930:** 356
Society of the Genesee, **1930:** 122; **1931:** 51; **1932–33:** 30, 445
Sockeye Salmon Fisheries Treaty, **1931:** 433
Soldiers' Home, United States, **1930:** 226, 227, 391
Sons of the American Revolution, **1932–33:** 164
Soper, Morris A., **1931:** 173
Sousa, John Philip, **1930:** 133
South Carolina
   Battle of Kings Mountain, anniversary, **1930:** 319
   Patronage investigation, **1930:** 87, 88
South Dakota
   Agricultural relief, **1931:** 275
   Child health and protection conference, **1932–33:** 5n.
South Pole, **1929:** 293
Southern Baptist Convention, **1931:** 191; **1932–33:** 162
Souza, Washington Luis Pereira de, **1930:** 337n.
Spain, **1929:** 44, 161, 247, 317
Spain, International Exposition at Seville, **1930:** 201; **1931:** 434
Spalding, Lt. Col. G. S., **1930:** 223
Spangler, Harrison E., **1932–33:** 314, 325

Spanish War veterans' pension bill, **1930:** 168, 173, 174

Sparks, Jared, **1931:** 59

Sparks, Ruth Lyle, **1931:** 314

Spaulding, Huntley, **1929:** 242n.

Special Business Committee.
    See National Business Survey Conference.

Special Committee on Expedition of Public Utilities Construction to Assist Employment, **1930:** 71n.

Special Congressional Medal, **1931:** 23

Special interest groups, **1931:** 13, 116, 117, 226, 324, 325, 341, 358, 359, 397, 398; **1932–33:** 9, 10, 137, 146, 147, 148, 182, 183, 245, 366, 439, 440, 465

Special International Niagara Board, **1930:** 109; **1931:** 37

Speculation, **1929:** 272

Spingarn, J. E., **1932–33:** 41n.

Spokane, Wash., **1930:** 367

Sports
    Army-Navy football game, **1932–33:** 415
    Comiskey, Charles A., death, **1931:** 382
    Hunting season, ducks, **1931:** 299
    Olympic Games, **1931:** 98, 241; **1932–33:** 200, 253, 318
    Opening baseball game, **1932–33:** 111
    Rockne, Knute, death, **1931:** 119
    World Series, **1931:** 327

Spillsbury, P. G., **1931:** 299

Sprague, Frank Julian, **1932–33:** 242

Springfield, Ill., **1931:** 232, 233; **1932–33:** 377

SS *Santa Rosa*, **1932–33:** 91

Stafford, Wendell P., **1931:** 174

Standard of living.
    See under Economy, national.

Standards, Bureau of, **1930:** 158; **1932–33:** 423

Standstill agreement.
    See London Conference of Ministers.

Stanford University, **1930:** 24n., 167, 326, 327n.; **1932–33:** 392

Star Pro Juventute, **1932–33:** 312

State compacts, **1929:** 132, 133

State cooperation in solving unemployment, **1929:** 286

State, Department of
    Acting Secretary, **1930:** 42, 49, 53, 75, 79, 90, 109, 136, 138, 172, 221
    Appropriations, **1930:** 86, 181; **1931:** 11, 25, 28, 87; **1932–33:** 207, 421
    Armistice Day comments on role of, **1929:** 275
    Assistant Secretary, **1931:** 189; **1932–33:** 3n.
    Budget message, **1929:** 296
    Chief of Division of Western European Affairs, **1930:** 11n.
    Foreign loan policy, **1930:** 194
    Foreign relations, message to Congress, **1931:** 433

State, Department of — *continued*
    Foreign Service, **1930:** 25, 34, 53, 158, 303, 303n., 313
    Great Lakes-St. Lawrence Deep Waterway, treaty, **1932–33:** 235n.
    Immigration, **1931:** 113
    Report, **1930:** 288
    Secretary of (Henry L. Stimson), **1929:** 6, 49n., 61, 241, 306; **1930:** 9, 11n., 12, 18, 22, 28, 31, 37, 83, 94n., 123, 139, 152, 172, 181, 194, 337, 405, 414, 417, 419; **1931:** 11, 25, 28, 35, 37, 71, 263, 266, 267, 268, 383n., 411, 433, 434; **1932–33:** 3n., 23, 25, 34, 35, 111, 112, 206, 214, 228, 235n., 380, 395, 396, 444, 446, 449n., 454
    Special International Niagara Board, **1931:** 37
    Under Secretary, **1929:** 6, 84, 113; **1931:** 97, 116, 189, 392; **1932–33:** 34

State and local governments.
    See also specific state.
    Agricultural credit corporations, **1929:** 121
    Boulder Dam settlement, **1930:** 326, 328
    Child health, **1930:** 369, 376; **1931:** 22, 137
    Conference of Governors, **1932–33:** 137
    Conferences on child health and protection, **1932–33:** 5
    Corporations, jurisdiction based on diversity of citizenship, **1932–33:** 69
    County health units, funding, **1932–33:** 348
    Drought relief, **1930:** 253, 255, 258, 259, 261, 265, 266, 271, 272, 276, 334, 406, 418
    Expenditures, **1932–33:** 9, 10
    Governors, **1930:** 3, 4, 130, 144, 157, 258, 259, 261, 265, 266, 271, 272, 276, 301, 331, 332, 338, 339, 369, 376, 377n., 390; **1931:** 43, 44, 91n., 94, 283, 284
    Governors' Conference, **1930:** 215
    Great Lakes-St. Lawrence Deep Waterway, **1932–33:** 219
    Hoarding of currency, **1932–33:** 36, 41
    Illinois State Legislature, address, **1931:** 232
    Interstate Conference of Legislators, **1932–33:** 461
    Juvenile delinquency, jurisdiction, **1932–33:** 69, 193
    Law enforcement, **1930:** 19, 135, 380, 381; **1931:** 27, 355; **1932–33:** 335, 379
    Lincoln's Birthday, address, **1931:** 58
    Mortgage laws, **1930:** 249
    Oil, regulation, **1931:** 99
    Power production, Federal regulation, **1932–33:** 259, 358, 366
    Prohibition, **1932–33:** 259
    Property taxes, **1932–33:** 292, 322, 377
    Public works, **1932–33:** 14, 175, 187, 221, 337, 358
    Railroad consolidation, **1930:** 428, 429
    Regulatory functions, **1930:** 311

State and local governments — *continued*
  Relief efforts, **1931:** 248, 275, 283, 284, 303, 319,
    329, 357, 360, 421, 431, 436, 437; **1932–33:**
    1, 157, 175, 186, 187, 208, 209, 215, 217,
    221, 233, 259, 294, 305, 337, 347, 380, 419,
    470
  Roads program, **1931:** 248, 302
  San Francisco Bay Bridge agreement, **1930:** 261,
    262
  Streets and highways, **1930:** 130, 166, 397
  Topographic maps, **1930:** 3
  Unemployment relief, **1930:** 3, 4, 76, 76n., 77,
    215, 224, 315, 331, 332, 334, 336, 338, 339,
    390, 397
State Parks, National Conference on, **1930:** 197
State of the Union message, **1929:** 295; **1930:** 390;
    1931: 430; **1932–33:** 419
State University of Iowa, **1930:** 217
Statements by the President.
  See also White House statements.
  Advisory Committee on Unemployment Statis-
    tics, **1930:** 247
  Agricultural tariffs, **1932–33:** 385
  American Bar Association convention, welcom-
    ing foreign guests, **1930:** 277
  American Legion employment drive, **1932–33:**
    40
  Apportionment under the 15th Decennial Cen-
    sus, **1930:** 374
  Appropriations for the Executive Office and
    independent establishments, **1929:** 218n.
  Army Chief of Staff, appointment of Gen.
    Douglas MacArthur, **1930:** 254
  Army Reserve Corps, appointment of Benedict
    Crowell, **1931:** 32
  Automobile sales, **1932–33:** 107
  Bankruptcy law and judicial reform, **1932–33:** 64
  Bankruptcy law and practice, investigation,
    1930: 246
  Better Homes Week, **1931:** 151; **1932–33:** 134
  Bonus marchers, **1932–33:** 246, 250, 285
  Boulder Canyon project, **1929:** 133
  Boulder Dam, **1930:** 328
  Budget, **1932–33:** 77, 93, 113, 148, 453
  Cabinet committee on unemployment relief,
    1930: 332
  California water resources, **1929:** 178
  Campaign plans, **1932–33:** 200
  Canadian Prime Minister Richard B. Bennett,
    visit, **1931:** 40
  China, famine relief, **1931:** 304
  Colorado River Basin interstate compact, **1929:**
    133
  Columbus Day, **1931:** 354; **1932–33:** 331
  Commerce Department, resignation of Secretary
    Lamont, **1932–33:** 257
  Commission on Conservation and Administra-
    tion of the Public Domain, **1929:** 242

Statements by the President — *continued*
  Commodity markets, speculation, **1931:** 257
  Congress, possibility of special session, **1931:** 197
  Cruiser construction, suspension, **1929:** 162
  Deaths
    Booth, Ralph Harmon, **1931:** 237
    Burton, Sen. Theodore E., **1929:** 263
    Cotton, Joseph P., **1931:** 97
    Eastman, George, **1932–33:** 84
    Edison, Thomas Alva, **1931:** 362, 366
    Foch, Marshall Ferdinand, **1929:** 11
    Good, James W., Secretary of War, **1929:** 283
    Herrick, Myron T., **1929:** 21, 29
    Marshall, Louis, **1929:** 199
    Morrow, Sen. Dwight W., **1931:** 335
    Rosenwald, Julius, **1932–33:** 6
    Straus, Nathan, **1931:** 14
    Warren, Sen. Francis E., **1929:** 287
  District of Columbia, Commissioner, appoint-
    ment of Herbert B. Crosby, **1930:** 45
  District of Columbia, unemployment relief,
    1931: 388
  Domestic credit conditions, **1931:** 389
  Drought relief, **1930:** 255, 259, 272
  Economic problems, conference with certain
    Members of Congress, **1931:** 342
  Economic recovery program, **1931:** 437, 447;
    1932–33: 36, 157, 159, 251
  "Economy Act," **1932–33:** 199, 212
  Economy in Government, **1931:** 454
  Electric incandescent lamp, 50th anniversary,
    1929: 157
  Emergency Adjusted Compensation Act, 1931,
    1931: 80
  Emergency relief and construction legislation of
    1932, **1932–33:** 183, 209, 217, 233
  Employment and business surveys, **1930:** 77
  Employment Stabilization Act of 1931, **1931:** 55
  Executive branch appropriations legislation, dis-
    approval, **1932–33:** 482
  Executive branch reorganization, **1932–33:** 59,
    290, 440, 453
  Farm relief, **1929:** 42, 98, 117, 121
  Federal budget, **1931:** 148, 398
  Federal expenditures, **1931:** 325, 359; **1932–33:**
    10
  Federal Farm Board, **1929:** 117, 121
  Federal Farm Loan Act, amendments, **1932–33:**
    28
  Federal Home Loan Bank Act, **1932–33:** 239
  Federal Government expenditures, **1929:** 156
  Federal prison reform, **1929:** 170, 182
  Federal Power Commission, appointments con-
    troversy, **1931:** 13
  Federal Reserve Act, amendments, **1932–33:** 66
  Federal Reserve Board, appointments, **1930:** 285
  Federal Reserve District Banking and Industrial
    Committees, conference, **1932–33:** 264

Statements by the President — *continued*
  Federal taxes and expenditures, **1931:** 117
  Financial and economic problems, **1931:** 333,
    343
  Flag Day ceremonies, **1932–33:** 196
  Foreign relations, post-election conduct, **1932–
    33:** 434
  Foreign trade, Commerce Department report,
    1930: 295
  Franco-Italian naval agreement, **1931:** 89
  French Prime Minister Pierre Laval, visit, **1931:**
    370
  General Disarmament Conference, **1932–33:** 25,
    112, 205, 304
    U.S. delegation, **1931:** 449
  German economic situation, **1931:** 236
  German war reparations, **1929:** 99, 126
  Government employees, holiday weekends,
    1931: 448
  Government employees' retirement fund, **1930:**
    60
  Government expenditures, **1930:** 67, 237, 274,
    403
  Great Lakes-St. Lawrence Deep Waterway,
    1932–33: 226, 235
  Helium exports, **1930:** 323
  Hoarding of currency, **1932–33:** 49, 81
  Home loan discount bank system, proposed,
    1931: 408
  House of Representatives, cancellation of recep-
    tion, **1930:** 68
  House Select Committee on Economy, meetings,
    1932–33: 124
  Income tax revenues, **1930:** 103
  Indian affairs, **1930:** 5
  Intergovernmental debts, **1932–33:** 407
  Interior Department appropriations act, bill
    signing, **1932–33:** 133
  Interior Department, Secretary Ray Lyman
    Wilbur, **1930:** 327
  Interstate Commerce Commission, appoint-
    ments, **1930:** 6
  Koch, Dr. Robert, tribute, **1932–33:** 89
  Labor Department, appointment of Secretary
    William N. Doak, **1930:** 384
  Library, University of Louvain, Belgium, **1929:**
    243
  Lindbergh kidnaping, **1932–33:** 160
  London Conference of Ministers, **1931:** 263, 266
  London Naval Conference, **1930:** 11, 113
  London Naval Treaty, **1930:** 162, 184, 241
  MacDonald, Prime Minister J. Ramsay, conver-
    sations with, **1929:** 228
  McNab, John, appointment to study and for-
    mulate plans for improvement of prohi-
    bition law enforcement, **1929:** 220
  Mellon-Berenger Agreement, France's ratifica-
    tion of, **1929:** 163

Statements by the President — *continued*
  Military expenditures, **1929:** 160
  Mississippi River flood control, **1929:** 85, 197
  Missouri, unemployment relief, **1931:** 329
  Moratorium on intergovernmental debts, **1931:**
    239, 252, 450
  Muscle Shoals Commission, **1931:** 416
    Legislation, **1931:** 82
  National business and economic situation, **1929:**
    257
  National Commission on Law Observance and
    Enforcement, **1930:** 210
  National employment system, disapproval of
    legislation, **1931:** 94
  National Hospital Day, **1932–33:** 140
  National Pharmacy Week, **1932–33:** 329
  Naval reduction, **1929:** 68, 193, 198
  Navy Day, **1931:** 380; **1932–33:** 356
  Navy Department, budget, **1931:** 406
  Navy League, investigation, **1931:** 385, 390
  New England Conference on Reemployment,
    meeting with the President, **1932–33:** 240
  New York appointments, **1930:** 163
  New York Banking and Industrial Committee,
    1932–33: 170
  New York Stock Exchange, **1932–33:** 55
  New Jersey Republican senatorial candidate,
    1930: 187, 191
  Nicaragua, bandit activities, **1931:** 141
  Oil conservation policies, **1929:** 9
  Oil imports and production, **1931:** 100
  Oil shale lands controversy, **1930:** 343
  Patronage investigations, **1930:** 88
  Philippines
    Governor Generalship, **1932–33:** 11
    Independence, **1931:** 379
    Interim appointment of Vice General, **1930:**
      245
    Sugar exports, **1932–33:** 384
  Porto Rico and the Virgin Islands, **1931:** 112
  President's Commission for the Study and Re-
    view of Conditions in the Republic of
    Haiti, **1930:** 39, 51, 93
  President's Organization on Unemployment Re-
    lief, appointment of Walter S. Gifford,
    1931: 295
  President's vacation plans, **1930:** 263
  Prohibition enforcement incidents at the Cana-
    dian border, **1929:** 127
  Public building projects, **1931:** 307, 394
  Public debt, retirement, **1930:** 379
  Public vs. private financing of relief efforts,
    1931: 44
  Public works program, **1932–33:** 283
  Railroad consolidation, **1930:** 429
  Railroad reconstruction, **1932–33:** 88
  Railroads, financial assistance, **1931:** 442

Statements by the President — *continued*
 Reconstruction Finance Corporation, **1932–33:**
  24, 27, 78, 94, 243
 Renunciation of War Treaty, first anniversary,
  1929: 184
 Report of the President's Research Committee
  on Social Trends, **1932–33:** 437
 Republican Party in the South, reorganization,
  1929: 16
 Revenue Act of 1932, bill signing, **1932–33:** 188
 River and Harbor Act, bill signing, **1930:** 223
 San Francisco Bay Bridge, **1929:** 178
 San Francisco Bay Bridge Commission, **1930:**
  262
 Secretary to the President, resignation of George
  E. Akerson, **1931:** 2
 Senate Minority Leader Robinson, meeting,
  1932–33: 156
 Spanish War veterans' pension bill, override of
  veto, **1930:** 174
 State law enforcement, **1930:** 381
 Street and highway traffic safety, **1930:** 130
 Taft, William Howard
  House of Representatives, cancellation of re-
   ception, **1930:** 68
  Resignation as Chief Justice, **1930:** 41
 Tariff, **1929:** 98, 216
 Tariff legislation, **1930:** 188
 Tax reduction, **1929:** 141
 Treasury Department
  Appointment of Secretary and Undersecre-
   tary, **1932–33:** 39
  Resignation of Assistant Secretary Walter E.
   Hope, **1931:** 68
 Unemployment and public works, **1930:** 4, 339
 Unemployment relief, organization, **1931:** 284
 United Kingdom, U.S. Ambassador, **1932–33:** 37
 United States Employment Service, appoint-
  ment, **1931:** 101
 United States Junior Chamber of Commerce,
  "Get Out the Vote" drive, **1932–33:** 96
 United States Shipping Board, **1929:** 225; **1932–
  33:** 108
 United States Tariff Commission, appointments,
  1930: 294
 U.S. Navy, reduction in force, **1930:** 322
 Veterans' Administration, establishment, **1930:**
  227
 Veterans' bonus, **1932–33:** 102, 293
 Veterans' hospitals, construction, bill signing,
  1929: 321
 Virgin Islands, reorganizaion, **1931:** 41
 White House Conference on Child Health and
  Protection, **1929:** 142
 White House Conference on Drought Relief,
  1930: 265
 White House Conference on Home Building and
  Home Ownership, **1930:** 250; **1931:** 314

Statements by the President — *continued*
 White House conferences with business, indus-
  try, agriculture, and labor leaders, **1929:**
  281
 White House executive offices, repair, **1930:** 7
 World Court protocols, **1930:** 385
 World War veterans' bill, **1930:** 203
 Yale Daily News, **1929:** 33
Statements other than Presidential.
 See also White House statements.
 American Electric Railway Association, J. N.
  Shannahan, **1929:** 285n.
 American Gas Association, B. J. Mullaney,
  1929: 285n.
 Association of Railway Executives, R. H.
  Aishton, **1929:** 285n.
 National Commission on Law Observance and
  Enforcement, Attorney General Mitchell,
  1929: 92n.
  Chairman Wickersham, **1929:** 92n.
 National Electric Light Association, M. Sloane,
  1929: 285n.
 President's conference with agricultural leaders,
  Secretary of Agriculture, **1929:** 285n.
 United States position on disarmament, Ambas-
  sador Gibson, **1929:** 48n.
Statistics, Advisory Committee on Unemployment,
  1930: 244, 247
Statistics, President's Advisory Committee on Em-
  ployment, **1931:** 60n.
Statistics, Bureau of Labor, **1930:** 76n., 244, 247,
  334
Steamboat Inspection, Bureau of Navigation and,
  1932–33: 423
Steamfitters, United States Association of Plumb-
  ers and, **1931:** 101
Stearns, Myron, **1931:** 33
Stedman, Repr. Charles M., **1930:** 300
Steed, H. Wickham, **1930:** 119
Steel Construction, American Institute of, **1929:**
  278; **1930:** 344, 345; **1932–33:** 180n.
Steiwer, Sen. Frederick, **1932–33:** 234
Stelzle, Charles, **1929:** 269
Stephenson, Gilbert T., **1931:** 66
Sterling, Ross D., **1931:** 91n.
Stern, Alfred K., **1931:** 314
Steuart, William M., **1930:** 244, 247
Steuben, Gen. Frederick von, **1930:** 235
Steuben County Society, **1930:** 35
Steuben Society, **1931:** 171n.
Stevens, Henry L., **1932–33:** 38, 40
Stewart, Ethelbert, **1930:** 244, 247
Stewart, Rev. G. E., **1930:** 290n.
Stimson, Henry L., **1929:** 6, 49n., 61, 241, 306;
  1930: 11n., 94n., 123, 337, 405, 414n.;
  1931: 11, 25, 28, 35, 37, 71, 263, 266, 267,
  268, 383n., 411, 433, 434; **1932–33:** 3n.,
  23, 25, 34, 214, 228, 235n., 396, 444,
  449n., 454

Stock Exchange, New York, **1929:** 272, 282; **1932–33:** 54, 55
Stokes, Edward C., **1932–33:** 372
Stone, Harlan F., **1929:** 54
Stone, James C., **1929:** 136, 140; **1930:** 265n.; **1931:** 92
Storrs, Lucius S., **1929:** 285n.
Stout, J. Robert, **1932–33:** 18, 21, 455
Stowe, Harriet Beecher, **1930:** 186
Straus, Nathan, **1931:** 14, 96
Strauss, Lewis, **1931:** 107; **1932–33:** 374n.
Street and Highway Safety, Third National Conference on, **1930:** 130, 166
Streets and highways, **1930:** 49, 130, 166, 307, 390, 391, 423
  Federal expenditures, **1931:** 147, 148, 248, 319
  Safety, **1931:** 356
Strong, Lt. Col. George V., **1932–33:** 25n.
Strong, Walter A., **1929:** 146n.; **1931:** 179
Strother, French, **1931:** 116
Sugar trade, **1932–33:** 384, 387
Sukesli, Col. G., **1930:** 223
Sullivan, Mark, **1929:** 144
Sulzer, Mayor Marcus A., **1929:** 254n.
Summerall, Gen. Charles P., **1930:** 253, 254
Summers, Jean, **1932–33:** 368
Sunday, William F., **1931:** 374
Supervising Architect, Office of, **1932–33:** 423
Supplements—Public Statements by Mr. Hoover From the Nomination to the Inauguration, **1929:** p. 495
Supply Committee, General, **1932–33:** 423
Supreme Court of the District of Columbia, **1931:** 173, 174; **1932–33:** 250n.
Supreme Court of the United States, **1930:** 40, 41, 92; **1931:** 65, 75, 95, 400, 433
  American Bar Association, address, **1932–33:** 335
  Associate Justice, **1932–33:** 15, 16
  Chief Justice, **1932–33:** 335
  Independent status, **1932–33:** 358, 363, 366
  Judicial procedure, reform, **1932–33:** 69, 475
Svinhufvud, Pehr Evind, **1932–33:** 417
Swanson, Sen. Claude A., **1929:** 161; **1931:** 238, 239; **1932–33:** 3n., 25n.
Sweden, **1929:** 3n., 161, 317
  King Gustaf V, **1930:** 104; **1931:** 230
Swedish-Americans, **1932–33:** 381
Swift, Ernest J., **1929:** 108
Switzerland, **1929:** 161
  Arbitration and conciliation treaty, **1931:** 433
  Trade relations, **1931:** 426
  U.S. Ambassador, **1932–33:** 25n.
  U.S. Minister to, **1930:** 11n.
Syracuse Post-Standard, **1929:** 208

Taber, Louis, J., **1930:** 259
Tacna-Arica, **1930:** 133
  Dispute, **1929:** 77, 89, 167, 295
Taft, Chief Justice William H., **1929:** 1n.; **1930:** 40, 41, 68, 79, 80n., 81, 244, 247
Takamatsu, Prince of Japan, **1931:** 146, 217
Tamblyn, George O., **1932–33:** 61
Tannenbaum, A., **1929:** 190n.
Tanners' Council, **1929:** 316
Tardieu, André, **1932–33:** 150
Tariff Act of 1922, **1929:** 216
Tariff Act of 1930, amendments, **1932–33:** 155
Tariff Commission, United States.
  See United States Tariff Commission.
Tariff legislation
  Congressional leadership, meeting, **1930:** 55
  Export debenture plan, **1930:** 147
  Foreign protests, transmittal to Senate, **1930:** 172
  Imports, temporary effect on, **1930:** 273, 274
  Tariff Act of 1930, **1930:** 188, 190
Tariffs
  Agricultural, **1932–33:** 384, 385
  Commodity investigations, **1931:** 122, 258, 412, 426; **1932–33:** 237, 336, 349, 357
  Flexible tariff, **1929:** 38, 215, 216, 267, 295
  Glass (window) increases, **1929:** 75
  Legislation, **1929:** 98, 267
  Linseed increases, **1929:** 75
  Milk and cream increases, **1929:** 75
  Oil, **1932–33:** 342
  President's views, **1929:** 212
  Protective, **1932–33:** 155, 259, 322, 328, 337, 342, 344, 346, 347, 357, 358, 360, 363, 364, 366, 371, 376, 377, 378, 379, 380, 386, 387, 388, 390, 457
  Revision, **1929:** 4, 38, 267; **1931:** 226
  State of the Union message, **1931:** 430
  United Kingdom, policies, **1931:** 420, 436
Tate, Hugh McCall, **1930:** 6n.
Tax Association, National, **1932–33:** 292
Taxation
  Budget message, **1930:** 391; **1931:** 432
  Capital gains, **1930:** 311, 390
  Conference of Governors, **1932–33:** 137
  Customs, **1932–33:** 450
  Excise, **1932–33:** 186, 346, 419, 421, 450
  Federal expenditures and revenues, message to Congress, **1932–33:** 450
  Federal refunds, **1932–33:** 402, 456
  Gasoline tax, **1932–33:** 421
  Income, **1932–33:** 186, 450
  Increase, **1929:** 46; **1930:** 65, 103, 200, 402, 403 408; **1931:** 78, 116, 117, 385, 436, 437
  International Chamber of Commerce, **1931:** 162, 168
  Property, **1932–33:** 292, 322, 377, 461
  Publication of Internal Revenue tax refund decisions, **1929:** 7, 10

Taxation — *continued*
　Reduction, continuation of, **1929:** 28, 140, 141,
　　218, 295, 296; **1930:** 273, 274, 379n., 390,
　　391
　Revenues, **1930:** 103; **1931:** 214, 302, 318, 430;
　　1932–33: 1, 9, 10, 31, 92, 93, 123, 126, 137,
　　146, 148, 154, 175, 186, 188, 208, 209, 259,
　　287, 322, 347
　Veterans, exemptions, **1930:** 222
Taylor, Alfred A., **1931:** 423
Taylor, Amos, **1932–33:** 317
Taylor, John Thomas, **1932–33:** 38
Taylor, Marshall, **1929:** 33
Teachers, National Congress of Parents and, **1931:**
　314
Teachers Association, Parent-, **1931:** 246
Teachers in Colored Schools, National Association
　of, **1931:** 272
Teagle, Walter C., **1932–33:** 404
Teague, Charles C., **1929:** 140; **1931:** 92, 210, 283;
　1932–33: 342
Telephone and Telegraph Corporation, Interna-
　tional, **1929:** 32
Temperance, **1929:** 210
Tennessee
　Child health and protection conference, **1932–
　　33:** 5n.
　Drought relief, **1931:** 121
　Governor, **1930:** 265n.
　Muscle Shoals Commission, **1931:** 88, 260, 416,
　　430, 440
　Republican primary, **1930:** 243
　Roads program, **1931:** 248
Tennessee Valley, **1931:** 82
Tercentenary of the Founding of the Colony of
　　Massachusetts, Commission for the Cel-
　　ebration of the, **1930:** 233
Terra, Gabriel, **1931:** 85, 300; **1932–33:** 271
Terrell, William D., **1929:** 8
Texas
　Child health and protection conference, **1932–
　　33:** 5n.
　Governor, **1931:** 91n.
　Intracoastal Canal Association of Louisiana and,
　　1931: 399
　Oil resources, **1931:** 100
　Pipeline, gas, **1931:** 1
　Roads program, **1931:** 248
Texas and Pacific Railway Co., **1929:** 19
Textile Foundation Act, **1930:** 182
Textile Institute, Cotton, **1932–33:** 341
Thacher, Thomas Day, **1931:** 301
Thanksgiving Day, **1931:** 422
Theodore Roosevelt Island, **1932–33:** 425
Third National Conference on Street and Highway
　　Safety, **1930:** 130, 166
Thirteen Club, **1930:** 70n.
Thomas, Sen. Elmer, **1930:** 172

Thomas Jefferson Memorial Foundation, **1930:** 54,
　114
Thomas Prize, M. Carey, **1931:** 165
Thompson, Samuel H., **1930:** 259; **1931:** 106
Thompson, William B., **1930:** 214
Thompson, William O., **1930:** 16
Three Power Naval Conference, 1927, **1929:** 48n.
Thrift Committee, National, **1932–33:** 41n.'
Thrift Week, National, **1932–33:** 21
Thwing, Alfred L., **1931:** 70
Tientsin, China, **1930:** 133
Tiffany, R. K., **1929:** 242
Tiffereth Israel Congregation, **1930:** 164
Tilson, Repr. John Q., **1929:** 12, 97; **1930:** 147;
　1931: 238, 239
Tilton, Frederic A., **1929:** 108, 147; **1931:** 200, 201
Timber Conservation Board, **1932–33:** 135
Tinkham, Edward, **1931:** 199
Tobacco, crop production loans, **1932–33:** 309n.
Tolan, Eddie, **1932–33:** 318
Toledo, Ohio, **1932–33:** 346
Tomb of the Unknown Soldier, **1932–33:** 393
Topographic maps, **1930:** 3
Towner, Horace M., **1929:** 84
Townsend, Wallace, **1929:** 242n.
Trade.
　See also Exports; Imports; Tariff.
　Agricultural exports, **1931:** 264, 303, 313
　　Reconstruction Finance Corporation, financ-
　　　ing, **1932–33:** 221, 322
　Arms and munitions
　　Exports, **1931:** 86
　　Restrictions, **1932–33:** 446, 470
　Commerce Department report, **1930:** 293, 295
　European crisis, impact, **1931:** 238, 239, 264
　Expansion, **1930:** 119, 131, 188, 314
　Fourth Pan American Commercial Conference,
　　1931: 347
　Government supplies, imports, **1932–33:** 31, 32
　Great Lakes-St. Lawrence Deep Waterway,
　　1932–33: 235, 322
　Imports, domestic impact, **1932–33:** 259, 322,
　　328, 337, 342, 344, 346, 347, 357, 358, 360,
　　363, 364, 366, 371, 376, 377, 378, 379, 380,
　　386, 387, 388, 457, 462, 465
　Indiana Republican Editorial Association,
　　remarks, **1931:** 226
　International Chamber of Commerce, address,
　　1931: 162
　International conference, possibility of, **1931:**
　　313n., 315; **1932–33:** 155
　Merchant marine, **1932–33:** 91
　National Foreign Trade Convention, message,
　　1930: 158
　Oil, **1931:** 91, 99, 100
　Philippines, **1932–33:** 384, 449
　Porto Rico, **1931:** 111

Trade — *continued*
  Union of Soviet Socialist Republics, **1930:** 244, 380, 390
  United Kingdom, **1931:** 320, 420, 436
Trade, New York Board of, **1930:** 110
Trade Association Executives, American, **1931:** 160; **1932–33:** 41n., 296
Trade Commission, Federal, **1931:** 100
Trade Convention, National Foreign, **1930:** 160
Trade Council, National Foreign, **1932–33:** 143
Trade Exhibition and Congress, International Fur, **1930:** 18
Trammell, Sen. Park, **1930:** 403n.
Transatlantic Fliers Committee, **1931:** 126
Transatlantic flights, **1932–33:** 173, 252
Transcontinental Air Transport, **1930:** 273n.
Trans-Lux movie theatres, message, **1931:** 193
Transportation
  Bonus army veterans, travel expenses, **1932–33:** 225
  Common carriers, **1932–33:** 358
  Great Lakes-St. Lawrence Deep Waterway, **1932–33:** 219, 226, 235, 259, 273, 322, 470
  Mississippi River, 9-foot waterway, **1932–33:** 321
  Safety, **1932–33:** 320
Transportation Act of 1920, **1930:** 311
Travel, President's.
  See President's travel.
Traylor, Melvin A., **1930:** 272
Treadway, Repr. Allen T., **1931:** 238, 239
Treadway, Dr. W. L., **1931:** 103
Treasury, Department of the
  Appropriations, **1930:** 128, 193, 391, 395n.; **1932–33:** 29, 421
  Assistant Secretary, **1929:** 256; **1930:** 158, 165; **1931:** 67
  Bureau of the Budget, **1930:** 55, 58, 65n., 72, 78, 86, 103, 125, 128, 140, 142, 193, 390, 395, 397, 401, 410; **1931:** 39, 41; **1932–33:** 26, 29, 83, 109, 119, 154n., 207, 218n., 225n., 287, 289, 290, 423
  Bureau of Customs, **1930:** 391; **1932–33:** 237, 423
  Bureau of Internal Revenue, **1930:** 266
  Bureau of the Mint, **1930:** 121
  Bureau of Narcotics, **1930:** 183n., 299, 390; **1931:** 103
  Bureau of the Public Health Service, **1930:** 55n., 165, 265; **1931:** 43, 44, 103, 297, 298, 430; **1932–33:** 2, 294, 311, 337, 358, 419, 423
  Collector of Customs, Los Angeles, **1931:** 218
  Comptroller of the Currency, **1932–33:** 238, 239, 284
  Convict produced imports, regulations, **1930:** 380
  Executive branch reorganization, **1932–33:** 423
  Export debenture plan analysis, **1929:** 46
  Federal Farm Loan Bureau, **1930:** 258, 259, 265, 265n., 271, 272, 390

Treasury, Department of the — *continued*
  Office of Supervising Architect, **1931:** 453
  Officials, meeting with the President, **1932–33:** 36n.
  Post Office site, selection, **1932–33:** 224
  Prohibition Bureau, transfer to Justice Department, **1930:** 135, 165
  Prohibition enforcement, **1929:** 125, 127
  Public building projects, reports, **1931:** 184, 277, 278, 307, 394
  Public construction projects, equal employment opportunity policy, **1932–33:** 354
  Recovery efforts, **1932–33:** 123
  Rubber imports, investigation, **1932–33:** 336
  Secretary (Andrew Mellon), **1929:** 7n., 10, 46, 281; **1930:** 17, 74, 200, 206, 267, 273, 274, 331, 332, 395; **1931:** 120, 251, 263, 266, 268, 299, 333, 433; **1932–33:** 37, 38, 39, 44, 73n., 119n., 154n., 156n., 186, 220, 221, 251, 264, 267ftn., 282, 283, 322, 347, 399, 421, 454
  Under Secretary, **1930:** 271, 272, 273, 274; **1932–33:** 38, 39, 41, 220
Treaties and other international agreements.
  See also specific treaty.
  Arbitration and conciliation treaties, **1930:** 365, 390
  Foreign relations, message to Congress, **1931:** 433
  Great Lakes-St. Lawrence Deep Waterway, treaty with Canada, **1932–33:** 219, 226, 235, 259, 273, 322, 470
  International Convention for the Suppression of International Trade in Arms and Ammunition and Implements of War, **1932–33:** 446
  International Load Lines convention, **1931:** 57
  London Naval Treaty, **1930:** 143
  Mixed Claims Commission, United States and Germany, settlement on costs of U.S. Army of Occupation, **1930:** 74
  Niagara Falls convention, **1930:** 109
Treaty of 1915, Republic of Haiti, **1930:** 38, 39
Tremaine, C. M., **1929:** 55n.
Trenton, N.J., **1932–33:** 363
  250th anniversary, **1929:** 260
Trigg, Ernest T., **1931:** 314
Tripp, Louis H., **1931:** 118ftn.
Tropical Radio Telegraph Company, **1930:** 141
Trujillo, Rafael Leonidas, **1930:** 268, 286, 425; **1931:** 81
Trust Companies Division, American Bankers Association, **1931:** 66
Trusts, benevolent, **1932–33:** 322
Ts'ao Jung-k'uan, **1931:** 36
Tschudi, Harold, **1932–33:** 41n.
Tuberculosis, **1932–33:** 89
Tuberculosis Association, National, **1930:** 382, 392; **1931:** 424; **1932–33:** 408

Tuck, S. Pinkney, **1932–33:** 25n.
Tucumcari, N. Mex., **1932–33:** 397
Turkey, **1929:** 3n., 161, 265
  President Mustapha Kemal, **1930:** 346; **1931:**
    279, 386; **1932–33:** 361
  Treaty with United States, **1931:** 433
Turner, Gov. Daniel W., **1932–33:** 313
Turner, Comdr. Richmond K., **1932–33:** 25n.
Tuskegee Institute, **1930:** 50, 51, 106; **1931:** 136;
    1932–33: 353
Tuttle, Charles H., **1930:** 308
Twelfth Exposition of Chemical Industries, **1929:**
    66
Tygel, Z., **1931:** 77

Ubico, Jorge, **1932–33:** 300
Udall, W. V., **1932–33:** 227
Uncle Robert, **1931:** 178; **1932–33:** 118
Uncle Robert Foundation, **1930:** 424n.
Underwood tariff, **1930:** 188
Unemployment.
  See Employment and unemployment.
Unemployment Relief
  Cabinet Committee on, **1930:** 331, 332, 334, 390,
    395
  President's Organization on, **1931:** 294, 295, 297,
    299, 303, 324, 360 387, 388, 430, 436
  See also President's Organization on
    Unemployment Relief.
Unemployment Relief Committee of New York
    City, Emergency, **1932–33:** 351
Unemployment Statistics, Advisory Committee on,
    1930: 244, 247; **1932–33:** 135
Union League, Philadelphia, Pa., **1931:** 204
Union of South Africa, **1929:** 161
Union of Soviet Socialist Republics, **1929:** 161, 317
  Nonrecognition, **1931:** 57
  Trade, **1930:** 244, 380, 390
  Wheat production, **1931:** 303
  U.S. Embassy, former, **1930:** 181
  U.S. relations with, **1930:** 83
Union Square, New York City, **1932–33:** 130
United Avigation Corporation, **1930:** 273n.
United Brethren in Christ, **1929:** 78
United Campaign Appeal of Philadelphia, **1931:**
    431
United Kingdom
  Ambassador to U.S., **1932–33:** 395
  American Bar Association convention, guests,
    1930: 276, 277
  Claim against U.S., **1930:** 37
  Convention for safety of life at sea, **1929:** 317
  Counselor of U.S. Embassy, **1930:** 11n.
  Dirigible *R-101*, crash, **1930:** 317
  Disarmament, **1930:** 8, 112, 113, 115, 143, 183,
    184, 221, 225, 341

United Kingdom — *continued*
  Financial crisis, **1931:** 299, 320, 387, 389, 420
  Foreign Minister Arthur Henderson, **1931:** 89
  Intergovernmental debts, **1932–33:** 228n., 395,
    431, 452, 454
  Kellogg-Briand pact, **1929:** 161, 229
  King George V, **1929:** 107; **1930:** 8, 109, 175,
    317; **1931:** 216
  London Conference of Ministers, **1931:** 263,
    266–268
  Naval disarmament discussions, **1929:** 162, 202,
    224, 229
  Payment of claim to, **1929:** 312
  Prime Minister James Ramsay MacDonald,
    1930: 115, 133, 341; **1931:** 266
  Prime Minister's visit to the United States, **1929:**
    116, 162, 209, 218, 222, 224, 226, 227,
    228, 229, 240
  Tariffs and trade, **1931:** 320, 420, 426, 436
  Unemployment, **1930:** 315
  U.S. Ambassador to, **1930:** 10n., 11n., 158, 231;
    1931: 211, 238, 239, 446, 449, Supp. I;
    1932–33: 3n., 37, 38, 39, 44
United Mine Workers, **1931:** 244
United Press Association, **1930:** 124
United States Association of Plumbers and
    Steamfitters, **1931:** 101
United States Battle of the Monongahela Com-
    mission, **1932–33:** 135
United States Building and Loan League, **1931:**
    293, 314; **1932–33:** 41n., 274
United States Bureau of Efficiency, **1930:** 55,
    261; **1932–33:** 423
United States-Canada dam investigation, joint,
    1930: 42
United States Chamber of Commerce, **1929:** 284,
    285, 292, 297, 304; **1930:** 250; **1931:** 160n.,
    314
United States Civil Service Commission, **1930:** 48,
    338, 373; **1931:** 150, 403, 413n.
  Executive branch reorganization, **1932–33:** 423
  Federal employees, political activity, **1932–33:**
    275, 276
  President, **1932–33:** 212, 275, 276
  Retirement and Disability Fund, appropriations,
    1932–33: 421
United States Coast Guard, **1930:** 55n., 117, 139,
    152, 190, 391
United States Commission on Education in Haiti,
    1930: 50, 51n.; **1932–33:** 135
United States Courts.
  See Courts, United States.
United States Customs Court, **1930:** 299
United States Employees' Compensation Commis-
    sion, **1932–33:** 423
United States Employment Service, **1931:** 61, 94,
    101, 277
United States Flag Association, **1929:** 36

United States George Washington Bicentennial
Commission, **1931:** 59
United States and Germany, Mixed Claims Commission, **1930:** 74
United States Junior Chamber of Commerce,
1932–33: 96
United States League of Building and Loan Associations, **1930:** 250
United States Marine Corps, **1930:** 38, 39, 55n., 92,
133, 236, 253; **1931:** 36, 71n., 138, 297;
1932–33: 34
United States Mediation Board, **1931:** 196
U.S. Shipping Board, **1929:** 104, 224, 225, 295;
1930: 176, 177, 231, 347, 391; **1931:** 147,
148, 430, 432, 453
Appropriations, **1932–33:** 421
Reorganization, proposed, **1932–33:** 106, 108,
423
Shipping lines operation, suspension, **1932–33:**
119
Vice Chairman, **1932–33:** 106, 108
United States Soldiers' Home, **1930:** 226, 227, 391
United States Supreme Court, **1931:** 65, 75, 95, 400,
433
United States Tariff Commission, **1929:** 38, 75,
216; **1930:** 147, 188, 195, 236, 273, 276,
293, 294, 390; **1931:** 122, 226, 258, 270,
403, 411, 412, 420, 426, 430
Appointments
Interim, **1930:** 195, 236
Preparation, **1931:** 403
Chairman, **1930:** 273; **1931:** 122, 270, 411, 412,
420; **1932–33:** 237, 349
Commodity investigations, **1931:** 122, 258, 412,
426; **1932–33:** 237, 336, 349, 357
Flexibility, **1931:** 226, 430; **1932–33:** 155, 259,
322, 337, 346, 347, 358, 360, 363, 364, 366,
371, 376, 377, 378, 379, 380, 387
Members, **1930:** 276, 293, 294
Reorganization, **1930:** 188, 390
United States Veterans' Bureau
Appropriations, **1930:** 140, 391
Consolidation, **1930:** 226, 227
Director, **1930:** 200, 202, 203, 206, 222
Universal Bible Sunday, **1931:** 427; **1932–33:** 362
Universal Draft Commission, **1932–33:** 135
Universities.
See Colleges and universities.
University of Chicago, **1930:** 335n.
Upham, Rear Adm. F. B., **1930:** 145, 146
Urban League, National, **1930:** 84
Urban League of New York City, **1932–33:** 353
Urban planning, **1930:** 249, 250
Uriburu, José Francisco, **1931:** 203
Uruguay, **1929:** 251
President Juan Çampisteguy, **1930:** 101, 239, 278
President Gabriel Terra, **1931:** 85, 300; **1932–33:**
271

Uruguay — *continued*
Radiotelephonic service, **1930:** 101
U.S. Ambassador to, **1930:** 303n.
U.S.S. *Arizona*, **1931:** 102
Utah, **1929:** 134, 185n.
President's visit, **1932–33:** 386, 387, 388
Utilities Committee, Electrical, **1930:** 145

Vallance, William R., **1932–33:** 467
Valley Forge, Pa., Memorial Day address, **1931:**
205
Van Keuren, Capt. A. H., **1932–33:** 25n.
Van Orsdel, Josiah A., **1932–33:** 164
Van Petten, E. C., **1929:** 242n.
Van Rensselaer, Martha, **1931:** 314; **1932–33:** 184
Van Sweringen, Mantis J., **1930:** 428, 429
Van Sweringen, Oris P., **1930:** 428, 429
Van Valkenburg, Edwin A., **1932–33:** 410
Vance, R. B., **1930:** 88
Vandenberg, Sen. Arthur H., **1929:** 267n.; **1931:**
238, 239
Vargas, Getulio, **1930:** 337n., 371, 407
Vasquez, Horacio, **1930:** 66ftn.
Veiller, Lawrence, **1931:** 314
Venemann, Robert M., **1929:** 149
Venezuela, **1929:** 3n., 145, 161
Vergil, **1930:** 375
Vest, Christine, **1930:** 64
Vestal, Repr. Albert R., **1931:** 226
Veteran Preference, Advisory Committee on,
1932–33: 135
Veteran Preference, President's Advisory Committee on, **1931:** 150
Veterans, **1929:** 295, 321
American Legion, **1932–33:** 38, 40, 51 101, 102,
256, 293
Address, **1930:** 314; **1931:** 318
Army Day, message, **1930:** 105
Benefits, budget increases, **1930:** 65, 66, 67, 236,
237, 391
Bonus bill, **1932–33:** 101, 102, 123, 126, 154, 293,
358
Bonus loans, **1931:** 147, 148, 214, 302, 324, 325,
430, 432
Bonus marchers, **1932–33:** 218, 225, 246, 248,
249, 250, 256, 275, 276, 285
"Buddy Poppy" campaign, message, **1931:** 145
Christmas message to disabled, **1930:** 420
Civil War Veterans' Act, **1930:** 182
Conference on the hoarding of currency, **1932–
33:** 36
Cornell University War Memorial, remarks,
1931: 199
Disability preference, **1931:** 150
Disabled, **1932–33:** 51, 365, 432
Messages, **1931:** 64, 444

Veterans — *continued*
  District of Columbia War Memorial, address,
    1931: 404
  Emergency Adjusted Compensation Act, 1931,
    1931: 63, 67, 78, 79, 80
  Employment, **1931:** 63, 78, 79, 80, 277n.
  Federal expenditures, **1932–33:** 9, 10, 92, 119,
    419, 421
  Imperial Order of the Dragon, **1932–33:** 47
  Military Order of the World War, **1932–33:** 67
  Pensions, **1931:** 358, 359
    Bill, **1932–33:** 138
  Spanish War veterans' pension bill, **1930:** 168,
    173, 174
  State of the Union message, **1930:** 390
  Tomb of the Unknown Soldier, dedication cer-
    emonies, **1932–33:** 393
  World War Shrine, Hoboken, N.J., message,
    1931: 202
  World War Veterans' Act, 1924, Amendments,
    1930: 200, 202, 203, 206, 222
Veterans' Administration, **1930:** 226, 227, 331, 390,
    391
  Administrator of Veterans' Affairs, **1931:** 63, 72,
    78, 79, 80, 147, 148, 214, 430, 453, 454;
    1932–33: 76, 77, 119, 218, 225n.
  Appropriations, **1931:** 432; **1932–33:** 218, 225,
    421
  Committee to study the disposition of U. S.
    Army posts, **1931:** 181
  Reorganization, **1932–33:** 423
Veterans' Bureau
  Medical Council, **1929:** 321
  United States, **1930:** 140, 200, 202, 203, 206, 222,
    226, 227, 391
Veterans of Foreign Wars, **1930:** 200, 222; **1931:**
    145, 166, 419; **1932–33:** 41n.
Veterans Services, Committee on Coordination of,
    1932–33: 135
Veto messages.
  See also Legislation.
  Deficiency and supplemental appropriations bill,
    1932–33: 456
  Emergency Adjusted Compensation Act, 1931,
    1931: 78
  Emergency relief and construction bill, **1932–33:**
    221
  Executive branch appropriations bill, statement
    on disapproval, **1932–33:** 482
  Gadsden Purchase coinage bill, **1930:** 121
  Indian claims bills, **1932–33:** 136, 458
  Indian claims legislation, **1931:** 65, 75
  Malheur and Harney Lakes, Oreg., **1930:** 179
  Muscle Shoals resolution, **1931:** 88
  National employment system legislation, state-
    ment of disapproval, **1931:** 94
  Philippine Islands, independence, **1932–33:** 449
  Quartermaster Corps civilian employees benefits
    bill, **1931:** 72; **1932–33:** 152

Veto messages — *continued*
  Relief of private citizens, **1931:** 49, 73; **1932–33:**
    65
  Spanish War veterans' pension bill, **1930:** 168
  Tariff Act of 1930, amendments, **1932–33:** 155
  Veterans' pensions bill, **1932–33:** 138
  Wage rates for workers employed by contractors
    on public buildings, **1932–33:** 213
  World War veterans' bill, **1930:** 206
Vezina, Elie, **1930:** 50, 51
Victoria, Queen of Sweden, **1930:** 104
Virgin Islands
  Administration, **1931:** 39, 41, 111, 112
  Governor, **1931:** 39, 41; **1932–33:** 425
  President's visit, **1931:** 102, 106, 110, 111, 112
Virginia, **1929:** 172, 180
  Drought relief, **1930:** 258, 265n., 266, 271, 276
  President's visit, **1931:** 360, 364, 365; **1932–33:**
    57, 137
  University of, **1931:** 164
Virginia State Conservation and Development
    Commission, **1929:** 172n.
Visas, **1930:** 22, 288, 380, 390; **1931:** 113, 189
Vittorio Emmanuele III, King (Italy), **1929:** 148,
    330; **1930:** 242
Vocational Education, Federal Board for, **1932–33:**
    119, 423
Volunteers of America, Inc., **1929:** 58

Wade, B. F., **1932–33:** 302
Wadsworth, Eliot, **1930:** 299; **1931:** 392
Wages, **1929:** 284n. 297; **1930:** 76, 77, 133, 144, 188,
    224, 238, 311, 315, 422; **1931:** 1, 43, 44,
    226, 271, 430
  Cabinet and President's salary, reductions,
    1932–33: 119, 127, 231
  Furlough plan for Federal employees, **1932–33:**
    119, 126, 127, 132, 133, 137, 146, 175, 198,
    199, 208, 212, 240, 307, 337, 419, 421
  Mississippi River flood control projects, **1932–
    33:** 353
  Public buildings, laborers, **1932–33:** 213
  Purchasing power, **1932–33:** 337, 346, 357, 358,
    360, 363, 364, 379, 380, 388
Wagner, Sen. Robert F., **1931:** 54, 55, 238, 239;
    1932–33: 221
Wagner bill.
  See National employment system legislation.
Wagner-Garner bill.
  See Emergency Relief and Construction Act of
    1932.
Wakatsuki, Reijiro, **1929:** 331n.
Wakerman, S. W., **1929:** 193n.
Walcott, Sen. Frederic C., **1930:** 388
Wald, Lillian D., **1932–33:** 30
Waldorf-Astoria Hotel, **1931:** 328

Walker, Alfred, **1931:** 182
Walker, Mayor James J., **1929:** 120
Wallace, Hugh C., **1931:** 3
Wallace, L. W., **1932–33:** 41n.
Walsh, Sen. David I., **1930:** 403n.; **1931:** 238, 239
Walsh, Frank P., **1931:** 383
Walsh, James L., **1932–33:** 41n.
Walsh, Sen. Thomas J., **1931:** 238, 239; **1932–33:** 480
War, Department of
  Acting Secretary, **1932–33:** 235
  Appropriations, **1930:** 58, 65, 66, 67, 238, 391, 395n.; **1931:** 432; **1932–33:** 83, 421
  Army Air Corps, maneuvers, **1931:** 211, 212
  Army Corps of Engineers, **1930:** 218n., 223, 261, 262; **1931:** 88, 185, 260, 319, 416, 430, 440, 453
  Army Reserve Corps, **1931:** 31, 32
  Assistant Secretary, **1929:** 6, 302; **1930:** 126; **1932–33:** 265
  Aviation, **1930:** 261, 391
  Chief of Cavalry, **1930:** 45
  Chief of Staff, **1930:** 253, 254
  General Staff, **1931:** 181, 185
    Chief of Staff, **1932–33:** 34
  Economy drive, **1931:** 173, 181
  Inland Waterways Corporation, **1932–33:** 423
  Interoceanic Canal Board, **1932–33:** 423
  Mississippi River flood control projects, charges of unfair labor practices, **1932–33:** 353
  Office of Chief of Engineers, **1930:** 132; **1932–33:** 251, 353n., 423
  Office of the Judge Advocate General, **1931:** 260, 416, 440
  Panama transports, proposed abolition, **1932–33:** 119
  Pay increase, **1930:** 55n., 65, 66, 67
  Quartermaster Corps, **1931:** 72; **1932–33:** 152
  Procurement policy, **1932–33:** 32
  Public works projects, **1932–33:** 282
  Research achievements, **1931:** 127
  San Francisco Bay Bridge agreement, **1930:** 261, 262
  Secretary (James W. Good), **1929:** 178, 196, 197
  Secretary (Patrick J. Hurley), **1929:** 304; **1930:** 109, 223, 253, 254, 266, 331, 332, 395; **1931:** 73, 82n., 173, 211, 212, 324, 378, 379; **1932–33:** 34, 83, 187n., 206, 246n., 403, 444, 449n.
  Soldiers' Home, transfer to Veterans' Administration, **1930:** 226, 227
  Special International Niagara Board, **1931:** 37
  Surgeon General, **1931:** 144n., 181
  Survey of military establishment, **1929:** 159, 160
  U.S. Army of Occupation, Germany, **1930:** 74
War, General Pact for the Renunciation of, **1929:** 1, 94, 161, 184, 229, 275, 295
War debt, French, **1929:** 163, 296

War debts, **1930:** 74, 133, 200n., 273, 274, 378, 379, 390, 391, 402
  See also Economy, national; Intergovernmental debts.
War memorials, dedications
  Cornell University, **1931:** 199
  District of Columbia, **1931:** 404
  World War Shrine, Hoboken, N.J., **1931:** 202
War Mother magazine, American, **1932–33:** 479
War reparations, German, **1929:** 97, 99, 109, 125, 126, 295
Warburg, Felix M., **1930:** 54, 80, 114, 151, 455; **1931:** 18; **1932–33:** 339
Warburg, Paul F., **1929:** 45n.
Ward, Albert N., **1930:** 91
Ward, Joseph, **1930:** 229
Warner, Henry Edward, **1931:** 206
Warren, Sen. Francis E., **1929:** 287, 302
Warren, Whitney, **1929:** 241, 243
Washburn, Albert Henry, **1930:** 102
Washington, Booker T., **1931:** 136
Washington, George, **1929:** 223, 253; **1931:** 59, 170, 205, 364
  Bicentennial Commission, United States, **1931:** 59
  Bicentennial Commission of the New York Board of Jewish Ministers, **1932–33:** 142
  Bicentennial of birth, **1932–33:** 35, 54, 56, 57, 58, 122, 142, 174, 181, 194, 196, 262, 335
Washington, **1929:** 185n.
  California Society of Washington, D.C., address, **1932–33:** 371
  Child health and protection conference, **1932–33:** 5n.
  Lincoln's Birthday, message, **1932–33:** 45n.
Washington, D.C.
  See District of Columbia.
Washington Cathedral, **1929:** 325
Washington Disarmament Conference, **1931:** 228
Washington Naval Conference, **1930:** 115, 184, 214n.
Washington Naval Treaty, **1930:** 117, 183, 391
Water Commission
  California, **1932–33:** 135
  United States and Mexico, International, **1931:** 11
Water Power Act, amendments, **1930:** 240
Water resources, **1929:** 132, 133, 134, 177, 178, 185, 241, 242, 253; **1930:** 158, 182; **1931:** 11, 13
Waterfowl, conservation, **1931:** 299
Waterton-Glacier International Peace Park, **1932–33:** 201
Waterways, **1929:** 211, 250, 274, 295
  See also Rivers, harbors, and waterways.
Waterways Association, Atlantic Deeper, **1931:** 346; **1932–33:** 352
Waterways Commission, Inland, **1929:** 250
Waterways Corporation, Inland, **1932–33:** 423

[References are to items except as otherwise indicated]

Watson, Chief Engineer George S., **1929:** 328

Watson, Sen. James E., **1929:** 97; **1930:** 222; **1931:** 226, 238, 239; **1932–33:** 135, 157, 357, 358

Watson, Thomas J., **1931:** 51

Waverly, Ohio, **1932–33:** 346

WCAU Radio building, **1932–33:** 463

Weather Bureau, **1930:** 391; **1932–33:** 423

Weaver, Gov. Arthur J., **1930:** 265n.

Weber, Joe, **1932–33:** 306

Welch, Dr. William Henry, **1929:** 266; **1930:** 107

Welfare, District of Columbia Board of, **1932–33:** 423

Welfare Association, Catholic, **1932–33:** 41n.

Welfare Board, Jewish, **1932–33:** 41n.

Welfare and Relief Mobilization Conference, **1932–33:** 294

Welfare and Relief Mobilization of 1932, **1932–33:** 338

Wellsboro, Ind., **1932–33:** 376

West, James E., **1932–33:** 244

West Liberty, Iowa, **1932–33:** 321

West Virginia
    Drought relief, **1930:** 258, 259, 265n.
    President's campaign, **1932–33:** 336, 346, 357, 360
    President's visit, **1931:** 223, 224

Westchester County World Affairs Institute, **1931:** 414

Western Air Express, **1930:** 273n.

Western Governors Conference on Public Land Questions, **1929:** 185, 186

Westinghouse, George, **1930:** 318

Westinghouse Electric and Manufacturing Corporation, **1930:** 351

Wharton, Arthur O., **1930:** 247n.

Wheat, Alfred A., **1929:** 37n.

Wheat, **1931:** 256, 257, 264, 297, 299, 303, 304, 387, 389
    Crop production loans, **1932–33:** 309

Wheeler, Sen. Burton K., **1932–33:** 366, 378

Wheeler, Harry A., **1931:** 314, 403

Whistler, James, **1931:** 187

Whitaker, Jane T., **1929:** 82

White, Charles L., **1929:** 62

White, Edward D., **1930:** 92

White, Gov. George, **1931:** 229n.

White, Robe Carl, **1931:** 189

White, Repr. Wallace H., Jr., **1929:** 17

White, Dr. William A., **1931:** 439

White, William Allen, **1930:** 50, 51

White House Conference on Child Health and Protection, **1930:** 204n., 369, 376, 389; **1931:** 22, 137, 182, 206, 231, 246, 321; **1932–33:** 135, 171, 184, 259, 311, 312, 328, 380, 383, 441
    Announcement, **1929:** 140, 142
    Planning Committee, remarks to, **1929:** 164

White House Conference on Drought Relief, **1930:** 258, 259, 261, 265, 270, 301, 390

White House Conference on Home Building and Home Ownership, **1930:** 249, 250, 302; **1931:** 149, 313, 314, 344, 395, 425; **1932–33:** 99, 135, 180, 184, 259, 311, 328, 358, 380

White House Correspondents Association, **1929:** 2; **1932–33:** 76

White House executive offices, repair, **1930:** 3, 7, 116

White House fire, **1929:** 328

White House staff
    Administrative Assistant to the President, **1931:** 116
    Secretary to the President, **1931:** 1, 2, 7; **1932–33:** 154n., 439

White House statements.
    See also Statements by the President.
    Agricultural relief, **1931:** 275
    Agriculture Department, economy conference, **1931:** 213
    Budget increases, **1930:** 65
    Cabinet members, salary reductions, **1932–33:** 231
    Caribbean tour, **1931:** 102
    China, International Settlement at Shanghai, protection of U.S. citizens, **1932–33:** 34
    Committees and commissions, **1932–33:** 135
    Communist demonstration, **1929:** 313
    Conference with certain members of Congress on economic problems, **1931:** 337
    Conference on the Limitation of the Manufacture of Narcotic Drugs, U.S. delegation, **1931:** 103
    Conferences with industrial and business leaders, **1929:** 281n., 284n.
    Congresssional Members, meeting with the President, **1932–33:** 400
    Crop production loans, **1932–33:** 309
    Currency hoarding, conference, **1932–33:** 41
    Domestic health conditions, **1932–33:** 2
    Drought relief campaign, **1931:** 26
    Emergency relief and construction legislation, **1932–33:** 216, 230
    Equal employment opportunity, **1932–33:** 354
    Executive branch, reorganization, **1932–33:** 79
    Executive department appropriations bills, **1932–33:** 459
    Federal budget, **1932–33:** 402
    Federal employees, furlough plan, **1932–33:** 127
    Federal expenditures, **1931:** 214
    French Prime Minister Pierre Laval, visit, **1931:** 368
    General Disarmament Conference
        Appropriations, **1932–33:** 441
        U.S. delegation, instructions, **1932–33:** 206
    Government expenditures, **1930:** 238
    Immigration restriction, **1931:** 113
    International monetary and economic conference, appropriations, **1932–33:** 441

White House statements — *continued*
Joint select committee to study prohibition enforcement, proposed, **1930:** 15
Latin American debts, **1931:** 243
London Conference of Ministers, **1931:** 267
Mississippi River flood control projects, charges of unfair labor practices, **1932–33:** 353
Muscle Shoals Commission, appointment of members, **1931:** 260
National economy program, **1932–33:** 119
Navy, U.S., changes in chain of command, **1930:** 146
Navy Department, economy conference, **1931:** 219
Navy League, investigation, **1931:** 392
Norris-La Guardia Act, **1932–33:** 90
Polish Corridor, **1931:** 373
Post Office Department, economy conference, **1931:** 200, 201
President-elect Roosevelt, meetings with the President, **1932–33:** 399, 405, 454
Presidential receptions, **1932–33:** 43
President's vacation plans, **1930:** 234
Prohibition enforcement in the District of Columbia, **1929:** 214
Public building projects, **1931:** 184, 278
Public works and drought relief, **1931:** 319
Public works and unemployment relief, **1930:** 127, 357, 423
Railroad reconstruction conferences, **1932–33:** 87
Reconstruction Finance Corporation, **1932–33:** 187
Research Committee on Social Trends, **1929:** 318
Roads program, State and Federal expenditures, **1931:** 248
Senate cooperation on appropriations legislation, **1930:** 368
Sinclair, Harry F., **1929:** 213
Tariff legislation, **1929:** 212, 267
Unemployment relief efforts of the Association of Community Chests and Councils, **1931:** 290
United States Tariff Commission, **1931:** 258, 270, 426
Wage levels, maintenance, **1931:** 271
White House Conference on Home Building and Home Ownership, **1931:** 395
World trade conference, possibility of, **1931:** 315
Yellowstone National Park Boundary Commission, **1929:** 31
Whitehead, Lt. Comdr. Richard P., **1931:** 435
Whitlock, Ward B., **1932–33:** 274
Whitman, Walt, **1931:** 187
Whitney, A. F., **1932–33:** 41n.
Whitney, A. W., **1930:** 130n.
Whitney, Harry Payne, **1931:** 415
Whitney Museum of American Art, **1931:** 415

Whitsitt, Vincent, **1932–33:** 41n.
Wickersham, George W., **1929:** 92n.; **1931:** 27
Wilbur, Ray L., **1929:** 140, 142, 164, 241, 242; **1930:** 3, 5, 326, 327, 342, 343, 376; **1931:** 72, 75, 100, 120, 324; **1932–33:** 119n., 167n., 232n., 392n., 411n.
Wildlife, **1930:** 388
Wile, Frederic W., **1929:** 206n.
Wiley, Louis, **1929:** 101; **1930:** 35, 122; **1932–33:** 30, 445
Wilkerson, James H., **1932–33:** 15, 418
Willard, Adm. A. L., **1930:** 146
Willard, Daniel, **1929:** 281n.; **1930:** 428
Willebrandt, Mabel W., **1929:** 90, 91
William Penn Commemoration Committee, **1932–33:** 350
Williams, Albert C., **1929:** 177
Williams, Carl, **1929:** 136
Williams, Frank M., **1929:** 125n.
Williams, George, **1932–33:** 330
Williams, L. B., **1932–33:** 264
Williams, Michael, **1932–33:** 117
Williams, Ralph E., **1929:** 194
Williams, Roger Q., **1929:** 148n.
Williams, Thomas J., **1930:** 29n.
Williams, Repr. Thomas S., **1929:** 237
Williams, W. T. B., **1930:** 51n.
Williams, Dr. Walter, **1929:** 71n.; **1930:** 154
Williamson, Ralph B., **1931:** 13
Williamson, Sidney B., **1929:** 125n.
Willingdon, Viscount, **1931:** 19
Willits, Joseph H., **1930:** 247n.
Willys, John N., **1931:** 249n.; **1932–33:** 346
Wilmer, Dr. William H., **1929:** 239
Wilmer Institute of Ophthalmology, **1929:** 239
Wilmington, Del., **1932–33:** 363
Wilson, Charles S., **1929:** 140ftn., p. 207; **1930:** 265n.
Wilson, Ferman, **1930:** 372n.
Wilson, Francis, **1929:** 242n.
Wilson, Hugh R., **1930:** 11n.; **1932–33:** 25n.
Wilson, Thomas E., **1929:** 26
Wilson, President Woodrow, **1929:** 18ftn., p. 47; **1930:** 244, 247, 405; **1931:** 68, 249
Wilson tariff, **1930:** 188
Winant, Gov. John G., **1932–33:** 240
Winslow, Francis A., **1929:** 37
Wisconsin
Great Lakes-St. Lawrence Deep Waterway, **1932–33:** 235
President's campaign, **1932–33:** 379
Roads program, **1931:** 248
Wittpenn, Mrs. H. Otto, **1932–33:** 416
Wolman, Leo, **1930:** 247n.
Woman, Pioneer, **1930:** 129
Woman's Christian Temperance Union, National, **1929:** 210; **1930:** 370

Women
 American National Red Cross, address, **1931:** 195
 American War Mother magazine, **1932–33:** 479
 Aviation, **1931:** 23
 Campaign remarks, **1932–33:** 328, 380, 389
 Child health, **1930:** 376
 Employment, **1931:** 161
 Equal opportunity, **1930:** 319
 Frontier, **1930:** 129
 General Disarmament Conference, U.S. delegation, **1931:** 446, 449
 Housing, **1931:** 314
 Red Cross Chapter House, dedication, **1930:** 89
 Service clubs, conference on hoarding of currency, **1932–33:** 36
Women, National Council of Catholic, **1931:** 340
Women's Clubs, General Federation of, **1930:** 250; **1931:** 314; **1932–33:** 41n.
Women's Clubs, Inc., National Federation of Business and Professional, **1932–33:** 41n., 71
Women's Clubs, Westchester County Federation of, **1931:** 414
Women's Conference on Current Problems, **1932–33:** 311
Women's Education League, Chenango County Republican, **1932–33:** 333
Women's International League for Peace and Freedom, **1931:** 351
Women's National Farm and Garden Association, **1930:** 250; **1931:** 314
Women's Week, National Business, **1932–33:** 71
Wood, **1931:** 189, 190
Wood, George H., **1930:** 226, 227
Wood, Leonard, **1932–33:** 265
Wood, Repr. William R., **1930:** 125; **1931:** 226, 238, 239
Woodlock, D. J., **1932–33:** 41n.
Woodlock, Thomas F., **1930:** 249
Woodring, Harry H., **1931:** 91n.
Woods, A. F., **1931:** 181ftn.
Woods, Col. Arthur, **1930:** 334, 338, 339, 347, 413; **1931:** 295; **1932–33:** 294, 337ftn.
Woodville, Ind., **1932–33:** 376
Woolsey, John M., **1929:** 37n.
Wooley, Mark, **1931:** 70n.
Woolley, Clarence M., **1930:** 190
Woolley, Mary Emma, **1930:** 233; **1932–33:** 3n., 25n., 380
WOR Radio station, **1932–33:** 473
Work, Dr. Hubert, **1929:** 111, 194
World Affairs Institute, Westchester County, N.Y., **1931:** 414
World Alliance for Friendship Through the Churches, **1930:** 365
World Alliance for International Friendship, **1929:** 269n.
World Conference on Narcotic Education, **1930:** 61; **1931:** 69

World Conference of the Young Men's Christian Association, **1931:** 286
World Court, **1929:** 12, 275; **1930:** 115, 119, 133, 365, 383, 385, 390, 405; **1931:** 191n., 433
World Disarmament Conference.
 See General Disarmament Conference.
World economic conference
 Appropriations, **1932–33:** 207, 441
 Campaign remarks, **1932–33:** 259, 322, 337, 347, 377, 380, 387, 388
 Goals, **1932–33:** 457, 465
 Intergovernmental debts, **1932–33:** 395, 407, 431, 434
 Silver interests, representation, **1932–33:** 269, 343, 388
 State of the Union message, **1932–33:** 419
World Narcotic Defense Association, **1932–33:** 52
World Power Conference, **1930:** 192
World Series, **1931:** 327
World War, **1930:** 119, 133, 297, 314, 408
World War, Military Order of the, **1932–33:** 67
World War bonus bill.
 See Bonus, veterans.
World War Foreign Debt Commission, **1931:** 433; **1932–33:** 407
World War Shrine, Hoboken, N.J., **1931:** 202
World War Veterans' Act, 1924, Amendments, **1930:** 200, 202, 203, 206, 222
World's Fair, Chicago, **1930:** 158, 417
World's Fair Centennial Celebration, Chicago, **1932–33:** 135
Wright, J. Butler, **1930:** 303n.
Wright Brothers National Memorial, N.C., **1932–33:** 403
Wriston, Henry M., **1929:** 258
Writings of George Washington from Original Manuscript Sources, foreword, **1931:** 59
Wyman, A. Lee, **1929:** 37n.
Wyoming, **1929:** 134, 185n.
 Child health and protection conference, **1932–33:** 5n.
 Election, **1930:** 48n.
 President's campaign, **1932–33:** 344, 386

Yale Bowl, **1931:** 428
Yale Daily News, **1929:** 33
Yancey, Lewis A., **1929:** 148n.; **1931:** 126
Yangtze Valley, China, flood disaster, **1931:** 296
Yao Ah-Ken, **1931:** 36
Yellow Bird (monoplane), **1929:** 119
Yellowstone National Park, **1930:** 153
Yellowstone National Park Boundary Commission, **1929:** 31; **1931:** 5; **1932–33:** 135
Yiddish Art Theatre, **1932–33:** 474
Yorktown, Battle of, **1932–33:** 301
Yorktown, Va., **1931:** 364, 365

Yorktown Sesquicentennial Commission, **1931:** 365
Yost, Lenna L., **1931:** 224
Young, Dr. Alton M., **1929:** 58
Young, Arthur H., **1931:** 287; **1932–33:** 223
Young, Gov. Clement C., **1929:** 177, 178
Young, John R., **1929:** 2
Young, Roy A., **1930:** 271, 272, 279, 284, 285
Young, Sanborn, **1931:** 103
Young, Walker R., **1932–33:** 396
Young Men's Christian Association, **1931:** 286;
    1932–33: 22, 41n., 68, 330
Young Plan, **1930:** 74n.
Young reparations agreement.
   See War reparations *under* Germany.
Young Republican League, **1932–33:** 366, 368
Youngquist, G. Aaron, **1929:** 270
Youngstown, Ohio, **1932–33:** 336
Youth
   Athletics, **1931:** 241
   American Indians, **1930:** 3, 5
   Association for Childhood Education, **1932–33:**
    145
   Boy Scouts of America, **1931:** 33; **1932–33:** 165,
    244
    Address, **1930:** 81
   Boys Club of America, **1932–33:** 178
   Boys Week, message, **1930:** 134
   Camp Directors of America, **1932–33:** 414
   Catholic Boys' Brigade of the United States,
    1932–33: 312
   Child labor, **1932–33:** 311
   Childrens' Charter, **1931:** 124
   Children's Hour, message, **1931:** 206
   Conference on the Crisis in Education, **1932–33:**
    442
   Delinquent, **1930:** 165, 376
   Disadvantaged, **1930:** 424
   Education, **1930:** 64, 213
   Girl's Service League of America, **1931:** 161
   Handicapped, **1930:** 376

Youth — *continued*
   Health, **1930:** 204, 369, 376, 382, 389, 390; **1931:**
    22, 137, 149, 182, 206, 231, 246, 321, 430;
    1932–33: 2, 5, 8, 135, 171, 184, 259, 311,
    312, 328, 348, 358, 380, 383, 441
   International Save the Children Fund, **1932–33:**
    447
   Juvenile delinquency, **1932–33:** 69, 193
   Kips Bay Boys' Club, message, **1931:** 105
   Musical education, **1932–33:** 110
   National Boys' Week, **1931:** 152
   Opportunity, **1930:** 319
   Parent-Teachers Association, **1931:** 246
   Parents' Day, **1931:** 178; **1932–33:** 118
   Porto Rico Child Feeding Committee, **1932–33:**
    433
   Recreation, **1931:** 291
   Scholastic magazine, **1932–33:** 277
   Sixth Pan American Child Congress, **1930:** 75
   Support for Republican Party, **1932–33:** 465
Young, Owen D., **1929:** 97, 99, 109; **1930:** 74n.;
    1931: 238, 239, 299; **1932–33:** 170n., 264,
    366, 434
Yrigoyen, Hipolito.
   See Irigoyen, Hipolito.
Yugoslavia, King Alexander I, **1930:** 415; **1931:**
    441; **1932–33:** 430

Zaimis, Alexander, **1932–33:** 95
Zangara, Giuseppe, **1932–33:** 466n.
Zelienople, Pa., **1932–33:** 336
Zeta Beta Tau, **1930:** 155
Ziegler, Matilda, **1932–33:** 70
Zionism, **1930:** 400n.
Zionist Organization of America, **1929:** 139, 190n.;
    1932–33: 19, 374
Zonta International, **1932–33:** 41n.
Zukor, Adolph, **1931:** 24

INDEX FROM

PROCLAMATIONS AND EXECUTIVE ORDERS

A

Abernethy, Marie V. (EO 5695)

Abraham, Eli (EO 5474)

Absaroka National Forest, Mont. (EO 5800, 5801)

Abuyog Naval Reservation, Philippine Islands (EO 5139)

Acker, William Bertrand (EO 5897, 5940)

Administration and Conservation of Public Domain, Committee on the (EO 5358)

Agricultural Economics, Bureau of (EO 5200)

Agriculture, Department of

Civil service, exceptions to certain requirements (EO 5093, 5100, 5186, 5329, 5390, 5628, 5635, 5720, 5781, 5802, 6000, 6026, 6041, 6070)

Civil service rules, Schedule A, positions excepted from examinations (EO 5123, 5198, 5662, 5901)

Cooperative Marketing in the Bureau of Agricultural Economics, Division of, transfer to the Federal Farm Board (EO 5200)

Land utilization agencies, consolidation (EO 5963)

Lands, transfer of jurisdiction in Alaska to the Interior Department (EO 6039)

Retirement, compulsory, exemption of certain individuals (EO 5872)

Weather Bureau, Department of Agriculture, Porto Rico (Proc. 1983)

Aiea Military Reservation, Hawaii (EO 5692)

Air Mail Service, Transcontinental (EO 5162)

Air navigation. *See main heading* Navigation

Alaska

Aleutian Islands

Kiska, closing of port (EO 5281)

Reservation (EO 5243, 5318)

Amaknak Island (EO 5243, 5457, 6044)

Business, establishment of a commission for the more economical and effective conduct of (EO 5260)

Cold Bay-Dolgoi Island (EO 5214)

Customs collection district no. 31 (EO 5385)

Education

Schools, lands reserved for building (EO 5289, 5391)

Vocational schools (EO 5365)

Ketchikan radio station (EO 5419)

Lands

Fur farming (EO 5097)

Opening to ex-servicemen (EO 5207)

Restoration to public domain (EO 5207, 5243, 5378, 5457, 5461, 5517, 5568, 5574, 5641, 5673, 5779, 5806, 5856, 5947, 5950, 6011)

Transfer of jurisdiction

Agriculture Department (EO 6039)

Interior Department (EO 6039)

Withdrawals (EO 5125, 5289, 5352, 5359, 5361, 5364, 5365, 5384, 5391, 5450, 5458, 5500, 5582, 5754, 5784, 5813, 5815, 5858, 6006, 6039, 6044; Proc. 1950)

Military reservations

Chilkoot Barracks (EO 5784)

Fort Davis (EO 5219)

Fort St. Michael (EO 5832)

Fort William H. Seward (EO 5784)

Alaska—Continued
National forests, parks, and monuments
Chugach National Forest (EO 5102, 5402, 5517, 5568, 5574)
Katmai National Monument (Proc. 1950)
Tongass National Forest (EO 5199, 5227, 5409, 5425, 5439, 5449, 5673, 5779, 5856, 5947, 5950, 6011, 6045, 6050)
Nenana (EO 5136, 5441)
Nunivak Island Reservation (EO 5095, 5470)
Port Graham (EO 5214)
Power site reserves (EO 5378, 5461)
Railroad lines, construction and operation (EO 5125)
Salmon Hatchery Reservation (EO 5641)
Semidi Islands Wildlife Refuge (EO 5858)
Seward (EO 5447)
Sitka dock site (EO 6045)
Washington-Alaska Military Cable and Telegraph System (EO 5450)
Water reserves, public (EO 5106, 5754, 6006)
Wide Bay (EO 5214)
Yakutat Bay (EO 5214)
Alaska Game Commission (EO 6039)
Alaska Railroad (EO 5441)
Alaska Railroad townsite regulations (EO 5136)
Alaska Reindeer Service (EO 5219)
Alaska Road Commission (EO 5361, 5500, 5784)
Aleutian Islands, Alaska
Kiska, closing of port (EO 5281)
Reservation (EO 5243, 5318)
Alexander, Cecil (EO 5604)
Alien Property Custodian, Office of the
Delegation of Presidential authority (EO 5113–A, 5645, 6018)
Stock, authorization for the sale of United States Metals Refining Co. (EO 5263)

Alien Property Custodian, Office of the—Continued
Succession, order of, during the absence of the Alien Property Custodian (EO 5113–A, 5645, 6018)
Transfer of functions to the Justice Department (EO 5968)
Aliens
Chinese, admission to United States (EO 5110)
Entry into the United States
Control (Proc. 1872)
Documents required (EO 5426, 5869)
Naturalization and citizenship, regulations governing females (EO 5417, 5621)
Oriental ports, restriction on the transportation of passengers from certain (EO 5143, 6064)
Quotas (Proc. 1872, 1953)
Visas (EO 5427)
Allen, Thomas H. (EO 6067)
Alsimin, change of duty rate (Proc. 2002)
Aluminum or wood, folding rules for, change of duty rate (Proc. 2020)
Amaknak Island, Alaska (EO 5243, 5457, 6044)
American Metal Co., Ltd. (EO 5263)
Arapaho National Forest, Colo. (Proc. 1906, 1910)
Arches National Monument, Utah (Proc. 1875)
Architect of the Capitol, retirement, compulsory, exemption of certain individuals (EO 5872, 5954)
Argentina, exports to U.S., flaxseed, change of duty rate (Proc. 1881)
Arizona
Boulder Canyon Project (Proc. 1882)
Customs collection district no. 26 (EO 5322, 5608)
Fort Huachuca Military Reservation (EO 5147)
Lands
Opening to ex-servicemen (EO 5262)

Arizona—Continued
  Lands—Continued
    Restoration to public domain (EO
      5262, 5379, 5655, 5780)
    Withdrawals (EO 5341, 5404, 5438,
      5462, 5522, 5571, 5611, 5712,
      5726, 5850, 5889, 5898, 5958,
      6002, 6065; Proc. 1911, 1927,
      1975, 2011, 2022, 2032)
  National forests, parks, and monu-
    ments
    Canyon De Chelly National Monu-
      ment (Proc. 1945, 2036)
    Coconino National Forest (Proc.
      1911)
    Coronado National Forest (EO
      5147; Proc. 2032)
    Crook National Forest (EO 5092,
      5404, 5618)
    Grand Canyon National Monument
      (Proc. 2022)
    Petrified Forest National Monu-
      ment (Proc. 1927, 1975, 2011)
    Prescott National Forest (EO 5726)
    Saguaro National Monument (Proc.
      2032)
    Sunset Crater National Monument
      (Proc. 1911)
  Navajo Indian Reservation (Proc.
    1945)
  San Carlos Indian irrigation project
    (EO 5611, 5889)
  Water reserves, public (EO 5370,
    5379, 5655, 5780)
  Wildlife refuges
    Boulder Canyon Wildlife Refuge
      (EO 6065)
    Grand Canyon National Game
      Preserve (Proc. 1971)
  Willow administrative site (EO 5726)
Arkansas
  Army and Navy General Hospital,
    rates for medical care (EO 5429)
  Hot Springs Reservation (EO 5913)
  Lands
    Opening to ex-servicemen (EO
      5743)
    Restoration to public domain (EO
      5448, 5743)

Arkansas—Continued
  Lands—Continued
    Withdrawals (EO 5116, 5194, 5342,
      5747; Proc. 1964)
  National forests, parks, and monu-
    ments
    Hot Springs National Park (EO
      5913)
    Ouachita National Forest (EO
      5820; Proc. 1964)
  Power site reserve (EO 5448)
Armed Forces
  See also Navy, Department of the *and*
    War, Department of
  Army and Navy General Hospital,
    Ark., rates for medical care (EO
    5429)
  Enlisted personnel
    Pay and subsistence allowances
      (EO 5256, 5866)
    Quarters (EO 5256, 5288)
    Rations (EO 5256, 5288)
  Flight regulations (EO 5865)
  Military and naval reservations. *See*
    main heading Military reserva-
    tions
  Officers, rental and subsistence allow-
    ances (EO 5099, 5355, 5583, 5878)
  Veterans. *See main heading* Veterans
Armistice Day (Proc. 1897, 1924, 1973,
  2014)
Arms and munitions, exportation
  Brazil (Proc. 1923, 1939)
  Mexico (Proc. 1885)
Army department. *See main heading*
  War, Department of
Army and Navy General Hospital, Ark.,
  rates for medical care (EO 5429)
Ashley National Forest, Utah and Wyo-
  ming (Proc. 1903, 2030)
Asylum, political, U.S. policy (EO 5956)
Astoria, Oreg., customs port of entry,
  extension of limits (EO 5193)
Augur Barracks Military Reservation,
  Philippine Islands (EO 5493)
Austria, exports to United States, pig-
  skin leather (Proc. 1935)

Aviation
  Airspace reserved for governmental
    purposes (EO 5211, 5281, 5710,
    6023)
  Armed Forces, flight regulations (EO
    5865)
  Oregon and California railroad grant
    lands, withdrawal of, for mainte-
    nance of air navigation facilities
    (EO 5160, 5980)
Aztec Ruins National Monument, N.
  Mex. (Proc. 1928)

B

Baguio Naval Reservation, Philippine
  Islands (EO 5139)
Baker, Mary (EO 5087)
Bamforth Lake Migratory Bird Refuge,
  Wyo. (EO 5783)
Bandelier National Monument, N. Mex.
  (Proc. 1991)
Barber, Jessie N. (EO 6058)
Barracks Lot Military Reservation,
  Hawaii (EO 5715)
Barrett, Marguerite (EO 5235)
Battese (EO 5299)
Bear River Migratory Bird Refuge,
  Utah (EO 5871; Proc. 2012)
Bearskin family (EO 5306)
Beartooth National Forest, Mont. (EO
  5800, 5801)
Beaverhead National Forest, Mont.
  (EO 5757)
Beck, William H. (EO 5171)
Belgium, exports to United States
  Glass, cylinders, crowns, and sheet
    (Proc. 1981)
  Metal, cylinders, crowns, and sheet
    (Proc. 1879)
Bells, change of duty rate (Proc. 1954)
Benicia Arsenal Military Reservation,
  Calif. (EO 5465)
Benjamin, Warren (EO 5847)
Bennett, Mrs. James R. (EO 5442)
Bent, James Lawrence (EO 5164)
Benton Lake Bird Refuge, Mont. (EO
  5228)
Bentwood furniture, change of duty
  rate (Proc. 1958)

Bestor, Horace Paul (EO 5114, 5663)
Big Lake Reservation, Ark. (EO 5747)
Bingham, Pearl (EO 5302)
Binoculars, prism, change of duty rate
  (Proc. 2021)
Birch, Mabel V. (EO 5283)
Bird (EO 5301)
Bird Island Wildlife Refuge, Utah
  (EO 5349, 5515)
Birds, migratory. *See main heading*
  Migratory birds and certain game
  animals
Bishops Point Military Reservation,
  Hawaii (EO 5613)
Bitterroot National Forest, Idaho and
  Montana (EO 5646, 5761; Proc.
  1946, 1960)
Black Canyon of the Gunnison National
  Monument, Colo. (Proc. 2033)
Black Hill National Forest, S. Dak.
  (Proc. 1913)
Blandin, Lucy (EO 5299)
Board of Surveys and Maps (EO 5268)
Boggs, Samuel W. (EO 5171)
Boise National Forest, Idaho (EO 5925)
Border patrols (EO 5966)
Boulder Canyon Project (Proc. 1882;
  EO 5836)
Boulder Canyon Wildlife Refuge, Ari-
  zona and Nevada (EO 6065)
Brazil
  Arms and munitions, exportation
    from United States to (Proc.
    1923, 1939)
  U.S. Ambassador to (EO 5247)
Brock, Florence C. (EO 5781)
Bronche, Antoine (EO 5305)
Brown, Howard (EO 5306)
Brown, Minnie (EO 5302)
Brown, Rosanna J. (EO 5306)
Bryce Canyon National Park, Utah
  (Proc. 1930, 1952)
Budget, Bureau of, transfer of certain
  functions from the General Ac-
  counting Office and Bureau of Effi-
  ciency to (EO 5959)
Bulicek, Louis (EO 5161)
Bull, Nicholas (EO 5302)
Bureau. *See other part of title*

Burke, Guilia P. (EO 5209)
Burton, Florence F. (EO 5762)
Byrne, Daphne Mary (EO 6068)

C

Cabinet National Forest, Mont. (EO 5758)
Cadue, Earl (EO 5299)
California
  Benicia Arsenal Military Reservation (EO 5465)
  Boulder Canyon Project (Proc. 1882; EO 5836)
  Customs collection districts
    No. 25 (EO 5350)
    No. 27 (EO 5350)
    No. 28 (EO 5577, 5578)
  Government Island (EO 5722)
  Lands
    Opening to ex-servicemen (EO 5446, 5674, 5978)
    Railroad grants (EO 5160, 5980)
    Restoration to public domain (EO 5197, 5360, 5379, 5403, 5432, 5443, 5446, 5467, 5537, 5674, 5718, 5750, 5868, 5890, 5908, 5915, 5916, 5927, 5978, 5983, 5987)
    Transfer of jurisdiction
      Commerce Department (EO 6009)
      Navy Department (EO 6009)
    Withdrawals (EO 5117, 5121, 5166, 5182, 5202, 5218, 5222, 5229, 5233, 5237, 5319, 5326, 5331, 5339, 5362, 5380, 5401, 5408, 5465, 5472, 5478, 5489, 5498, 5512, 5542, 5550, 5581, 5585, 5623, 5631, 5633, 5640, 5681, 5709, 5714, 5729, 5732, 5789, 5794, 5827, 5836, 5843, 5902, 5936, 5945; Proc. 1904, 2005, 2028)
  Los Angeles
    Boulder Canyon Project, power transmission lines (EO 5836)
    Water supply system, protection (EO 5117, 5229, 5319, 5380, 5401, 5472, 5512)

California—Continued
  Napa, water supply system, protection (EO 5222, 5233)
  National forests, parks, and monuments
    California National Forest (EO 5885)
    Death Valley National Monument (Proc. 2028)
    Mendocino National Forest (EO 5885)
    Pinnacles National Monument (Proc. 1948)
    Shasta National Forest (EO 5714)
    Yosemite National Park (Proc. 1904, 2005)
  Naval Reserve No. 1 (EO 5239)
  Power site reserves (EO 5197, 5360, 5403, 5443, 5915, 5916, 5927)
  Reservoir site reserves (EO 5467, 5686, 5868, 5906, 6053)
  Trust period extensions on Indian land allotments
    Klamath River Reservation (EO 5416)
    Mission Indians, Agua Caliente Band (EO 5580)
    Pechanga Reservation (EO 5768)
    Round Valley Reservation (EO 5953)
    Temecula Reservation (EO 5768)
  Water reserves, public (EO 5379, 5432, 5478, 5489, 5717, 5902)
  Wildlife refuges
    Salton Sea Wildlife Refuge (EO 5498)
    Tule Lake Wildlife Refuge (EO 5945)
California National Forest, Calif. (EO 5885)
Camel hair, bonded (Proc. 2023)
Canacao-Sangley Point Naval Reservation, Philippine Islands (EO 5139)
Canada
  Exports to the United States
    Feldspar (Proc. 1980)
    Maple sugar and sirup (Proc. 1933)
    Milk, fresh and cream (Proc. 1880)

Canada—Continued
  Exports to the United States—Con.
    Pipe organs (Proc. 1957)
    Sperm oil, crude (Proc. 2034)
  National forests, parks, and monu-
      ments
    Waterton Lakes National Park
        (Proc. 2003)
    Waterton-Glacier International
        Peace Park (Proc. 2003)
Canal Zone. *See main heading* Panama
    Canal Zone
Canyon De Chelly National Monument,
    Ariz. (Proc. 1945, 2036)
Cape Bojeador Naval Reservation, Phi-
    lippine Islands (EO 5139)
Cape Romain Migratory Bird Refuge,
    S.C. (Proc. 2000)
Capozio, Eugene R. (EO 5861)
Captain, Bertha (EO 5306)
Carlsbad Caverns National Park, N.
    Mex. (Proc. 2031)
Carpet wool, bonded (Proc. 2023)
Carran, Charles (EO 5992)
Carver, Wanda Coolidge (EO 5811)
Casanovas, Jose T. (EO 5269)
Cavite Naval Reservation, Philippine
    Islands (EO 5139)
Cedar Keys Bird Refuge, Fla. (EO
    5158)
Census, decennial (EO 5187; Proc.
    1898)
Centenary of Chicago (Proc. 1896)
Century of Progress, A (Proc. 1896)
Cerro Tigre Ordnance Depot Military
    Reservation, Panama Canal Zone
    (EO 5369)
Challis National Forest, Idaho (EO
    5925)
Chaney, Dirrelle (EO 5997)
Chapman, Bushman (EO 5474)
Charles Sheldon Wildlife Refuge, Nev.
    (EO 5540)
Cherloe, David (EO 5306)
Cheyenne River Indian Reservation,
    S. Dak. (EO 5546, 5768)
Chicago World's Fair (Proc. 1896)
Child Health Day (Proc. 1873, 1902,
    1947, 1995)

Chilkoot Barracks, Alaska (EO 5784)
China
  Chinese persons, admission to United
      States (EO 5110)
  Exports to United States, eggs, dried
      (Proc. 1956)
  Ports, transportation restriction on
      passengers coming to United
      States (EO 5143)
Chippewa Indians, Minn. (EO 5466,
    5575)
Choteau, Lillian (EO 5306)
Choteau, Sidney (EO 5306)
Christie, Emerson B. (EO 5171)
Christmas, closing of executive depart-
    ments and government agencies
    (EO 5238, 5514, 5763, 5977)
Chromite reserves (EO 5690)
Chugach National Forest, Alaska (EO
    5102, 5402, 5517, 5568, 5574)
Cibola National Forest, N. Mex. (EO
    5752)
Civil service
  See also Federal employees
  Age limit, waiver (EO 5084, 5821,
      5853)
  Appointments without compliance
      with civil service rules
    Agencies
      Agriculture Department (EO
          5093, 5100, 5186, 5329, 5390,
          5628, 5635, 5720, 5781, 5802,
          6000, 6026, 6041, 6070)
      Census Bureau (EO 5340)
      Commerce Department (EO 5112,
          5113, 5145, 5161, 5377, 5527,
          6048)
      Federal Radio Commission (EO
          5338)
      Federal Trade Commission (EO
          5333, 5553)
      General Accounting Office (EO
          5134, 5374, 5503, 6058)
      Interior Department (EO 6029)
      Interstate Commerce Commission
          (EO 5330, 5554)
      Justice Department (EO 5431,
          5437, 5762, 5766, 5767, 5822,
          6005)

Civil service—Continued
Appointments without compliance
with civil service rules—Con.
Agencies—Continued
Labor Department (EO 5204,
5387, 5620, 5893, 6028, 6061,
6063, 6067)
Navy Department (EO 5131,
5164, 5167, 5617, 5665, 5742,
5811, 5831, 5852, 6003)
Post Office (EO 5442, 5604, 5997,
5998, 5999, 6031, 6032, 6033,
6034, 6035, 6036, 6037, 6042,
6057, 6062)
Public Buildings and Public
Parks of the National Capital (EO 5103, 6049)
Smithsonian Institution (EO
5311)
State Department (EO 5310, 5839,
6022-A, 6056)
Treasury Department (EO 5094,
5101, 5146, 5175, 5180, 5205,
5209, 5210, 5225, 5259, 5283,
5325, 5259, 5325, 5335, 5347,
5348, 5335, 5347, 5348, 5399,
5520, 5563, 5649, 5659, 5695,
5697, 5706, 5847, 5851, 5879,
5972, 5986, 6007, 6052, 6069)
Veterans' Administration (EO
5738, 5804, 5861, 5905, 6038,
6068)
War Department (EO 5269, 5285,
5334, 5591)
Individuals
Abernethy, Marie V. (EO 5695)
Alexander, Cecil (EO 5604)
Allen, Thomas H. (EO 6067)
Barber, Jessie N. (EO 6058)
Bassford, Wallace D. (EO 6028)
Benjamin, Warren (EO 5847)
Bennett, Mrs. James R. (EO
5442)
Bent, James Lawrence (EO 5164)
Birch, Mabel V. (EO 5283)
Brock, Florence C. (EO 5781)
Brown, Ervin F. (EO 6028)
Bulicek, Louis (EO 5161)
Burke, Guilia P. (EO 5209)

Civil service—Continued
Appointments without compliance
with civil service rules—Con.
Individuals—Continued
Burton, Florence F. (EO 5762)
Byrne, Daphne Mary (EO 6068)
Capozio, Eugene R. (EO 5861)
Carran, Charles (EO 5992)
Carver, Wanda Coolidge (EO
5811)
Casanovas, Jose T. (EO 5269)
Chaney, Dirrelle (EO 5997)
Chisum, W. Woodruff (EO 6028)
Coffey, Ida A. (EO 5145)
Cogley, Eugene (EO 5338)
Coons, Mary Edwina (EO 5333)
Costello, Lamar (EO 5893)
Cowing, Amy (EO 5628)
Crossette, Marie (EO 5113)
Curtiss, Sarah L. (EO 5905)
Dartt, Ruth Bascot (EO 5831)
Decker, Laura Mae (EO 5329)
Demshock, Elsie K. (EO 5617)
de Vio, Carlo (EO 6028)
Dickstein, Abraham (EO 6028)
Dinger, Selma F. (EO 5334)
Doak, Edward S. (EO 6028)
Edington, Jean N. (EO 5100)
Eldridge, Gladys W. (EO 5720)
Finley, Germaine M. (EO 5231)
Floyd, Yetta B. (EO 5766)
Ford, William L. (EO 6028)
Forsythe, A. D. (EO 5665)
Freeman, Adelle B. (EO 6041)
Freeman, Mrs. Robert D. (EO
5431)
Gallagher, Charles (EO 5998)
Gallivan, Louise A. (EO 5738)
Gambaro, Joseph (EO 6061)
George, J. Theodore (EO 6028)
Gilbert, A. Louise (EO 5390)
Gillespie, Paula (EO 6003)
Glancy, Kathleen M. (EO 6005)
Goldbarth, Irvin S. (EO 6059)
Goodwin, Alice W. (EO 6031)
Gregg, Isaac (EO 6032)
Haldeman, Frances D. (EO 5149)
Halloran, Ann (EO 5804)

Civil service—Continued
  Appointments without compliance
    with civil service rules—Con.
    Individuals—Continued
      Hangliter, Mary J. A. (EO 5706)
      Harring, Juliette V. (EO 5112)
      Henning, Ida Elizabeth (EO 5186)
      Hess, Clara L. (EO 6057)
      Higgins, James W., Jr. (EO 5986)
      Hillyard, Margaret B. (EO 5706)
      Hoes, Laurence Gouverneur (EO
        6038)
      Hollister, Mabel P. (EO 5311)
      Hooe, John M. (EO 6069)
      Hoover, James (EO 6028)
      Hopkins, Florence R. (EO 5347,
        5659)
      Horigan, Josephine (EO 6000)
      Howe, A. Blondell (EO 5879)
      Israel, Solomon (EO 6061)
      Jackley, Josephine (EO 5210)
      Jett, Ewile K. (EO 5338)
      Joynes, Bell Scarburgh (EO
        5399)
      Kaley, Marie K. (EO 6052)
      Kammerer, Ann F. (EO 6033)
      Kane, Frances N. (EO 5706)
      Kane, Margaret (EO 5563)
      Kearney, Frances (EO 5437)
      Keatley, G. Harold (EO 6056)
      Kehoe, Mary V. (EO 5134)
      Kennedy, William A. (EO 5094)
      Kerkam, Robert F. (EO 5167)
      Kinnahan, Joseph A. (EO 6034)
      Knight, Gladys L. (EO 5852)
      Krigbaum, Mae A. (EO 5150)
      Laddbush, Helen (EO 5330)
      Landt, Arthur B. (EO 5635)
      Lehmkuhl, Catherine (EO 5706)
      Lewis, Thomas A. (EO 6028)
      Long, Nesta Stephens (EO 5851)
      Macpherson, Kenneth C. (EO
        6035)
      Malone, George Henry (EO 5131)
      Marsh, Ida K. (EO 5340)
      Martin, Edmond M. (EO 6036)
      Martin, Mary R. (EO 5374)
      May, Edna (EO 5146)
      May, Erwin G. (EO 5205)

Civil service—Continued
  Appointments without compliance
    with civil service rules—Con.
    Individuals—Continued
      Mays, Helen Terrill (EO 5649)
      McBride, Harry A. (EO 6022–A)
      McClung, Mary A. (EO 6070)
      McIntosh, Pearl (EO 5503)
      McInturff, Mildred Barnes (EO
        5527)
      Moncure, Liza B. (EO 5325)
      Morelock, Sterling L. (EO 6026)
      Moyer, Lottie C. (EO 5103)
      Mummenhoff, Alice (EO 6037)
      Noone, Marjorie M. (EO 5175)
      O'Connor, James H. (EO 6028)
      O'Reilly, Eliza C. (EO 5225)
      Owczarzak, Martha (EO 5999)
      Partridge, Mary Bernadine (EO
        5259)
      Plummer, Mrs. Nixon S. (EO
        5553)
      Porterfield, Mary Elizabeth (EO
        5101)
      Powell, Milton Harold (EO 6049)
      Purcell, Ellen T. (EO 6063)
      Rewman; Mabel (EO 6028)
      Ring, Andrew D. (EO 5338)
      Roberts, Estelle (EO 5204)
      Rollins, Geraldine (EO 5972)
      Roy, Thelma D. (EO 5335)
      Schaefer, Lessie L. (EO 5084)
      Scott, Fred (EO 5822)
      Shely, Myrtle B. (EO 5168)
      Shepard, Carl R. (EO 6007)
      Sinnott, Dorothy I. (EO 5620)
      Skilton, Caroline J. (EO 5697)
      Smith, Patia (EO 5377)
      Smythe, Grace F. (EO 6042)
      Spruks, H. Charles (EO 5310)
      Stewart, Mary (EO 6029)
      Stotler, Hallie D. (EO 5767)
      Strong, Ida (EO 5093)
      Tetlow, Harry L. (EO 6028)
      Timmis, Harry E. (EO 6048)
      Turnipseed, Lulie Hunt (EO
        5520)
      Tyndall, Grace McMahan (EO
        5591)

Civil service—Continued
Appointments without compliance with civil service rules—Con.
Individuals—Continued
Vallecer, Eustaquio (EO 5285)
Vaughan, Jeanette C. (EO 5180)
Vestal, Ralph A. (EO 5839)
Vincent, Mildred E. (EO 5387)
Webb, Ruby Mae (EO 6062)
White, Joseph B. (EO 5128)
White, William C. (EO 5742)
Williams, J. Elizabeth (EO 6063)
Williams, John W. (EO 6028)
Williams, Maude (EO 5232)
Wilson, Sinclair A. (EO 5802)
Witt, Helen R. (EO 5554)
York, Helen Hall (EO 5348)
Civil service rules
Amendments (EO 5107, 5111, 5123, 5124, 5153, 5170, 5171, 5198, 5213, 5230, 5236, 5248, 5388, 5471, 5479, 5513, 5544, 5545, 5560, 5570, 5584, 5588, 5610, 5636, 5657, 5662, 5680, 5691, 5696, 5724, 5731, 5753, 5764, 5774, 5776, 5777, 5787, 5817, 5984, 6043)
Schedule A (positions excepted from examinations)
Agriculture Department (EO 5123, 5198, 5662, 5901)
Federal Farm Board (EO 5230)
Federal Power Commission (EO 5560)
Indian Service (EO 5213, 5388, 5584)
Interior Department (EO 5680)
Justice Department (EO 5787)
Post Office (EO 5471, 5731, 5930)
State Department (EO 5171, 5657)
Treasury Department (EO 5236, 5544, 5859, 5974, 6047)
United States Employees' Compensation Commission (EO 5107)
Veterans' Administration (EO 5691, 5724, 5774)

Civil service—Continued
Civil service rules—Continued
Schedule A (positions excepted from examinations)—Con.
War Department (EO 6046)
Schedule B (positions filled upon noncompetitive examinations)
Commerce Department (EO 5817)
Federal Farm Board (EO 5248)
Indian Service (EO 5545)
Navy Department (EO 5170)
Post Office (EO 5922)
State Department (EO 5171, 5513)
Veterans' Administration (EO 5636)
War Department (EO 5696, 5777)
Classified service, inclusion of certain individuals and agencies (EO 5163, 5171, 5459, 5523, 5599, 5609, 5622, 5775)
District of Columbia government employees, authorization to maintain a register of eligibles for positions (EO 5491)
Examinations, waiver of (EO 5168, 5248)
Furloughs, administrative (EO 5887)
Leave
Holidays. *See main heading* Holidays
Sick (EO 5871, 6021)
Veterans, disabled, for medical treatment (EO 5396)
Military and naval academies, authorization to test applicants for (EO 5918)
Reinstatements
Agencies
General Accounting Office (EO 5142)
Navy Department (EO 6024)
Post Office (EO 6020)
State Department (EO 5286)
Treasury Department (EO 5083, 5135, 5149, 5150, 5152, 5154, 5235, 5501)

Civil service—Continued
  Reinstatements—Continued
    Individuals
      Barrett, Marguerite (EO 5235)
      Davis, Lulu M. (EO 5152)
      Dingley, Edward N., Jr. (EO
        6024)
      Dodge, H. Percy (EO 5286)
      Gordon, Birdie E. (EO 5154)
      Knight, Richard H. (EO 6020)
      Liscombe, Walter K. (EO 5135)
      MacFate, Eva (EO 5501)
      Stedman, Ralph Ely (EO 5142)
      Tasker, Alice (EO 5224)
    Retirement, compulsory, exemption of
      certain individuals (EO 5872,
      5873, 5874, 5875, 5881, 5896, 5897,
      5911, 5912, 5917, 5921, 5940, 5946,
      5954, 5981, 5982, 5988, 5989, 6004,
      6013, 6022, 6027, 6030)
    Travel regulations, Government em-
      ployees (EO 5605, 5870)
    Vacancies
      Furloughed and dropped Federal
        employees, priority filling (EO
        5924)
      Postmaster, method of filling (EO
        5104)
    Wages and salaries
      International Joint Commission,
        American members (EO 5376)
      War Claims Arbiter (EO 5267)
Clearwater National Forest, Idaho (EO
  5615)
Coal reserves (EO 5336, 5359, 5499,
  5582, 5598, 5713, 5733, 5813, 5815,
  5876, 5985, 6015)
Coast Guard Service, merger of the Im-
  migration Border Patrol and the
  Customs Patrol in (EO 5966)
Cochetopa National Forest, Colo. (EO
  5990; Proc. 1097, 1908)
Cocoa-fiber mats, change of duty rate
  (Proc. 2018)
Coconino National Forest, Ariz. (Proc.
  1911)
Coffey, Ida A. (EO 5145)
Cogley, Eugene (EO 5338)

Cold Bay-Dolgoi Island, Alaska (EO
  5214)
Colomb, Joseph (EO 5302)
Colon Naval Radio Station, Canal Zone
  (EO 5185)
Colonial National Monument, Va. (Proc.
  1929)
Colorado
  Boulder Canyon Project (Proc. 1882)
  Colorado School of Mines (EO 5559)
  Lands
    Opening to ex-servicemen (EO 5195,
      5418, 5420, 5422, 5488, 5506,
      5524, 5587, 5688, 5698, 5819,
      5823, 5877, 5883, 5934, 5943,
      6008)
    Restoration to public domain (EO
      5195, 5252, 5271, 5379, 5418,
      5420, 5422, 5460, 5488, 5492,
      5524, 5587, 5653, 5688, 5698,
      5744, 5819, 5823, 5877, 5883,
      5934, 5943, 6008)
    Withdrawals (EO 5089, 5109, 5165,
      5201, 5241, 5251, 5257, 5270,
      5297, 5304, 5328, 5395, 5424,
      5538, 5559, 5593, 5652, 5654,
      5672, 5751, 5791, 5807, 5846,
      5862, 5894, 5990, 6054, 6055;
      Proc. 1917, 1985, 1994, 2033,
      2037)
  National forests, parks, and monu-
    ments
    Arapaho National Forest (Proc.
      1906, 1910)
    Black Canyon of the Gunnison Na-
      tional Monument (Proc. 2033)
    Cochetopa National Forest (EO
      5990; Proc. 1907, 1908)
    Colorado National Forest (EO
      5826; Proc. 1910)
    Colorado National Monument
      (Proc. 2037)
    Great Sand Dunes National Monu-
      ment (Proc. 1994)
    Gunnison National Forest (Proc.
      1907, 1908)
    Hayden National Forest (Proc.
      1888)

Colorado—Continued
National forests, parks, and monuments—Continued
Holy Cross National Monument (Proc. 1877, 1906)
Hovenweep National Monument (EO 5201)
Leadville National Forest (Proc. 1906, 1909)
Mesa Verde National Park (Proc. 1998)
Pike National Forest (Proc. 1909)
Rocky Mountain National Park (Proc. 1917, 1985)
Roosevelt National Forest (EO 5826)
Routt National Forest (Proc. 1888, 1906, 1910)
San Juan National Forest (EO 5749)
O'Connor ranger station (EO 5422)
Petroleum reserves (EO 5252, 5460)
Power site reserves (EO 5271, 5653, 5744)
Water reserves, public (EO 5379, 5492, 5593, 5672)
Colorado National Forest, Colo. (EO 5826; Proc. 1910)
Colorado National Monument, Colo. (Proc. 2037)
Colorado School of Mines (EO 5559)
Colorow, Jimmie (EO 5552)
Commerce, Department of
Acting Secretary of Commerce, designation of Clarence M. Young (EO 5242)
Census, decennial (Proc. 1898; EO 5187)
Civil service, exceptions to certain requirements (EO 5112, 5113, 5145, 5161, 5340, 5377, 5527, 6040)
Civil service rules, Schedule B, positions filled upon noncompetitive examinations (EO 5817)
Classified service, inclusion of certain agencies and individuals in (EO 5599, 5775)
Commerce activities, governmental policies, consolidation (EO 5960)

Commerce, Department of—Continued
Lands, transfer of jurisdiction in California to the Navy Department (EO 6009)
Lighthouse Service (EO 5097)
Lighthouses, Bureau of (EO 5268)
Merchant marine activities, consolidation and grouping (EO 5965)
Transfer of records
President's Emergency Committee to (EO 6060)
President's Organization for Unemployment Relief to (EO 6060)
Radio Division, transfer to the Federal Radio Commission (EO 5892)
Retirement, compulsory, exemption of certain individuals (EO 5872, 5873, 5896, 5921, 5946, 5982)
State and local offices, holding of, by employees (EO 5666)
Tax returns, authorization for inspection (EO 5321)
Commerce Commission, Interstate
Civil service, exceptions to certain requirements (EO 5330, 5554)
Retirement, compulsory, exemption of certain individuals (EO 5872, 5873)
Committee. *See other part of title*
Congress
Convening of (Proc. 1870)
Senate, convening, special sessions (Proc. 1915, 2029)
Conservation of Public Domain, Committee on the Administration and (EO 5358)
Consular regulations. *See main heading* State Department
Cook, Judith (EO 5087)
Coolidge, Calvin (Proc. 2024)
Coons, Mary Edwina (EO 5333)
Cooper, Joseph S. (EO 5366)
Cooperative Marketing in the Bureau of Agricultural Economics, Division of, transferred from the Agriculture Department to the Federal Farm Board (EO 5200)

Copyright protection, extension to
  Greece (Proc. 1990)
  Irish Free State (Proc. 1981)
Cornwallis, Lord, Sesquicentennial of
  the Surrender of, at Yorktown
  (Proc. 1967)
Coronado National Forest, Ariz. (EO
  5147; Proc. 2032)
Costello, Lamar (EO 5893)
Cotton velvet, change of duty rate
  (Proc. 2019)
Coulter, Eliot B. (EO 5171)
Council. *See other part of title*
Courts, United States
  District Court for Porto Rico, acting
    judges, designations (EO 5156,
    5394, 5705, 5842)
  Supreme Court of the District of Co-
    lumbia, retirement, compulsory,
    exemption of certain individuals
    (EO 6030)
Covered Wagon Centennial (Proc. 1900)
Cowing, Amy (EO 5628)
Crater National Forest, Oreg. (EO
  5882)
Craters of the Moon National Monu-
  ment, Idaho (Proc. 1916)
Crescent Lake Wildlife Refuge, Nebr.
  (EO 5579)
Crook National Forest, Ariz. (EO 5092,
  5404, 5618)
Crossette, Marie (EO 5113)
Crow, Angeline (EO 5306)
Crow, Jennie (EO 5306)
Crow Indian Reservation, Mont. (EO
  5301, 5768)
Crow Creek Indian Reservation, S. Dak.
  (EO 5768)
Crowley, John T. (EO 5981)
Cuba
  Exports to United States
    Eggplants (Proc. 1977)
    Peppers (Proc. 1978)
    Sponges, sheepswool (Proc. 2008)
  Guantánamo Naval Station, closing of
    port (EO 5281)
Cumming, Hugh S., Jr. (EO 5171)
Cunningham, Edwin Sheddan (EO
  6066)

Curtiss, Sarah L. (EO 5905)
Custer National Forest, Montana and
  South Dakota (EO 5801; Proc.
  1913)
Customs Bureau
  Customs collection districts
    No. 4, Massachusetts (EO 5096,
      5444)
    No. 8, New York (EO 5455)
    No. 9, New York (EO 5192, 5320)
    No. 15, North Carolina (EO 5159,
      5291, 5317)
    No. 18, Florida (EO 5284, 5770)
    No. 20, Louisiana (EO 5130, 5392,
      5993)
    No. 21, Louisiana and Texas (EO
      5392, 5475)
    No. 25, California (EO 5350)
    No. 26, Arizona (EO 5322, 5608)
    No. 27, California (EO 5350)
    No. 28, California (EO 5577, 5578)
    No. 29, Oregon (EO 5193, 5445)
    No. 30, Washington (EO 5081, 5206,
      5835)
    No. 31, Alaska (EO 5385)
    No. 34, North Dakota and Min-
      nesota (EO 5137, 5169, 5835)
    No. 36, Minnesota and Wisconsin
      (EO 5530)
    No. 42, Kentucky (EO 5507)
    No. 45, Missouri (EO 5453)
    No. 46, Nebraska (EO 5078)
  Customs ports of entry
    Ambrose, N. Dak. (EO 5835)
    Andrade, Calif. (EO 5350)
    Astoria, Oreg. (EO 5193)
    Baton Rouge, La. (EO 5993)
    Blaine, Wash. (EO 5835)
    Calexico, Calif (EO 5350)
    Carbury, N. Dak. (EO 5137)
    Fort Pierce, Fla. (EO 5284)
    Lake Charles, La. (EO 5474)
    Lawrence, Mass. (EO 5444)
    Lewiston, N.Y. (EO 5192)
    Lincoln, Nebr. (EO 5078)
    Longview, Wash. (EO 5193)
    Manteo, N.C. (EO 5291, 5317)
    Marshfield, Oreg. (EO 5193, 5445)
    New Bern, N.C. (EO 5291, 5317)

Customs Bureau—Continued
Customs ports of entry—Con.
Noyes, Minn. (EO 5835)
Oakland, Calif. (EO 5577)
Oroville, Wash. (EO 5206)
Paducah, Ky. (EO 5507)
Port Everglades, Fla. (EO 5770)
Portland, Oreg. (EO 5193)
Reidsville, N.C. (EO 5159)
Roche Harbor, Wash. (EO 5081)
St. John, N. Dak. (EO 5835)
St. Michael, Alaska (EO 5385)
San Luis, Ariz. (EO 5322)
San Ysidro, Calif. (EO 5350)
Sasabe, Ariz. (EO 5608)
Souris, N. Dak. (EO 5169)
Tecate, Calif. (EO 5350)
Two Harbors, Minn. (EO 5530)
Wichita, Kans. (EO 5453)
Customs Patrol, merger with the Immigration Border Patrol in the Coast Guard Service (EO 5966)
Cuyo Naval Reservation, Philippine Islands (EO 5139)
Czechoslovakia, exports to United States
Bentwood furniture (Proc. 1958)
Rubber-soled and rubber footwear (Proc. 2027)
Turn shoes (Proc. 1979)

D

Darity, Lavina (EO 5306)
Darmstädter und Nationalbank, Germany (EO 5263)
Dartt, Ruth Bascot (EO 5831)
Datil National Forest, N. Mex. (EO 5752, 5765)
Davis, Albert D. (EO 5917)
Davis, Lulu M. (EO 5152)
Days of observance
Armstice Day (Proc. 1897, 1924, 1973, 2014)
Child Health Day (Proc. 1873, 1902, 1946, 1995)
Cornwallis, Lord, Sesquicentennial of the Surrender of, at Yorktown (Proc. 1967)

Days of observance—Continued
Covered Wagon Centennial (Proc. 1900)
Fire Prevention Week, National (Proc. 1890, 1921, 1962, 2009)
Pan American Day (Proc. 1912)
Pulaski (General) Memorial Day (Proc. 1884, 1968, 2010)
Thanksgiving Day (Proc. 1895, 1925, 1974, 2015)
Washington, George, Bicentennial of Birth of (Proc. 1986)
de Aldrey, Hon. Pedro (EO 5394)
Death of a noted person
Coolidge, Calvin (Proc. 2024)
Longworth, Nicholas (EO 5595)
Taft, William Howard (Proc. 1901)
Death Valley National Monument, Calif. (Proc. 2028)
Decker, Laura Mae (EO 5329)
Deep Creek ranger station, Mont. (EO 5280)
Deerlodge National Forest, Mont. (EO 5619, 5759, 5757)
Del Toro, Hon. Emilio (EO 5842)
Demshock, Elsie K. (EO 5617)
Deschutes National Forest, Oreg. (EO 5928, 5991)
Devil's Garden, Utah (Proc. 1875)
Devils Lake Indian Reservation, N. Dak. (EO 5303, 5768, 5953)
Dick, Flora (EO 5306)
Didier, Vernon (EO 5302)
Dietz, Leafie E. (EO 5529)
Dinger, Selma F. (EO 5334)
Dingley, Edward N., Jr. (EO 6024)
Diplomatic instructions. *See main heading* State Department
District of Columbia
Airspace reservation (EO 6023)
Civil service, authorization to maintain register of eligibles for positions (EO 5491)
Governmental departments and agencies, closing (EO 5353)
Retirement, compulsory, exemption of certain individuals (EO 5872, 5873, 5896, 6030)

Dixie National Forest, Nev. (EO 5294)

Dodge, H. Percy (EO 5286)

Double Island, Wash. (EO 5151)

Duck Creek administrative site, Mont. (EO 5654)

Duties. *See main heading* Imports and exports

E

Eastern Shawnee Indian Reservation, Okla. (EO 5768)

Edington, Jean N. (EO 5100)

Education

    Colorado School of Mines (EO 5559)

    Schools, building of, Alaska (EO 5289, 5391)

    Vocational schools, Alaska (EO 5365)

Efficiency, Bureau of, transfer of certain functions to the Bureau of Budget (EO 5959)

Eggplant, change of duty rate (Proc. 1977)

Eggs, dried whole, yolk, and albumen, change of duty rate (Proc. 1956)

Eldridge, Gladys W. (EO 5720)

Emergency Fleet Corp., United States (EO 5722)

Employees, Federal. *See main headings* Civil service ; Federal employees

Employees' Compensation Commission, United States

    Civil service rules, Schedule A, positions excepted from examinations (EO 5107)

    Transfer of certain functions from the Labor Department to (EO 5961)

Ena Road, Hawaii (EO 5155)

Evans, Curtle (EO 5306)

Everlasting Sky (EO 5383)

Executive orders and proclamations, style and form, uniformity (EO 5220, 5658)

Expatriation (EO 5417, 5973)

Expenditures, Government, Treasury Department, reporting (EO 5614)

Exports. *See main heading* Imports and exports

F

Fallon Wildlife Refuge, Nev. (EO 5606)

Farm Board, Federal

    Civil service rules

        Schedule A, positions excepted from examinations (EO 5230)

        Schedule B, positions filled upon noncompetitive examinations (EO 5248)

    Cooperative Marketing in the Bureau of Agricultural Economics, Division of, transferred from the Agriculture Department to (EO 5200)

Farm Loan Board, Federal, Commissioners (EO 5114, 5663)

Farrell, Minnie (EO 5302)

Federal employees

    Classified service, inclusion of certain individuals and agencies (EO 5163, 5171, 5459, 5523, 5599, 5609, 5622, 5775)

    Employment, nonofficial, limitation on (EO 5221)

    Furloughs, administrative (EO 5887)

    Holidays. *See main heading* Holidays

    Philippines, inclusion in the classified service (EO 5622)

    Retirement, compulsory, exemption of certain individuals (EO 5872, 5873, 5874, 5875, 5881, 5896, 5897, 5911, 5912, 5917, 5921, 5940, 5946, 5954, 5981, 5982, 5988, 5989, 6004, 6013, 6022, 6027, 6030)

    Saturday working hours, closing of Federal agencies in the District of Columbia (EO 5353)

    State and local offices, holding of (EO 5133, 5627, 5666, 5700)

    Travel regulations (EO 5605, 5870)

    Virgin Islands, holding of positions in the local colonial councils (EO 6051)

    Wages and salaries

        International Joint Commission, American members (EO 5376)

        War Claims Arbiter (EO 5267)

Federal Farm Board
Civil service rules
Schedule A, positions excepted from examinations (EO 5230)
Schedule B, positions filled upon noncompetitive examinations (EO 5248)
Cooperative Marketing in the Bureau of Agricultural Economics, Division of, transfer from the Agriculture Department to (EO 5200)
Federal Farm Loan Board, Commissioners (EO 5114, 5663)
Federal Power Commission, civil service rules, Schedule A, positions excepted from examinations (EO 5560)
Federal Radio Commission
Civil service, exceptions to certain requirements (EO 5338)
Radio Division, transferred from the Commerce Department to (EO 5892)
Federal Trade Commission, civil service, exceptions to certain requirements (EO 5333, 5553, 5872)
Feldspar, change of duty rate (Proc. 1980)
Ferrin, Frank (EO 5302)
Ferroaluminum silicon, change of duty rate (Proc. 2002)
Ferrosilicon aluminum, change of duty rate (Proc. 2002)
Findlay, James G. (EO 5239)
Finley, Beatrice (EO 5306)
Finley, Claude (EO 5306)
Finley, Germaine M. (EO 5231)
Fire Prevention Week, National (Proc. 1890, 1921, 1962, 2009)
Fisher, Alfred (EO 5306)
Fisher, Eva (EO 5306)
Fisher, Lena (EO 5306)
Fisher, Minerva (EO 5306)
Fisheries, Northern Pacific Halibut Fishery (EO 5854)
Fishlake National Forest, Utah (EO 5307)
Flag, Office of the Secretary of State (EO 6005–A)

Flathead Indian Reservation, Mont. (EO 5953)
Flaxseed and various forms, change of duty rate (Proc. 1881, 1883)
Florida
Customs collection district no. 18 (EO 5284, 5770)
Lands
Homestead entry of Charley McMillan (EO 5191)
Opening to ex-servicemen (EO 5569)
Restoration to public domain (EO 5351, 5569, 5895)
Withdrawals (EO 5191, 5278, 5740, 5814)
National forests, parks, and monuments
Ocala National Forest (EO 5814; Proc. 1918)
Osceola National Forest (Proc. 1961)
Tampa, closing of port (EO 5281)
Wildlife refuges
Cedar Keys Bird Refuge (EO 5158)
Ocala National Game Refuge (EO 5814; Proc. 1918)
St. Marks Migratory Bird Refuge (EO 5740; Proc. 1982)
Flour, wood, change of duty rate (Proc. 1936)
Floyd, Yetta B. (EO 5766)
Folding rules of aluminum or wood, change of duty rate (Proc. 2020)
Foreign Service. *See main heading* State, Department of
Forests, national. *See main heading* National forests, parks, and monuments
Forsythe, A. D. (EO 5665)
Fort Armstrong Military Reservation, Hawaii (EO 5487)
Fort Davis, Alaska (EO 5219)
Fort De Russy Military Reservation, Hawaii (EO 5155)
Fort Huachuca Military Reservation, Ariz. (EO 5147)
Fort Keogh Military Reservation, Mont. (EO 5122)

Fort Randolph Military Reservation, Panama Canal Zone (EO 6010)

Fort Ruger Military Reservation, Hawaii (EO 5266)

Fort St. Michael Military Reservation, Alaska (EO 5832)

Fort Shafter Military Reservation, Hawaii (EO 5132, 5521, 5607)

Fort William H. Seward Military Reservation, Alaska (EO 5784)

France, exports to United States, cotton velvet (Proc. 2019)

France Field Military Reservation, Panama Canal Zone (EO 6010)

Frazier, Starr (EO 5474)

Freeman, Adelle B. (EO 6041)

Freeman, Mrs. Robert D. (EO 5431)

Fremont National Forest, Oreg. (EO 5991)

Fuller, Joseph V. (EO 5171)

Fuller, Sissy Bensell (EO 5087)

Fur farming (EO 5097)

Furloughs. *See main headings* Civil service ; Federal employees

Fyfe, Howard (EO 5163)

G

Gallagher, Charles (EO 5998)

Gallatin National Forest, Mont. (EO 5760, 5800)

Gallivan, Louise A. (EO 5738)

Gambaro, Joseph (EO 6061)

Gas reserves (EO 6016)

Gelatin, change of duty rate (Proc. 1942, 2007)

General Accounting Office

Civil service, exceptions to certain civil service rules (EO 5134, 5374, 5503, 6058)

Transfer of certain functions to the Budget Bureau (EO 5959)

Reinstatement of certain individuals (EO 5142)

General Land Office

Land offices, discontinuance of certain (EO 6001)

Land patents, signers designated (EO 5076, 5077)

General Land Office—Continued
United States v. *The Standard Oil Company of California* (EO 5239)

Geographic Board, United States (EO 5872)

George, John (EO 5416)

George Washington Bicentennial of Birth (Proc. 1986)

George Washington Birthplace National Monument, Va. (Proc. 1944)

George Washington National Forest, Virginia and West Virginia (EO 5867)

Georgia

Lands, withdrawal (EO 5748)

Nantahala National Forest (Proc. 1892)

Wildlife refuges

Savannah River Wildlife Refuge (EO 5743)

Wolf Island Wildlife Refuge (EO 5316)

Germany

Darmstädter und Nationalbank (EO 5263)

Exports to United States

Bells (Proc. 1954)

Binoculars, prism (Proc. 2021)

Folding rules for aluminum or wood (Proc. 2020)

Gelatin (Proc. 2007)

Glue (Proc. 2007)

Upholsterers' nails, chair glides, and thumb tacks (Proc. 2017)

Wire (Proc. 1934, 1940)

Nationalbank für Deutschland (EO 5263)

Gila National Forest, N. Mex. (EO 5765)

Gilbert, A. Louise (EO 5390)

Gillespie, Paula (EO 6003)

Ginder, John W. (EO 5911)

Girgam, Dorcas Johnson (EO 5306)

Gives Away With Buffalo (EO 5301)

Glacier National Park, Mont. (Proc. 2003)

Glancy, Kathleen M. (EO 6005)

Glass, cylinders, crowns, and sheet, change of duty rate (Proc. 1981)

Glue, change in duty rate (Proc. 2007)
Goldbarth, Irvin S. (EO 6059)
Goodwin, Alice W. (EO 6031)
Gordon, Birdie E. (EO 5154)
Government building contracts, regulations for the payment of the prevailing rate of wages for laborers and mechanics (EO 5778)
Government departments and agencies, closing (EO 5238, 5353, 5514, 5763, 5977; Proc. 1879, 1895, 1924, 1925, 1973, 1974, 2014, 2015)
Government Island, Calif. (EO 5722)
Government Printing Office, retirement, compulsory, exemption of certain individuals (EO 5872, 5921)
Grand Canyon National Game Preserve, Ariz. (Proc. 1971)
Grand Canyon National Monument, Ariz. (Proc. 2022)
Grand Portage Indian Reservation, Minn. (EO 5768)
Great Sand Dunes National Monument, Colo. (Proc. 1994)
Greece
  Copyright protection, extension to (Proc. 1990)
  U.S. Envoy to (EO 5519)
Green Mountain National Forest, Vt. (Proc. 1997)
Greenleaf administrative site, Wash. (EO 5976)
Gregg, Isaac (EO 6032)
Grinnell family (EO 5299, 5356)
Guam, closing of port (EO 5281)
Guantánamo Naval Station, Cuba (EO 5281)
Gunnison National Forest, Colo. (Proc. 1907, 1908)

H

Haldeman, Frances D. (EO 5149)
Hale, John (EO 5299)
Halloran, Ann (EO 5804)
Hangliter, Mary J. A. (EO 5706)
Hardy, Valentine (EO 5306)
Harlow, Charles J. (EO 5982)
Harney National Forest, S. Dak. (EO 5938; Proc. 1878, 1913, 1914, 1951)

Harring, Juliette V. (EO 5112)
Harris, George (EO 5087)
Harrison, John W. (EO 5701)
Hats and other head wear, change of duty rate (Proc. 1937, 1941)
Hawaii
  Ena Road (EO 5155)
  Kaena Point (EO 5119)
  Keaau Ridge (EO 5119)
  Lands
    Restoration to public domain (EO 5132, 5157, 5265, 5266, 5405, 5406, 5521, 5528, 5561, 5607, 5637, 5715, 5931)
    Transfer of U.S. lands to (Proc. 1871, 1926, 1972, 1984)
    Withdrawal (EO 5613)
  Military reservations
    Aiea Military Reservation (EO 5692)
    Barracks Lot Military Reservation (EO 5715)
    Bishops Point Military Reservation (EO 5613)
    Fort Armstrong Military Reservation (EO 5487)
    Fort De Russy Military Reservation (EO 5155)
    Fort Ruger Military Reservation (EO 5266)
    Fort Shafter Military Reservation (EO 5132, 5521)
    Hawaii Arsenal Military Reservation (EO 5132, 5521, 5607)
    Hawaiian Ordnance Depot (EO 5132)
    Kahauiki Military Reservation (EO 5132)
    Keaahala Military Reservation (EO 5637)
    Punch Bowl Hill Military Reservation (EO 5157, 5265, 5693)
    Puolo Point Military Reservation, Hawaii (EO 5405)
    Pupukea Military Reservation (EO 5174, 5240)
    Round Top Military Reservation (EO 5931)

Indians
Indian Service (EO 5188, 5213, 5388, 5545, 5584)
Navajo Indian Reservation, Ariz. (Proc. 1945)
San Carlos Indian irrigation project, Ariz. (EO 5611, 5889)
Trust period extensions on land allotments
Cheyenne River Reservation, S. Dak. (EO 5546, 5768)
Chippewa Indians, Minn. (EO 5466, 5575)
Crow Reservation, Mont. (EO 5301, 5768)
Crow Creek Reservation, S. Dak. (EO 5768)
Devils Lake Reservation, N. Dak. (EO 5303, 5768, 5953)
Eastern Shawnee Reservation, Okla. (EO 5768)
Flathead Reservation, Mont. (EO 5953)
Grand Portage Reservation, Minn. (EO 5768)
Kickapoo Indians, Kans. (EO 5414, 5626)
Kiowa Reservation, Okla. (EO 5953)
Klamath River Reservation, Calif. (EO 5416)
Mission Indians, Agua Caliente Band, Calif. (EO 5580)
Missouria Indians, Okla. (EO 5728, 5768)
Nez Perce Tribe, Idaho (EO 5305)
Niobrara Reservation, Nebr. (EO 5471)
Omaha Reservation, Nebr. (EO 5148, 5253)
Otoe Reservation, Okla. (EO 5728, 5768)
Pechanga Reservation, Calif. (EO 5768)
Pine Ridge Reservation, S. Dak. (EO 5557, 5768, 5953)
Ponca Reservation, Okla. (EO 5539)

Indians—Continued
Trust period extensions on land allotments—Continued
Potawatomi Indians, Prairie Band, Kans. (EO 5299, 5356, 5556)
Quinaielt Reservation, Wash. (EO 5768)
Red Lake Reservation, Minn. (EO 5383)
Rosebud Reservation, S. Dak. (EO 5302, 5768)
Round Valley Reservation, Calif. (EO 5953)
Sac and Fox Reservation, Kans., Nebr. (EO 5768)
Santee Reservation, Nebr. (EO 5474, 5768, 5953)
Seneca Tribe, Okla. (EO 5306)
Shoshone Reservation, Wyo. (EO 5768, 5953)
Siletz Reservation, Oreg. (EO 5087)
Standing Rock Reservation, N. Dak. (EO 5768, 5953)
Temecula Reservation, Calif. (EO 5768)
Uintah Indians, Utah (EO 5357)
Umatilla Reservation, Oreg. (EO 5516)
Uncompahgre Indians, Utah (EO 5357, 5552)
Walker River Reservation, Nev. (EO 5730)
Warm Springs Reservation, Oreg. (EO 5734)
White Earth Reservation, Minn. (EO 5768, 5953)
White River Bands, Ute Indians, Utah (EO 5357)
Wichita Reservation, Okla. (EO 5955)
Wind River Reservation, Wyo. (EO 5768, 5953)
Winnibigoshish Reservation, Minn. (EO 5768)
Yakima Reservation, Wash. (EO 5746)
Yankton Sioux Reservation, S. Dak. (EO 5173)

Interior, Department of the
Civil service, exceptions to certain requirements (EO 6029)
Civil service rules, Schedule A, positions excepted from examinations (EO 5680)
Education, health, and recreation activities, consolidation and grouping (EO 5962)
Field Service, working hours, Saturday (EO 5625)
Land patents, signers designated (EO 5076, 5077, 5529)
Lands, transfer of jurisdiction
Alaska (EO 6039)
Mississippi (EO 5505)
Nevada (EO 5660)
Oklahoma (EO 5975)
Washington (EO 5630)
Wyoming (EO 5592)
Public works activities, consolidation and grouping (EO 5964)
Retirement, compulsory, exemption of certain individuals (EO 5872, 5873, 5896, 5897, 5912, 5940, 5954)
Virgin Islands, government, transfer of jurisdiction from the Navy Department to (EO 5566)
War Minerals Relief Act, appointment of personnel under (EO 5830)
International Boundary Strip, United States-Mexico (EO 5689)
International Joint Commission, United States and Canada, American members, salaries (EO 5376)
Interstate Commerce Commission
Civil service, exceptions to certain requirements (EO 5330, 5554)
Retirement, compulsory, exemption of certain individuals (EO 5872, 5873)
Irish Free State, copyright protection, extension to (Proc. 1891)
Israel, Solomon (EO 6061)
Italy, exports to United States
Hats (Proc. 1937, 1941)

Italy, exports to United States—Con.
Hemp cordage (Proc. 1955)
Olive oil (Proc. 1959)

J

Jack, Susan (EO 5416)
Jack, Thomas (EO 5416)
Jackley, Josephine (EO 5210)
James, Charles J. (EO 6030)
Japan, exports to United States, rubber-soled and rubber footwear (Proc. 2027)
Jefferson National Forest, Mont. (EO 5834)
Jett, Ewile K. (EO 5338)
John, Albert (EO 5305)
John, Ida (EO 5305)
John, Stephen (EO 5474)
Johnson, Jackson (EO 5306)
Johnson, Lillian (EO 5306)
Johnson, Nellie (EO 5087)
Johnson, Robert A. (EO 5306)
Jones, John (EO 5474)
Joynes, Bell Scarburgh (EO 5399)
Justice, Department of
Civil service, exceptions to certain requirements (EO 5431, 5437, 5762, 5766, 5767, 5822, 6005)
Civil service rules, Schedule A, positions excepted from examinations (EO 5787)
Law Observance and Enforcement, National Commission on, transfer to (EO 5716)
Retirement, compulsory, exemption of certain individuals (EO 5872)
Transfer of certain functions
Office of the Alien Property Custodian to (EO 5968)
Veterans' Administration to (EO 5967)

K

Kabance (EO 5299)
Kahauiki Military Reservation, Hawaii (EO 5132, 5607)
Ka-ka Keese (EO 5383)
Ka-Kee-Ka Kee Sick (EO 5383)

Kaley, Marie K. (EO 6052)
Kammerer, Ann F. (EO 6033)
Kane, Frances N. (EO 5706)
Kane, Margaret (EO 5563)
Kansas
   Customs collection district no. 45 (EO 5453)
   Trust period extensions on Indian land allotments
      Kickapoo Indians (EO 5415, 5626)
      Potawatomi Indians, Prairie Band (EO 5299, 5356, 5556)
      Sac and Fox Reservation (EO 5768)
Kariho, Ruth (EO 5306)
Katmai National Monument, Alaska (Proc. 1950)
Keaahala Military Reservation, Hawaii (EO 5637)
Kearney, Frances (EO 5437)
Keatley, G. Harold (EO 6056)
Kehoe, Mary V. (EO 5134)
Kennedy, Emma E. (EO 5083)
Kennedy, William A. (EO 5094)
Kentucky, customs collection district no. 42 (EO 5507)
Ke o po wah quah (EO 5356)
Kerkam, Robert F. (EO 5167)
Ketchikan radio station, Alaska (EO 5419)
Ke-wah-quah (EO 5299)
Ke wan kah, Annie (EO 5299)
Ke yah (EO 5356)
Kickapoo Indians, Kans. (EO 5415, 5626)
Kills Him Short (EO 5302)
Kinnahan, Joseph A. (EO 6034)
Kiowa Indian Reservation, Okla. (EO 5953)
Klamath, Mary (EO 5087)
Klamath River Indian Reservation, Calif. (EO 5416)
Knight, Gladys L. (EO 5852)
Knight, Richard H. (EO 6020)
Knox sah Keesis (EO 5299)
Kootenai National Forest, Idaho and Montana (EO 5616)
Krighbaum, Mae A. (EO 5150)

L

Labor, Department of
   Civil service, exceptions to certain requirements (EO 5204, 5387, 5620, 5983, 6028, 6061, 6063, 6067)
   Immigration Border Patrol, transfer to the Treasury Department (EO 5966)
   Transfer of certain functions to the the United States Employees' Compensation Commission (EO 5961)
Labor disputes
   Louisiana, Arkansas, and Texas Railway Co. (Proc. 1992)
   Louisiana and Arkansas Railway Co. (Proc. 1949, 1992)
   Texas and Pacific Railway Co. (Proc. 1874)
Laddbush, Helen (EO 5330)
Lamb, Gertrude (EO 5955)
Land patents, signers designated (EO 5076, 5077, 5529)
Lands, public
   National, forests, parks, and monuments. See main heading National forests, parks, and monuments
   Opening to ex-servicemen
      Alaska (EO 5207)
      Arizona (EO 5262)
      Arkansas (EO 5743)
      California (EO 5446, 5674, 5978)
      Colorado (EO 5195, 5418, 5420, 5422, 5488, 5506, 5524, 5587, 5688, 5698, 5819, 5823, 5877, 5883, 5934, 5943, 6008)
      Florida (EO 5569)
      Idaho (EO 5223)
      Minnesota (EO 5651)
      Montana (EO 5433, 5434, 5619)
      Nevada (EO 5944)
      New Mexico (EO 5086, 5177, 5178, 5179, 5254, 5412, 5421, 5423, 5509, 5518, 5576, 5677, 5685, 5735, 5932)
      North Dakota (EO 5632)
      Oregon (EO 5699)

Lands, public—Continued
 Opening to ex-servicemen—Continued
  South Dakota (EO 5216)
  Utah (EO 5410, 5440, 5675, 5678)
  Washington (EO 5212, 5494)
  Wyoming (EO 5090, 5181, 5183,
   5184, 5215, 5411, 5413, 5679,
   5741, 5793, 5797, 5884, 5933,
   5935, 5995, 5996)
 Restoration to public domain
  Alaska (EO 5207, 5243, 5378, 5457,
   5461, 5517, 5568, 5574, 5641,
   5673, 5779, 5806, 5856, 5947,
   5950, 6011)
  Arizona (EO 5262, 5379, 5655, 5780)
  Arkansas (EO 5448, 5743)
  California (EO 5197, 5360, 5379,
   5403, 5432, 5443, 5446, 5467,
   5537, 5674, 5718, 5750, 5868,
   5890, 5908, 5915, 5916, 5927,
   5978, 5983, 5987)
  Colorado (EO 5195, 5252, 5271, 5379,
   5418, 5420, 5422, 5460, 5488,
   5492, 5524, 5587, 5653, 5688,
   5698, 5744, 5819, 5823, 5877,
   5883, 5934, 5943, 6008)
  Florida (EO 5351, 5569, 5895)
  Hawaii (EO 5132, 5157, 5265, 5266,
   5405, 5406, 5521, 5528, 5561,
   5607, 5637, 5715, 5931)
  Idaho (EO 5223, 5312, 5360, 5367,
   5393, 5543, 5739, 5769, 5926,
   5937)
  Michigan (EO 5366, 5368, 5386)
  Minnesota (EO 5651)
  Montana (EO 5293, 5363, 5430, 5433,
   5434, 5490, 5535, 5536, 5567,
   5590, 5619, 5669, 5816, 5878,
   5985, 6015)
  Nevada (EO 5197, 5294, 5496, 5944)
  New Mexico (EO 5086, 5177, 5178,
   5179, 5217, 5254, 5272, 5412,
   5421, 5423, 5485, 5497, 5509,
   5518, 5576, 5597, 5598, 5677,
   5685, 5735, 5785, 5932, 5939,
   5941, 5957, 5979)
  North Dakota (EO 5632)

Lands, public—Continued
 Restoration to public domain—Con.
  Oregon (EO 5360, 5372, 5486, 5541,
   5564, 5699, 5798, 5841, 5919)
  South Dakota (EO 5216)
  Utah (EO 5279, 5336, 5410, 5440,
   5454, 5456, 5499, 5515, 5552,
   5669, 5675, 5678, 5780, 5810,
   5971)
  Washington (EO 5212, 5494)
  Wyoming (EO 5090, 5181, 5183,
   5184, 5215, 5296, 5411, 5413,
   5510, 5679, 5703, 5741, 5745,
   5793, 5795, 5797, 5884, 5899,
   5933, 5935, 5995, 5996)
 Transfer of jurisdiction
  Agriculture Department, Alaska
   (EO 6039)
  Commerce Department, California
   (EO 6009)
  Interior Department
   Alaska (EO 6039)
   Mississippi (EO 5505)
   Nevada (EO 5660)
   Oklahoma (EO 5975)
   Washington (EO 5630)
   Wyoming (EO 5592)
  Navy Department
   California (EO 6009)
   Nevada (EO 5660)
   Washington (EO 5630)
  Treasury Department, Oklahoma
   (EO 5975)
  War Department, Wyoming (EO
   5592)
 Transfer of U.S. lands to
  Hawaii (Proc. 1871, 1926, 1972,
   1984)
  Porto Rico (Proc. 1889, 1983)
 Wildlife refuges. *See main heading*
  Wildlife refuges
 Withdrawals
  Alaska (EO 5125, 5289, 5352, 5359,
   5361, 5364, 5365, 5384, 5391,
   5450, 5458, 5500, 5582, 5754,
   5784, 5813, 5815, 5858, 6006,
   6039, 6044; Proc 1950)

Lands, public—Continued
  Withdrawals—Continued
    Arizona (EO 5341, 5404, 5438, 5462,
      5522, 5571, 5611, 5712, 5726,
      5850, 5889, 5898, 5958, 6002,
      6065; Proc. 1911, 1927, 2011,
      2022, 2032)
    Arkansas (EO 5116, 5194, 5342,
      5747; Proc. 1964)
    California (EO 5117, 5121, 5166,
      5182, 5202, 5218, 5222, 5229,
      5233, 5237, 5319, 5326, 5331,
      5339, 5362, 5380, 5401, 5408,
      5465, 5472, 5478, 5789, 5498,
      5512, 5542, 5550, 5581, 5585,
      5623, 5631, 5633, 5640, 5681,
      5709, 5714, 5729, 5732, 5789,
      5794, 5827, 5836, 5843, 5902,
      5936, 5945; Proc. 1904, 2005.
      2028)
    Colorado (EO 5089, 5109, 5165,
      5201, 5241, 5251, 5257, 5270,
      5297, 5304, 5328, 5395, 5424,
      5538, 5559, 5593, 5652, 5654,
      5672, 5751, 5791, 5807, 5846,
      5862, 5894, 5990, 6054, 6055;
      Proc. 1917, 1985, 1994, 2033,
      2037)
    Florida (EO 5191, 5278, 5740, 5814)
    Georgia (EO 5748)
    Hawaii (EO 5613)
    Idaho (EO 5277, 5481, 5482, 5504,
      5572, 5589, 5671; Proc. 1916)
    Illinois (EO 5796)
    Louisiana (EO 5282, 5511)
    Michigan (EO 5249, 5719, 5948;
      Proc. 1931, 1932, 1938)
    Minnesota (EO 5309, 5346, 5671,
      5833, 5994)
    Mississippi (EO 5562, 5721, 5755)
    Montana (EO 5172, 5280, 5344,
      5428, 5478, 5534, 5629, 5671,
      5711, 5907, 5949, 6025; Proc.
      2013)
    Nebraska (EO 5579; Proc. 1999)
    Nevada (EO 5105, 5141, 5182, 5208,
      5287, 5292, 5339, 5343, 5344,
      5534, 5540, 5594, 5596, 5606,

Lands, public—Continued
  Withdrawals—Continued
    Nevada—Continued
      5664, 5792, 5799, 5828, 5836,
      5903, 6065)
    New Mexico (EO 5091, 5120, 5144,
      5234, 5255, 5261, 5273, 5276,
      5300, 5315, 5370, 5452, 5478,
      5483, 5484, 5531, 5547, 5548,
      5551, 5555, 5558, 5682, 5790,
      5805, 5829, 5907, 5909, 5920,
      5942; Proc. 1928, 2025, 2031)
    North Dakota (EO 5258, 5586, 5671,
      5808, 5914)
    Oklahoma (Proc. 1964)
    Oregon (EO 5082, 5115, 5118, 5176,
      5190, 5196, 5203, 5313, 5344,
      5407, 5451, 5478, 5600, 5601,
      5650, 5667, 5671, 5683, 5694,
      5702, 5803, 5838, 5864, 5891,
      5900, 5907, 5923, 5928, 6014,
      6019, 6040)
    South Carolina (EO 5748)
    South Dakota (EO 5938; Proc. 1914,
      1951)
    Utah (EO 5274, 5275, 5344, 5508,
      5525, 5573, 5684, 5727, 6012,
      6019; Proc. 1903, 1930, 1952,
      2012, 2026, 2030)
    Vermont (Proc. 1997)
    Virginia (Proc. 1929)
    Washington (EO 5108, 5151, 5244,
      5397, 5671, 5818, 5976)
    Wisconsin (EO 5138, 5671, 5796,
      5929; Proc. 2035)
    Wyoming (EO 5085, 5098, 5140,
      5162, 5323, 5354, 5407, 5436,
      5480, 5494, 5595, 5603, 5639,
      5656, 5668, 5671, 5672, 5687,
      5782, 5783, 5886, 5904, 5907,
      5949, 6025)
Landt, Arthur B. (EO 5635)
LaPine administrative site, Oreg. (EO
  5928)
Larsh, Nellie (EO 5302)
Latranche, Ethel (EO 5299)
Latranche, Theodore (EO 5299)

Law Observance and Enforcement, National Commission on, transfer to the Justice Department (EO 5716)

Layne, Edna (EO 5306)

Leadville National Forest, Colo. (Proc. 1906, 1909)

Leather, pigskin, change of duty rate (Proc. 1935)

Leave, Federal employees. *See main heading* Civil service

Lehmkuhl, Catherine (EO 5706)

Lemhi National Forest, Idaho (Proc. 1922)

Levier, Oliver (EO 5356)

Lewis and Clark National Forest, Mont. (EO 5756, 5834)

Library of Congress, retirement, compulsory, exemption of certain individuals (EO 5872, 5988)

Lighthouse Service (EO 5097)

Lighthouses, Bureau of (EO 5268)

Linseed oil, change of duty rate (Proc. 1883)

Liscombe, Walter K. (EO 5135)

Little Crow (EO 5383)

Locomotive Springs Migratory Bird Refuge, Utah (EO 5727)

Lolo National Forest, Mont. (EO 5758, 5761)

Long, Nesta Stephens (EO 5851)

Long Lake Migratory Bird Refuge, N. Dak. (EO 5808, 5914)

Longview, Wash., customs port of entry, extension of limits (EO 5193)

Longworth, Hon. Nicholas (EO 5595)

Los Angeles

    Boulder Canyon Project, power transmission lines (EO 5836)

    Water supply system, protection (EO 5117, 5229, 5319, 5380, 5401, 5472, 5512)

Louisiana

    Customs collection districts

        No. 20 (EO 5130, 5392, 5993)

        No. 21 (EO 5392, 5475)

    Land withdrawals (EO 5282, 5511)

Louisiana, Arkansas, and Texas Railway Co. (Proc. 1992)

Louisiana and Arkansas Railway Co. (Proc. 1949, 1992)

Lucas, Samuel (EO 5474)

M

MacFate, Eva (EO 5501)

Ma-chock-a-rats (Chester) (EO 5552)

Mack, Alsea (EO 5087)

Macpherson, Kenneth C. (EO 6035)

Madison National Forest, Mont. (EO 5757, 5759, 5760)

Maine, White Mountain National Forest (Proc. 1894)

Makana (EO 5303)

Malone, George Henry (EO 5131)

Manzano National Forest, N. Mex. (EO 5752)

Maple sugar and sirup, change of duty rate (Proc. 1933)

Maps, Board of Surveys and (EO 5268)

Marquette National Forest, Mich. (Proc. 1938)

Marsh, Ida K. (EO 5340)

Marshall, Moses (EO 5302)

Marshfield, Oreg., customs port of entry, extension of limits (EO 5193, 5445)

Martin, Edmond M. (EO 6036)

Martin, Mary R. (EO 5374)

Martyn, John W. (EO 5523)

Maryland, airspace reserved for governmental purposes (EO 5211)

Masquat (EO 5299)

Massachusetts, customs collection district no. 4 (EO 5096, 5444)

Maxam, Oliver M. (EO 6004)

May, Edna (EO 5146)

May, Erwin G. (EO 5205)

Mays, Helen Terrill (EO 5649)

McBride, Harry A. (EO 6022–A)

McClellan Peak administrative site, Nev. (EO 5799)

McClung, Mary A. (EO 6070)

McCoy, Capt. Washington C. (EO 5599)

McDowell, John P. (EO 5912)

McIntosh, Pearl (EO 5503)

McInturff, Mildred Barnes (EO 5527)

McLeod, Helen V. (EO 5076)

McMillan, Charley (EO 5191)

Medicinal springs (EO 5389)

Medicine Bow National Forest, Wyo.
(Proc. 1888)
Meeker, Ezra (Proc. 1900)
Megginson, Jennie (EO 5087)
Mellon, Andrew W. (Proc. 1987, 1988)
Mendocino National Forest, Calif. (EO
5885)
Merchant marine activities, consolida-
tion and grouping in the Commerce
Department (EO 5965)
Mesa Verde National Park, Colo. (Proc.
1998)
Metal, cylinders, crowns, and sheet,
change of duty rate (Proc. 1879)
Mexico
Arms and munitions, exportation
from United States (Proc. 1885)
Exports to United States, peas (Proc.
1976)
Michigan
Lands
Homestead entry of Joseph S.
Cooper (EO 5366)
Restoration to public domain (EO
5366, 5368, 5386)
Withdrawals (EO 5249, 5719, 5948;
Proc. 1931, 1932, 1938)
National forests, parks, and monu-
ments
Hiawatha National Forest (Proc.
1931)
Huron National Forest (EO 5368,
5844)
Marquette National Forest (Proc.
1938)
Ottawa National Forest (Proc.
1932)
Migratory birds and certain game
animals
Regulations, amendments (Proc. 1876,
1899, 1905, 1920, 1943, 1966, 1969,
2004)
Waterfowl (Proc. 1965, 1989)
Wildlife refuges. *See main heading*
Wildlife refuges
Military reservations
Abuyog Naval Reservation, Philip-
pine Islands (EO 5139)

Military reservations—Continued
Aiea Military Reservation, Hawaii
(EO 5692)
Augur Barracks Military Reserva-
tions, Philippine Islands (EO
5493)
Baguio Naval Reservation, Philippine
Islands (EO 5139)
Barracks Lot Military Reservation,
Hawaii (EO 5715)
Benicia Arsenal Military Reserva-
tion, Calif. (EO 5465)
Bishops Point Military Reservation,
Hawaii (EO 5613)
Canacao-Sangley Point Naval Reser-
vation, Philippine Islands (EO
5139)
Cape Bojeador Naval Reservation,
Philippine Islands (EO 5139)
Cavite Naval Reservation, Philippine
Islands (EO 5139)
Cerro Tigre Ordnance Depot Military
Reservation, Panama Canal Zone
(EO 5369)
Chilkoot Barracks, Alaska (EO 5784)
Cuyo Naval Reservation, Philippine
Islands (EO 5139)
Fort Armstrong Military Reserva-
tion, Hawaii (EO 5487)
Fort Davis, Alaska (EO 5219)
Fort De Russy Military Reservation,
Hawaii (EO 5155)
Fort Huachuca Military Reservation,
Ariz. (EO 5147)
Fort Keogh Military Reservation,
Mont. (EO 5122)
Fort Randolph Military Reservation,
Panama Canal Zone (EO 6010)
Fort Ruger Military Reservation,
Hawaii (EO 5266)
Fort St. Michael Military Reserva-
tion, Alaska (EO 5832)
Fort Shafter Military Reservation,
Hawaii (EO 5132, 5521, 5607)
Fort William H. Seward Military
Reservation, Alaska (EO 5784)
France Field Military Reservation,
Panama Canal Zone (EO 6010)

Military reservations—Continued
Guantánamo Naval Station, Cuba (EO 5281)
Hawaii Arsenal Military Reservation, Hawaii (EO 5132, 5521, 5607)
Hawaiian Ordnance Depot, Hawaii (EO 5132)
Imus River Naval Reservation, Philippine Islands (EO 5139)
Keaahala Military Reservation, Hawaii (EO 5132, 5607)
Keaahala Military Reservation, Hawaii (EO 5637)
Naval Reservation No. 1, Calif. (EO 5239)
Punchbowl Hill Military Reservation, Hawaii (EO 5157, 5265, 5693)
Puolo Point Military Reservation, Hawaii (EO 5405)
Pupukea Military Reservation, Hawaii (EO 5174, 5240)
Romblon Naval Reservation, Philippine Islands (EO 5139)
Round Top Military Reservation, Hawaii (EO 5931)
San Fernando Naval Reservation, Philippine Islands (EO 5139)
San Juan Military Reservation, Porto Rico (Proc. 1889)
Schofield Barracks Military Reservation, Hawaii (EO 5771)
Upolu Point Military Reservation, Hawaii (EO 5406)
Waianae-Kai Military Reservation, Hawaii (EO 5414)
Milk and cream, change of duty rate (Proc. 1880)
Millington, Yale O. (EO 5171)
Mills, Ogden L. (Proc. 1987, 1988)
Minerals
Chromite (EO 5690)
Mineral rights in Alaska (EO 5365)
Phosphate (EO 5351, 5769)
Mines, Bureau of (EO 5775)
Mingo, Sophrina (EO 5306)
Minidoka Bird Reservation, Idaho (EO 5375)

Minnesota
Customs collection districts
No. 34 (EO 5835)
No. 36 (EO 5530)
Lands
Opening to ex-servicemen (EO 5651)
Restoration to public domain (EO 5651)
Withdrawals (EO 5309, 5346, 5671, 5833, 5994)
Superior National Forest (EO 5845)
Trust period extensions on Indian land allotments
Chippewa Indians (EO 5466, 5575)
Grand Portage Reservation (EO 5768)
Red Lake Reservation (EO 5383)
White Earth Reservation (EO 5768, 5953)
Winnibigoshish Reservation (EO 5768)
Mint (EO 5301)
Mission Indians, Agua Caliente Band, Calif. (EO 5580)
Mississippi
Lands
Transfer of jurisdiction, Interior Department (EO 5505)
Withdrawals (EO 5562, 5721, 5755)
Upper Mississippi River Wildlife and Fish Refuge (EO 5721)
Missoula National Forest, Mont. (EO 5080, 5759, 5761)
Missouri, customs collection district no. 45 (EO 5453)
Missouria Reservation, Okla. (EO 5728, 5768)
M-jis-sepe, Honnell (EO 5356)
M-joe-tah, Joseph (EO 5299)
M ko i gi mow (EO 5356)
M-ko-quah-wah (EO 5299)
M-nis-no-go quah Wah we as shuck (EO 5299)
M-nis-no-quah Chock-tuck (EO 5299)
Moessner, Ernest F. (EO 6022)
Moncure, Liza B. (EO 5325)

Montana
  Deep Creek ranger station (EO 5280)
  Duck Creek administrative site (EO 5654)
  Lands
    Opening to ex-servicemen (EO 5433, 5434, 5619)
    Restoration to public domain (EO 5293, 5363, 5430, 5433, 5434, 5490, 5535, 5536, 5567, 5590, 5619, 5669, 5816, 5878, 5985, 6015)
    Withdrawals (EO 5172, 5280, 5344, 5428, 5478, 5534, 5629, 5671, 5711, 5907, 5949, 6025; Proc. 2013)
  National forests, parks, and monuments
    Absaroka National Forest (EO 5800, 5801)
    Beartooth National Forest (EO 5800, 5801)
    Beaverhead National Forest (EO 5757)
    Bitterroot National Forest (EO 5646, 5761)
    Cabinet National Forest (EO 5758)
    Custer National Forest (EO 5801)
    Deerlodge National Forest (EO 5619, 5757, 5759)
    Gallatin National Forest (EO 5760, 5800)
    Glacier National Park (Proc. 2003)
    Helena National Forest (EO 5080, 5280, 5654, 5756, 5759)
    Jefferson National Forest (EO 5834)
    Kootenai National Forest (EO 5616)
    Lewis and Clark National Forest (EO 5756, 5834)
    Lolo National Forest (EO 5758, 5761)
    Madison National Forest (EO 5757, 5759, 5760)
    Missoula National Forest (EO 5080, 5759, 5761)
    Yellowstone National Park (EO 5296; Proc. 2013)

Montana—Continued
  Petroleum reserve (EO 5590)
  Power site reserves (EO 5363, 5430, 5490, 5535, 5536, 5567)
  Trust period extensions on Indian land allotments
    Crow Reservation (EO 5301, 5768)
    Flathead Reservation (EO 5953)
  Water reserves, public (EO 5293, 5344, 5478, 5534, 5629, 5669, 5907, 6025)
  Wildlife refuges
    Benton Lake Bird Refuge (EO 5228)
    Fort Keogh Bird Refuge (EO 5122)
Montgomery, Melissa Latta (EO 5087)
Monuments, national. *See main heading* National forests, parks, and monuments
Morelock, Sterling L. (EO 6026)
Morgan, Edwin V. (EO 5247)
Morrow, W. C. (EO 5239)
Mount Baker National Forest, Wash. (EO 5634)
Moyer, Lottie C. (EO 5103)
Mummenhoff, Alice (EO 6037)
M-zhick-ten-o (EO 5356)

N

Nantahala National Forest, Georgia, North Carolina, and South Carolina (Proc. 1892)
Napa, Calif., water supply system, protection (EO 5222, 5233)
Narcotic drugs, Virgin Islands, dispensation of (EO 5502)
National Commission on Law Observance and Enforcement, transfer to the Justice Department (EO 5716)
National Fire Prevention Week (Proc. 1890, 1921, 1962, 2009)
National forests, parks, and monuments
  Absaroka National Forest, Mont. (EO 5800, 5801)
  Arapaho National Forest, Colo. (Proc. 1906, 1910)
  Arches National Monument, Utah (Proc. 1875)

National forests, parks, and monuments—Continued

Ashley National Forest, Utah and Wyoming (Proc. 1903, 2030)

Aztec Ruins National Monument, N. Mex. (Proc. 1928)

Bandelier National Monument, N. Mex. (Proc. 1991)

Beartooth National Forest, Mont. (EO 5800, 5801)

Beaverhead National Forest, Mont. (EO 5757)

Bitterroot National Forest, Idaho and Montana (EO 5646, 5761; Proc. 1946, 1960)

Black Canyon of the Gunnison National Monument, Colo. (Proc. 2033)

Black Hills National Forest, S. Dak. (Proc. 1913)

Boise National Forest, Idaho (EO 5925)

Bryce Canyon National Park, Utah (Proc. 1930)

Cabinet National Forest, Mont. (EO 5758)

California National Forest, Calif. (EO 5885)

Canyon De Chelly National Monument, Ariz. (Proc. 1945, 2036)

Carlsbad Caverns National Park, N. Mex. (Proc. 2031)

Challis National Forest, Idaho (EO 5925)

Chugach National Forest, Alaska (EO 5102, 5402, 5517, 5568, 5574)

Cibola National Forest, N. Mex. (EO 5752)

Clearwater National Forest, Idaho (EO 5614)

Cochetopa National Forest, Colo. (EO 5990; Proc. 1907, 1908)

Coconino National Forest, Ariz. (Proc. 1911)

Colonial National Monument, Va. (Proc. 1929)

Colorado National Forest, Colo. (EO 5826; Proc. 1910)

National forests, parks, and monuments—Continued

Colorado National Monument, Colo. (Proc. 2037)

Coronado National Forest, Ariz. (EO 5147; Proc. 2032)

Crater National Forest, Oreg. (EO 5882)

Craters of the Moon National Monument, Idaho (Proc. 1916)

Crook National Forest, Ariz. (EO 5092, 5404, 5618)

Custer National Forest, Montana and South Dakota (EO 5801; Proc. 1913)

Datil National Forest, N. Mex. (EO 5752, 5765)

Death Valley National Monument, Calif. (Proc. 2028)

Deerlodge National Forest, Mont. (EO 5619, 5757, 5759)

Deschutes National Forest, Oreg. (EO 5928, 5991)

Dixie National Forest, Nev. (EO 5294)

Fishlake National Forest, Utah (EO 5307)

Fremont National Forest, Oreg. (EO 5991)

Gallatin National Forest, Mont. (EO 5760, 5800)

George Washington Birthplace National Monument, Va. (Proc. 1944)

George Washington National Forest, Virginia and West Virginia (EO 5867)

Gila National Forest, N. Mex. (EO 5765)

Glacier National Park, Mont. (Proc. 2003)

Grand Canyon National Monument, Ariz. (Proc. 2022)

Great Sand Dunes National Monument, Colo. (Proc. 1994)

Green Mountain National Forest, Vt. (Proc. 1997)

Gunnison National Forest, Colo. (Proc. 1907, 1908)

National forests, parks, and monuments—Continued

Harney National Forest, S. Dak. (EO 5938; Proc. 1878, 1913, 1914, 1951)

Hayden National Forest, Colorado and Wyoming (Proc. 1888)

Helena National Forest, Mont. (EO 5080, 5280, 5654, 5756, 5759)

Hiawatha National Forest, Mich. (Proc. 1931)

Holy Cross National Monument, Colo. (Proc. 1877, 1906)

Hot Springs National Park, Ark. (EO 5913)

Hovenweep National Monument, Colo. (EO 5201)

Huron National Forest, Mich. (EO 5368, 5844)

Jefferson National Forest, Mont. (EO 5834)

Katmai National Monument, Alaska (Proc. 1950)

Kootenai National Forest, Idaho, Mont. (EO 5616)

Leadville National Forest, Colo. (Proc. 1906, 1909)

Lemhi National Forest, Idaho (Proc. 1922)

Lewis and Clark National Forest, Mont. (EO 5756, 5834)

Lolo National Forest, Mont. (EO 5758, 5761)

Madison National Forest, Mont. (EO 5757, 5759, 5760)

Manzano National Forest, N. Mex. (EO 5752)

Marquette National Forest, Mich. (Proc. 1938)

Medicine Bow National Forest, Wyo. (Proc. 1888)

Mendocino National Forest, Calif. (EO 5885)

Mesa Verde National Park, Colo. (Proc. 1998)

Missoula National Forest, Mont. (EO 5080, 5759, 5761)

Mount Baker National Forest, Wash. (EO 5634)

National forests, parks, and monuments—Continued

Nantahala National Forest, Georgia, North Carolina, and South Carolina (Proc. 1892)

Nevada National Forest, Nev. (EO 5863)

Nezperce National Forest, Idaho (Proc. 1946, 1960)

Nicolet National Forest, Wis. (Proc. 2035)

Ocala National Forest, Fla. (EO 5814; Proc. 1918)

Osceola National Forest, Fla. (Proc. 1961)

Ottawa National Forest, Mich. (Proc. 1932)

Ouachita National Forest, Arkansas and Oklahoma (EO 5820; Proc. 1964)

Pend Oreille National Forest, Idaho (EO 5616)

Petrified Forest National Monument, Ariz. (Proc. 1927, 1975, 2011)

Pike National Forest, Colo. (Proc. 1909)

Pinnacles National Monument, Calif. (Proc. 1948)

Pisgah National Forest, North Carolina and Tennessee (Proc. 1892, 1893)

Prescott National Forest, Ariz. (EO 5726)

Rocky Mountain National Park, Colo. (Proc. 1917, 1985)

Rogue River National Forest, Oreg. (EO 5882)

Roosevelt National Forest, Colo. (EO 5826)

Routt National Forest, Colo. (Proc. 1888, 1906, 1910)

Saguaro National Monument, Ariz. (Proc. 2032)

St. Joe National Forest, Idaho (EO 5615)

Salmon National Forest, Idaho (Proc. 1922)

San Juan National Forest, Colo. (EO 5749)

National forests, parks, and monuments—Continued

Santa Fe National Forest, N. Mex. (EO 5809, 5840; Proc. 1991)

Sawtooth National Forest, Idaho (EO 5925)

Scotts Bluff National Monument, Nebr. (Proc. 1999)

Selway National Forest, Idaho (EO 5646)

Shasta National Forest, Calif. (EO 5714)

Shenandoah National Forest, Virginia and West Virginia (EO 5867)

Siuslaw National Forest, Oreg. (EO 5670, 5841)

Snoqualmie National Forest, Wash. (EO 5634)

Sunset Crater National Monument, Ariz. (Proc. 1911)

Superior National Forest, Minn. (EO 5845)

Tahoe National Forest, Nev. (EO 5799)

Targhee National Forest, Wyo. (EO 5296)

Toiyabe National Forest, Nev. (EO 5725, 5863)

Tongass National Forest, Alaska (EO 5199, 5227, 5409, 5425, 5439, 5449, 5673, 5779, 5856, 5947, 5950, 6011, 6045, 6050)

Uinta National Forest, Utah (Proc. 1887)

Wasatch National Forest, Utah (Proc. 1887, 2026)

Waterton-Glacier International Peace Park, Canada–U.S. (Proc. 2003)

White Mountain National Forest, Maine and New Hampshire (Proc. 1894)

White Sands National Monument, N. Mex. (Proc. 2025)

Yellowstone National Park, Montana and Wyoming (EO 5296; Proc. 2013)

Yosemite National Forest, Calif. (Proc. 1904, 2005)

National Home for Disabled Volunteer Soldiers (EO 5398, 5476, 5609)

National Mediation Board (Proc. 1874, 1949, 1992)

Nationalbank für Deutschland, Germany (EO 5263)

Natural resources. *See specific item*

Navajo Indian Reservation, Ariz. (Proc. 1945)

Naval reservations. *See main heading* Military reservations

Navigation

Air

Airspace reserved for governmental purposes (EO 5211, 5281, 5710, 6023)

Oregon and California railroad grant lands, withdrawal of, for maintenance of air navigation facilities (EO 5160)

Sea

Water and coastline areas reserved for governmental purposes (EO 5710, 5786)

Navy, Department of

See also Armed Forces

Civil service, exceptions to certain requirements (EO 5131, 5164, 5167, 5617, 5665, 5742, 5811, 5831, 5852, 6003)

Civil service rules, Schedule B, positions filled upon noncompetitive examinations (EO 5170)

Lands, transfer of jurisdiction

California (EO 6009)

Nevada (EO 5660)

Washington (EO 5630)

Naval academies, applicants, civil service authorization to test (EO 5918)

Naval reservations. *See main heading* Military reservations

Reinstatement of certain individuals (EO 6024)

Retirement, compulsory, exemption of certain individuals (EO 5872, 5873, 5896)

Navy, Department of—Continued
  Virgin Islands, government, transfer
    of jurisdiction to the Interior De-
    partment (EO 5566)
Nay-may-pack (EO 5383)
Nebraska
  Crescent Lake Wildlife Refuge (EO
    5579)
  Customs collection district no. 46 (EO
    5078)
  Lands
    Withdrawals   (EO   5579;   Proc.
      1999)
    Scotts Bluff National Monument
      (Proc. 1999)
    Trust period extensions on Indian
      land allotments
      Niobrara Reservation (EO 5474)
      Omaha   Reservation   (EO   5148,
        5253)
      Sac and Fox Reservation (EO
        5768)
      Santee Reservation (EO 5474, 5768,
        5953)
Nenana, Alaska (EO 5136, 5441)
Netherlands, exports to United States
  Flaxseed oil, raw, boiled, or oxidized
    (Proc. 1883)
  Gelatin, edible (Proc. 1942)
  Linseed oil (Proc. 1883)
Nevada
  Boulder Canyon Project (EO 5836;
    Proc. 1882)
  Lands
    Opening to ex-servicemen (EO
      5944)
    Restoration to public domain (EO
      5197, 5294, 5496, 5944)
    Transfer of jurisdiction
      Interior Department (EO 5660)
      Navy Department (EO 5660)
    Trust period extensions on Indian
      allotments, Walker River Res-
      ervation (EO 5730)
    Withdrawals (EO 5105, 5141, 5182,
      5208, 5287, 5292, 5339, 5343,
      5344, 5534, 5540, 5594, 5596,
      5606, 5664, 5792, 5799, 5828,
      5836, 5903, 6065)

Nevada—Continued
  McClellan administrative site (EO
    5799)
  National forests, parks, and monu-
    ments
    Dixie National Forest (EO 5294)
    Nevada National Forest (EO 5863)
    Tahoe National Forest (EO 5799)
    Toiyabe National Forest (EO 5725,
      5863)
  Power site reserve (EO 5197)
  Water reserves, public (EO 5292, 5344,
    5496, 5534, 5594)
  Wildlife refuges
    Boulder Canyon Wildlife Refuge
      (EO 6065)
    Charles Sheldon Wildlife Refuge
      (EO 5540)
    Fallon Wildlife Refuge (EO 5606)
Nevada National Forest, Nev. (EO
  5863)
New Hampshire, White Mountain Na-
  tional Forest (Proc. 1894)
New Mexico
  Boulder Canyon Project (Proc. 1882)
  Lands
    Opening to ex-servicemen (EO 5086,
      5177, 5178, 5179, 5254, 5412,
      5421, 5423, 5509, 5518, 5576,
      5677, 5685, 5735, 5932)
    Restoration to public domain (EO
      5086, 5177, 5178, 5179, 5217,
      5254, 5272, 5412, 5421, 5423,
      5485, 5497, 5509, 5518, 5576,
      5597, 5598, 5677, 5685, 5735,
      5785, 5932, 5939, 5941, 5957,
      5979)
    Withdrawals (EO 5091, 5120, 5144,
      5234, 5255, 5261, 5273, 5276,
      5300, 5315, 5370, 5452, 5478,
      5483, 5484, 5531, 5547, 5548,
      5551, 5555, 5558, 5682, 5790,
      5805, 5829, 5907, 5909, 5920,
      5942; Proc. 1928, 2025, 2031)
  National forests, parks, and monu-
    ments
    Aztec Ruins National Monument
      (Proc. 1928)

New Mexico—Continued
National forests, parks, and monu-
ments—Continued
Bandelier National Monument
(Proc. 1991)
Carlsbad Caverns National Park
(Proc. 2031)
Cibola National Forest (EO 5752)
Datil National Forest (EO 5752,
5765)
Gila National Forest (EO 5765)
Manzano National Forest (EO
5752)
Santa Fe National Forest (EO 5809,
5840; Proc. 1991)
White Sands National Monument
(Proc. 2025)
Power site reserves (EO 5497, 5957)
Water reserves, public (EO 5217,
5272, 5273, 5478, 5597, 5907, 5941)
New Year's, closing of executive depart-
ments and government agencies
(EO 5977)
New York
Customs collection districts
No. 8 (EO 5455)
No. 9 (EO 5192, 5320)
Nez Perce Indian Tribe, Idaho (EO
5305)
Nezperce National Forest, Idaho (Proc.
1946, 1960)
Nicolet National Forest, Wis. (Proc.
2035)
Niobrara Indian Reservation, Nebr.
(EO 5474)
Noone, Marjorie M. (EO 5175)
North Carolina
Customs collection district no. 15 (EO
5159, 5291, 5317)
National forests, parks, and monu-
ments
Nantahala National Forest (Proc.
1892)
Pisgah National Forest (Proc. 1892,
1893)
North Dakota
Customs collection district no. 34 (EO
5137, 5169, 5835)

North Dakota—Continued
Lands
Opening to ex-servicemen (EO
5632)
Restoration to public domain (EO
5632)
Withdrawals (EO 5258, 5586, 5671,
5808, 5914)
Long Lake Migratory Bird Refuge
(EO 5808, 5914)
Trust period extensions on Indian
land allotments
Devil's Lake Reservation (EO 5303,
5768, 5953)
Standing Rock Reservation (EO
5768, 5953)
Northern Pacific Halibut Fishery (EO
5854)
Norway, exports to U.S., wood flour
(Proc. 1936)
Nunivak Island Reservation, Alaska
(EO 5095, 5470)
N wahk tote (EO 5356)

O

Ocala National Forest, Fla. (EO 5814;
Proc. 1918)
Ocala National Game Refuge, Fla. (EO
5814; Proc. 1918)
O'Connor ranger station, Colo. (EO
5422)
Odell Lake Reservoir, Oreg. (EO 5533)
Office. *See other part of title*
O'Hardy, James (EO 5306)
Oil shale reserves (EO 5327, 5552, 6016)
Oklahoma
Lands
Transfer of jurisdiction
Interior Department (EO 5975)
Treasury Department (EO 5975)
Withdrawal (Proc. 1964)
Ouachita National Forest (Proc.
1964)
Salt Plains Wildlife Refuge (EO
5314)
Trust period extensions on Indian
land allotments
Eastern Shawnee Reservation (EO
5768)

Oklahoma—Continued
  Trust period extensions on Indian
    land allotments—Continued
    Kiowa Reservation (EO 5953)
    Missouria Indians (EO 5728, 5768)
    Otoe Reservation (EO 5728, 5768)
    Ponca Reservation (EO 5539)
    Seneca Tribe (EO 5306)
    Wichita Reservation (EO 5955)
Olive oil, change of duty rate (Proc.
  1959)
Omaha Indian Reservation, Nebr. (EO
  5148, 5253)
Oregon
  Customs collection district no. 29 (EO
    5193, 5445)
  Lands
    Opening to ex-servicemen (EO
      5699)
    Railroad grants (EO 5160, 5980)
    Restoration to public domain (EO
      5360, 5372, 5486, 5541, 5564,
      5699, 5798, 5841, 5919)
    Withdrawals (EO 5082, 5115, 5118,
      5176, 5190, 5196, 5203, 5313,
      5344, 5407, 5451, 5478, 5600,
      5601, 5650, 5667, 5671, 5683,
      5694, 5702, 5803, 5838, 5864,
      5891, 5900, 5907, 5923, 5928,
      6014, 6019, 6040)
  LaPine administrative site (EO 5928)
  National forests, parks, and monu-
    ments
    Crater National Forest (EO 5882)
    Deschutes National Forest (EO
      5928, 5991)
    Fremont National Forest (EO
      5991)
    Rogue River National Forest (EO
      5882)
    Siuslaw National Forest (EO 5670,
      5841)
  Odell Lake Reservoir (EO 5533)
  Power site reserves (EO 5360, 5372,
    5486, 5541, 5564, 5798, 5919)
  Railroad grant lands, reduction (EO
    5160, 5980)
  Reservoir site reserve (EO 5533)

Oregon—Continued
  Trust period extensions on Indian
    land allotments
    Siletz Reservation (EO 5087)
    Umatilla Reservation (EO 5516)
    Warm Spring Reservation (EO
      5734)
  Water reserves, public (EO 5344, 5407,
    5478, 5650, 5907, 6019, 6040)
O'Reilly, Eliza C. (EO 5225)
Osceola National Forest, Fla. (Proc.
  1961)
Otoe Indian Reservation, Okla. (EO
  5728, 5768)
Ottawa National Forest, Mich. (Proc.
  1932)
Ouachita National Forest, Arkansas
  and Oklahoma (EO 5820; Proc.
  1964)
Owczarzak, Martha (EO 5999)
O-zosh-quah (EO 5299)

P

Pan American Day (Proc. 1912)
Panama Canal Zone
  Cerro Tigre Ordnance Depot Military
    Reservation (EO 5369)
  Colon Naval Radio Station (EO
    5185)
  Federal personnel, retirement, com-
    pulsory, exemption of certain
    individuals (EO 5872)
  Hotel Tivoli, transfer of operations to
    the Panama Railroad Company
    (EO 5379)
  Judicial districts, delimiting (EO
    5704, 5880)
  Lands
    Transfer of jurisdiction
      Canal Zone authorities (EO 5849)
      Navy Department (EO 5849)
    Withdrawal (EO 5849)
  Liquor transportation (EO 5888)
  Military reservations
    Fort Randolph Military Reserva-
      tion (EO 6010)
    France Field Military Reservation
      (EO 6010)

Panama Canal Zone—Continued
Motor vehicles
Highways, public, regulations for the size, weight, and speed on (EO 5788)
Licensing (EO 5298)
Pardon Board, establishment (EO 5250)
Paymaster, authorization to advance funds to bonded employees (EO 5382)
Panama Railroad Company (EO 5379)
Pappan, John O. (EO 5299)
Parks, national. *See main heading* National forests, parks, and monuments
Parrots, restriction on the importation of (EO 5264)
Partridge, Mary Bernadine (EO 5259)
Passports (EO 5848, 5860, 5973)
Patents
Land patents, signers designated (EO 5076, 5077, 5529)
Plant patents (EO 5464)
Peanish, Mary (EO 5299, 5356)
Peas, change of duty rate (Proc. 1976)
Pechanga Indian Reservation, Calif. (EO 5768)
Pensions, Bureau of (EO 5398, 5476)
Peppers, change of duty rate (Proc. 1978)
Personnel Administration, Council of (EO 5612)
Personnel Classification Board (EO 5473)
Petrified Forest National Monument, Ariz. (Proc. 1927, 1975, 2011)
Petroleum reserves
Colorado (EO 5252, 5460)
Montana (EO 5590)
Philippine Islands
Augur Barracks Military Reservation (EO 5493)
Federal employees, civil service, authorization to be included in the classified service (EO 5622)
Jolo, municipality of, used for military purposes (EO 5129)

Philippine Islands—Continued
Lands
Restoration to public domain (EO 5493)
Withdrawals (EO 5129, 5139, 5308, 5690, 5736)
Malabang, municipality of, used for military purposes (EO 5308)
Naval reservations
Abuyog (EO 5139)
Baguio (EO 5139)
Canacao-Sangley Point (EO 5139)
Cape Bojeador (EO 5139)
Cavite (EO 5139)
Cuyo (EO 5139)
Imus River (EO 5139)
Romblon (EO 5139)
San Fernando (EO 5139)
Ports, transportation restriction on passengers coming to U.S. from (EO 5143)
Súbic Bay, closing of port (EO 5281)
Zamboango, city of, used for military purposes (EO 5129)
Phillips, Hon. Percy W. (EO 5133)
Phillirick, Clinton (EO 5474)
Phosphate reserves (EO 5351, 5769)
Pigskin leather, change of duty rate (Proc. 1935)
Pike National Forest, Colo. (Proc 1909)
Pine Ridge Indian Reservation, S. Dak. (EO 5557, 5768, 5953)
Pinnacles National Monument, Calif. (Proc. 1948)
Pipe organs, change of duty rate (Proc. 1957)
Pisgah National Forest, North Carolina and Tennessee (Proc. 1892, 1893)
Plant patents (EO 5464)
Plummer, Mrs. Nixon S. (EO 5553)
Political asylum, U.S. policy (EO 5956)
Ponca Indian Reservation, Okla. (EO 5539)
Port Graham, Alaska (EO 5214)
Porterfield, Mary Elizabeth (EO 5101)
Portland, Oreg., customs port of entry, extension of limits (EO 5193)

Porto Rico
  Culebra, Great Harbor, closing of port
      (EO 5281)
  District Court of the United States
      for Porto Rico, acting judges,
      designation (EO 5156, 5394, 5705,
      5842)
  Lands, transfer of U.S. lands to (Proc.
      1889, 1983)
  San Geronimo (Proc. 1889, 1970)
  Weather Bureau, Department of Agri-
      culture (Proc. 1983)
Ports and port facilities
  China and Philippine Islands, trans-
      portation restriction on passen-
      gers coming to United States
      from (EO 5143)
  Customs ports of entry and customs
      collection districts. See main
      heading Customs Bureau
Post Office Department
  Civil service, exceptions from certain
      requirements (EO 5442, 5604,
      5997, 5998, 5999, 6031, 6032,
      6033, 6034, 6035, 6036, 6037,
      6042, 6057, 6062)
  Civil service rules
      Schedule A, positions excepted from
          examinations (EO 5471, 5731,
          5930)
      Schedule B, positions filled upon
          noncompetitive examinations
          (EO 5922)
  Postmasters, selection procedures
      (EO 5104)
  Reinstatement of certain individuals
      (EO 6020)
  Retirement, compulsory, exemption
      of certain individuals (EO 5872,
      5874, 5946)
Potash reserve (EO 5537)
Potawatomi Indians, Prairie Band,
    Kans. (EO 5299, 5356, 5556)
Pot-ko-shuck, Mary (EO 5299)
Powell, Milton Harold (EO 6049)
Power Commission, Federal, Civil serv-
    ice rules, Schedule A, positions ex-
    cepted from examinations (EO
    5560)

Power site reserves
  Alaska (EO 5378, 5461)
  Arkansas (EO 5448)
  California (EO 5197, 5360, 5403, 5443,
      5915, 5916, 5927)
  Colorado (EO 5271, 5653, 5744)
  Idaho (EO 5312, 5360, 5367, 5393,
      5543, 5739, 5926, 5937)
  Montana (EO 5363, 5430, 5490, 5535,
      5536, 5567, 5816)
  Nevada (EO 5197)
  New Mexico (EO 5497, 5957)
  Oregon (EO 5360, 5372, 5486, 5541,
      5564, 5798, 5919)
  Utah (EO 5246, 5454, 5456, 5477)
  Wyoming (EO 5510, 5703, 5745, 5795)
Prescott National Forest, Ariz. (EO
    5726)
President's Emergency Committee,
    transfer of records to the Commerce
    Department (EO 6060)
President's Organization for Unemploy-
    ment Relief, transfer of records to
    the Commerce Department (EO
    6060)
Proclamations and executive orders,
    style and form, uniformity (EO
    5220, 5658)
Public Buildings and Public Parks of
    the National Capital, civil service,
    exceptions to certain requirements
    (EO 5103, 6027, 6049)
Public Domain, Committee on the Ad-
    ministration and Conservation of
    (EO 5356)
Public Health Service, employees, hold-
    ing of State and local offices (EO
    5700)
Puck kee (EO 5356)
Pugh, Viola B. (EO 5077)
Pulaski (General) Memorial Day (Proc.
    1884, 1968, 2010)
Punchbowl Hill Military Reservation,
    Hawaii (EO 5157, 5265, 5693)
Puolo Point Military Reservation,
    Hawaii (EO 5405)
Pupukea Military Reservation, Hawaii
    (EO 5174, 5240)
Purcell, Ellen T. (EO 6063)

Q

Qua she (EO 5356)

Quinaielt Indian Reservation, Wash. (EO 5768)

R

Radio Commission, Federal
  Civil service, exceptions from certain requirements (EO 5338)
  Radio Division, transferred from the Commerce Department to (EO 5892)

Radio and radio stations
  Colon Naval Radio Station, Canal Zone (EO 5185)
  Frequencies, assignment to Government stations (EO 5151–A, 5197–A, 5605–A, 5638, 5638–A, 5855, 5855–A)
  Ketchikan radio station, Alaska (EO 5419)
  Philippine Islands, naval radio stations (EO 5139)

Railroads
  Alaska Railroad (EO 5441)
  Director General of Railroads, Ogden L. Mills (Proc. 1987, 1988)
  Labor disputes
    Louisiana, Arkansas, and Texas Railway Co. (Proc. 1992)
    Louisiana and Arkansas Railway Co. (Proc. 1949, 1992)
    Texas and Pacific Railway Co. (Proc. 1874)
  Lines, construction and operation, Alaska (EO 5125)
  Oregon and California railroad grant lands, reduction (EO 5160, 5980)

Ramis, Pearl (EO 5302)

Reconstruction Finance Corporation, extension of date of expiration of lending powers (Proc. 2016)

Red Lake Indian Reservation, Minn. (EO 5383)

Refuges, for migratory birds and other wildlife. *See main heading* Wildlife refuges

Reindeer Service, Alaska (EO 5219)

Remick, Hon. James Waldron (EO 5267)

Reservations. *See other part of title*

Reservoir site reserves
  California (EO 5467, 5686, 5868, 5906, 6053)
  Oregon (EO 5533)
  Washington (EO 5532, 5676)

Ring, Andrew D. (EO 5338)

River Holding Corp., conveying of lands to Virginia for George Washington Birthplace National Monument (Proc. 1945)

Roberts, Estelle (EO 5204)

Rocks Island, Calif. (EO 5326)

Rocky Mountain National Park, Colo. (Proc. 1917, 1985)

Rogue River National Forest, Oreg. (EO 5882)

Rolfe, George H. (EO 5853)

Rollins, Geraldine (EO 5972)

Romblon Naval Reservation, Philippine Islands (EO 5139)

Roosevelt National Forest, Colo. (EO 5826)

Rosebud Indian Reservation, S. Dak. (EO 5302, 5768)

Ross, Nellie (EO 5302)

Ross, Solomon (EO 5474)

Rouillard, Joseph (EO 5474)

Round Top Military Reservation, Hawaii (EO 5931)

Round Valley Indian Reservation, Calif. (EO 5953)

Routt National Forest, Colo. (Proc. 1888, 1906, 1910)

Roy, Thelma D. (EO 5335)

Rubber-soled and rubber footwear, change of duty rate (Proc. 2027)

S

Sac and Fox Indian Reservation, Kansas and Nebraska (EO 5768)

Saguaro National Monument, Ariz. (Proc. 2032)

Sah gon ko shuck (EO 5415)

St. Joe National Forest, Idaho (EO 5615)

St. Marks Migratory Bird Refuge, Fla. (EO 5740; Proc. 1982)

Salaries. *See main heading* Wages and salaries

Salmon Hatchery Reservation, Alaska (EO 5641)

Salmon National Forest, Idaho (Proc. 1922)

Salt Plain Wildlife Refuge, Okla. (EO 5314)

Salton Sea Wildlife Refuge, Calif. (EO 5498)

San Carlos Indian irrigation project, Ariz. (EO 5611, 5889)

San Fernando Naval Reservation, Philippine Islands (EO 5139)

San Juan Military Reservation, Porto Rico (Proc. 1889)

San Juan National Forest, Colo. (EO 5749)

Santa Fe National Forest, N. Mex. (EO 5809, 5840; Proc. 1991)

Santee Indian Reservation, Nebr. (EO 5474, 5768, 5953)

Saunders, Nellie (EO 5416)

Savage, Carlton B. (EO 5171)

Savannah River Bird Refuge, S.C. (EO 5748)

Savannah River Wildlife Refuge, Georgia and South Carolina (EO 5748)

Sawtooth National Forest, Idaho (EO 5925)

Scallon, William (EO 5239)

Schaefer, Lessie L. (EO 5084)

Schofield Barracks Military Reservation, Hawaii (EO 5771)

Schrimpsher, Ida (EO 5306)

Scott, Fred (EO 5822)

Scotts Bluff National Monument, Nebr. (Proc. 1999)

Scissons, Lily (EO 5302)

Sea navigation. *See main heading* Navigation

Selway National Forest, Idaho (EO 5646)

Semidi Islands Wildlife Refuge, Alaska (EO 5858)

Senate, convening, special session (Proc. 1915, 2029)

Seneca Tribe, Okla. (EO 5306)

Seward, Alaska (EO 5447)

Shasta National Forest, Calif. (EO 5714)

Sheep Island, Wash. (EO 5151)

Shely, Myrtle B. (EO 5168)

Shenandoah National Forest, Virginia and West Virginia (EO 5867)

Shepard, Carl R. (EO 6007)

Shipping Board, United States (EO 5917)

Shipping Commissioner (EO 5459)

Shoes, change of duty rate (Proc. 1979)

Shopteese, Francis (EO 5299)

Shoshone Indian Reservation, Wyo. (EO 5768, 5953)

Sick leave. *See main hearing* Civil service

Siletz Indian Reservation, Oreg. (EO 5087)

Sinnott, Dorothy I. (EO 5620)

Sitka dock site, Alaska (EO 6045)

Siuslaw National Forest, Oreg. (EO 5670, 5841)

Skilton, Caroline J. (EO 5697)

Skinner, Robert Peet (EO 5519)

Skishkee (EO 5356)

Smith, Patia (EO 5377)

Smithsonian Institution
    Archaeological investigation in New Mexico (EO 5120)
    Civil service, exceptions to certain requirements (EO 5311)
    Retirement, compulsory, exemption of certain individuals (EO 5872, 5873, 5896)

Smythe, Grace F. (EO 6042)

Snoqualmie National Forest, Wash. (EO 5634)

Sperm oil, crude, and spermaceti wax, change of duty rate (Proc. 2034)

Spicer family (EO 5306)

Splitlog, Carrie B. (EO 5306)

Sponges, sheepswool, change of duty rate (Proc. 2008)

South Carolina
    Lands, withdrawal (EO 5748)
    Nantahala National Forest (Proc. 1892)

South Carolina—Continued
  Wildlife refuges
    Cape Romain Migratory Bird Refuge (Proc. 2000)
    Savannah River Bird Refuge (EO 5748)
    Savannah River Wildlife Refuge (EO 5748)
South Dakota
  Lands
    Opening to ex-servicemen (EO 5216)
    Restoration to public domain (EO 5216)
    Withdrawals (EO 5938; Proc. 1914, 1951)
  National forests, parks, and monuments
    Black Hills National Forest (Proc. 1913)
    Custer National Forest (EO 5801; Proc. 1913)
    Harney National Forest (EO 5938; Proc. 1878, 1913, 1914, 1951)
  Trust period extensions on Indian land allotments
    Cheyenne River Reservation (EO 5546, 5768)
    Crow Creek Reservation (EO 5768)
    Pine Ridge Reservation (EO 5557, 5768, 5953)
    Rosebud Reservation (EO 5302, 5768)
    Yankton Sioux Reservation (EO 5173)
Spruks, H. Charles (EO 5310)
Standard Oil Company of California (EO 5239)
Standing Rock Indian Reservation, N. Dak. (EO 5768, 5953)
State, Department of
  Accounts and returns (EO 5290, 5295, 5345, 5648)
  Aliens, female, regulations governing naturalization and citizenship (EO 5417, 5621)
  Chinese, admission to United States (EO 5110)

State, Department of—Continued
  Civil service, exceptions from certain requirements (EO 5163, 5171, 5310, 5839, 6022–A, 6056)
  Civil service rules
    Schedule A, positions excepted from examinations (EO 5171, 5657)
    Schedule B, positions filled upon noncompetitive examinations (EO 5171, 5513)
  Consular fees (EO 5110, 5345, 5417, 5737, 5837, 5848, 5910)
  Consular officers, authority to act for the Veterans' Administration (EO 6017)
  Consular regulations, amendments (EO 5110, 5127, 5226, 5290, 5345, 5417, 5469, 5526, 5621, 5642, 5648, 5661, 5737, 5773, 5812, 5825, 5837, 5857, 5973, 6017)
  Correspondence form (EO 5463, 5773)
  Diplomatic officers' instructions, amendments (EO 5126, 5295, 5463, 5468, 5549, 5642, 5648, 5825)
  Diplomatic visas (EO 5226)
  Flag, official, for the Office of the Secretary of State (EO 6005–A)
  Foreign Service, rules and regulations for administering (EO 5189, 5565, 5642, 5648, 5825)
  Inventory of Government property (EO 5468, 5469)
  Leaves of absence (EO 5126, 5217, 5642, 5825)
  Political asylum, U.S. policy (EO 5956)
  "Posts, unhealthful" (EO 5324, 5644)
  Quarters, Foreign Service (EO 5624, 5707)
  Representation and post allowances (EO 5400, 5643)
  Retention or reinstatement of individual Foreign Service officers (EO 5247, 5286, 5519, 6066)
  Retirement, compulsory, exemption of certain individuals (EO 5872, 5873, 5896)

State, Department of—Continued
Ship's papers, custody and return
(EO 5345)
Succession, order of, consular officers
during the absence of the princi-
pal officer (EO 5661)
State and local offices, holding of, by
Federal employees (EO 5133, 5627,
5666, 5700)
Stedman, Ralph Ely (EO 5142)
Stewart, Mary (EO 6029)
Storey, John (EO 6027)
Stotler, Hallie D. (EO 5767)
Strong, Ida (EO 5093)
Strout, L. E. (EO 5572)
Superior National Forest, Minn. (EO
5845)
Supervising Architect, Office of (EO
5094, 5135)
Suppur, Josie (EO 5416)
Surveys and Maps, Board of (EO 5268)
Switzerland, exports to U.S.
Alsimin, ferrosilicon aluminum, and
ferroaluminum silicon (Proc.
2002)
Shoes (Proc. 1979)

T

Taft, William Howard (Proc. 1901)
Tahoe National Forest, Nev. (EO 5799)
Targhee National Forest, Wyo. (EO
5296)
Tariff Commission, United States
Import quotas and fees on various
commodities. *See main heading*
Imports and exports
Retirement, compulsory, exemption of
certain individuals (EO 5872,
5989)
Tariffs. *See main heading* Imports and
exports
Tasker, Alice (EO 5224)
Taxes
Refunds, authorization for inspection
(EO 5079)
Returns, authorization for inspection
(EO 5321, 5647, 5824, 5970)
Temecula Indian Reservation, Calif.
(EO 5768)

Tennessee, Pisgah National Forest
(Proc. 1892, 1893)
Texas, customs collection district no. 21
(EO 5392, 5475)
Texas & Pacific Railway Co. (Proc.
1874)
Thanksgiving Day (Proc. 1895, 1925,
1974, 2015)
Timmis, Harry E. (EO 6048)
Toiyabe National Forest, Nev. (EO
5725, 5863)
Tom, Mary (EO 5087)
Tongass National Forest, Alaska (EO
5199, 5227, 5409, 5425, 5439, 5449,
5673, 5779, 5856, 5947, 5950, 6011,
6045, 6050)
Townsend, Dr. Charles Orrin (EO 5989)
Trade Commission, Federal, civil service, exceptions from certain requirements (EO 5333, 5553, 5872)
Transcontinental Air Mail Service (EO
5162)
Travel regulations, Government (EO
5605, 5870)
Treasury, Department of the
Civil service, exceptions from certain
requirements (EO 5094, 5101,
5146, 5175, 5180, 5205, 5209, 5210,
5225, 5259, 5283, 5325, 5335, 5347,
5348, 5399, 5520, 5563, 5649, 5659,
5695, 5697, 5706, 5847, 5851, 5879,
5972, 5986, 6007, 6052, 6069)
Civil service rules, Schedule A, positions excepted from examinations (EO 5236, 5544, 5859, 5974,
6047)
Coast Guard Service, merger of Immigration Border Patrol and Customs Patrol in (EO 5966)
Customs Patrol, merger with the Immigration Border patrol in the
Coast Guard Service (EO 5966)
Expenditures, Government, reporting
of (EO 5614)
Immigration Border Patrol, transfer
from the Labor Department to
(EO 5966)

Treasury, Department of the—Con.
Lands, transfer of jurisdiction in Oklahoma from the Interior Department to (EO 5975)
Public Health Service, employees, holding of State and local offices (EO 5700)
Reinstatement of certain individuals (EO 5083, 5135, 5149, 5150, 5152, 5154, 5235, 5501)
Retirement, compulsory, exemption of certain individuals (EO 5872, 5873, 5875, 5881, 5896, 5911, 5921, 5946, 6004, 6013, 6022)
Taxes
Refunds, authorization for inspection (EO 5079)
Returns, authorization for inspection (EO 5321, 5647, 5824, 5970)
Trudell, Emily (EO 5302)
Tule Lake Wildlife Refuge, Calif. (EO 5945)
Turnipseed, Lulie Hunt (EO 5520)
Tyndall, Grace McMahan (EO 5591)

U

Uinta National Forest, Utah (Proc. 1887)
Uinta Pipe Line Co. (EO 5245, 5246, 5477)
Uintah Indians, Utah (EO 5357)
Uintah Railroad Co. (EO 5708, 5723, 5772)
Umatilla Indian Reservation, Oreg. (EO 5516)
Uncompahgre Indians, Utah (EO 5357, 5552)
Unemployment Relief, President's Organization for, transfer of records to the Commerce Department (EO 6060)
United Kingdom, exports to United States
Infant's wool knit outerwear (Proc. 2001)
Spermaceti wax (Proc. 2034)
United States Emergency Fleet Corp. (EO 5722)

United States Employees' Compensation Commission
Civil service rules, Schedule A, positions excepted from examinations (EO 5107)
Transfer of certain functions from the Labor Department to (EO 5961)
United States Geographic Board (EO 5872)
United States Metals Refining Co., sale of stock by the Alien Property Custodian (EO 5263)
United States Shipping Board (EO 5917)
United States Soldiers' Home, retirement, compulsory, exemption of certain individuals (EO 5872)
United States Tariff Commission
Import quotas and fees on various commodities. *See main heading* Imports and exports
Retirement, compulsory, exemption of certain individuals (EO 5872, 5989)
United States v. *The Standard Oil Company of California* (EO 5239)
United States Veterans' Bureau (EO 5224, 5398, 5476)
Upholsterers' nail, chair glides, and thumb tacks, change of duty rate (Proc. 2017)
Upolu Airplane Landing Field, Hawaii (EO 5528)
Upolu Point Military Reservation, Hawaii (EO 5406)
Upper Mississippi River Wildlife and Fish Refuge, Miss. (EO 5721)
Utah
Boulder Canyon Project (Proc. 1882)
Devil's Garden (Proc. 1875)
Lands
Opening to ex-servicemen (EO 5410, 5440, 5675, 5678)
Restoration to public domain (EO 5279, 5336, 5410, 5440, 5454, 5456, 5499, 5515, 5552, 5669, 5675, 5678, 5780, 5810, 5971)

Utah—Continued
  Lands—Continued
    Withdrawals (EO 5274, 5275, 5344,
      5508, 5525, 5573, 5684, 5727,
      6012, 6019; Proc. 1903, 1930,
      1952, 2012, 2026, 2030)
    National forests, parks, and monu-
      ments
      Arches National Monument (Proc.
        1875)
      Ashley National Forest (Proc. 1903,
        2030)
      Bryce Canyon National Park (Proc.
        1930, 1952)
      Fishlake National Forest (EO
        5307)
      Uinta National Forest (Proc. 1887)
      Wasatch National Forest (Proc.
        1887, 2026)
    Power site reserves (EO 5246, 5454,
      5456, 5477)
    Trust period extensions on Indian
      land allotments
      Uintah Indians (EO 5357)
      Uncompahgre Indians (EO 5357,
        5552)
      White River Bands, Ute Indians
        (EO 5357)
    Uintah Railroad Co., authorization
      for right of way across certain
      lands (EO 5708, 5723, 5772)
    Water reserves, public (EO 5274,
      5344, 5669, 5780, 6019)
    Wildlife refuges
      Bear River Migratory Bird Refuge
        (EO 5971; Proc. 2012)
      Bird Island Wildlife Refuge (EO
        5349, 5515)
      Locomotive Springs Migratory Bird
        Refuge (EO 5727)
    Windows (Proc. 1875)
  Ute Indians, White River Bands, Utah
    (EO 5357)

                      V

Vallecer, Eustaquio (EO 5285)
Vaughan, Jeanette C. (EO 5180)
Velvet, cotton, change of duty rate
  (Proc. 2019)

Vermont
  Green Mountain National Forest
    (Proc. 1997)
  Land withdrawal (Proc. 1997)
Vestal, Ralph A. (EO 5839)
Veterans
  Armistice Day (Proc. 1897, 1924, 1973,
    2014)
  Employment, Federal
    Leave, for disabled veterans for
      medical treatment (EO 5396)
    Veterans preference in appoint-
      ments (EO 5610, 5776, 6043)
  Opening of lands to ex-servicemen
    Alaska (EO 5207)
    Arizona (EO 5262)
    Arkansas (EO 5743)
    California (EO 5446, 5674, 5978)
    Colorado (EO 5195, 5418, 5420, 5422,
      5488, 5506, 5524, 5587, 5688,
      5698, 5819, 5823, 5877, 5883,
      5934, 5943, 6008)
    Florida (EO 5569)
    Idaho (EO 5223)
    Minnesota (EO 5651)
    Montana (EO 5433, 5434, 5619)
    Nevada (EO 5944)
    New Mexico (EO 5086, 5177, 5178,
      5179, 5254, 5412, 5421, 5423,
      5509, 5518, 5576, 5677, 5685,
      5735, 5932)
    North Dakota (EO 5632)
    Oregon (EO 5699)
    South Dakota (EO 5216)
    Utah (EO 5410, 5440, 5675, 5678)
    Washington (EO 5212, 5494)
    Wyoming (EO 5090, 5181, 5183,
      5184, 5215, 5411, 5413, 5679,
      5741, 5793, 5797, 5884, 5933,
      5935, 5995, 5996)
Veterans' Administration
  Civil service, exceptions from certain
    requirements (EO 5738, 5804,
    5861, 5905, 6038, 6068)
  Civil service rules
    Schedule A, positions excepted from
      examinations (EO 5691, 5724,
      5774)

Veterans' Administration—Continued
Civil service rules—Continued
Schedule B, positions filled upon noncompetitive examinations (EO 5636)
Consular officers, authority to act for (EO 6017)
Establishment (EO 5398)
National Home for Disabled Volunteer Soldiers (EO 5398, 5476, 5609)
Pensions Bureau (EO 5398, 5476)
Retirement, compulsory, exemption of certain individuals (EO 5872, 5981)
Transfer of certain functions performed for veterans
Justice Department to (EO 5967)
War Department to (EO 5476)
Veterans' Bureau, United States (EO 5224, 5398, 5476)
Viles, Lily (EO 5305)
Vincent, Mildred E. (EO 5387)
Virgin Islands
Coastwise laws, exemption from (Proc. 1886, 1919, 1963, 2006)
Government
Appropriations (EO 5088, 5373)
Federal employees, holding of positions on the local colonial council (EO 6051)
Transfer of jurisdiction from the Navy Department to the Interior Department (EO 5566)
Lands
Transfer of jurisdiction
Interior Department (EO 5602)
Navy Department (EO 5602)
Narcotic drugs, dispensation of (EO 5502)
Virginia
Federal employees, holding of local offices in Arlington (EO 5627)
Land withdrawal (Proc. 1929)
National forests, parks, and monuments
Colonial National Monument (Proc. 1929)

Virginia—Continued
National forests, parks, and monuments—Continued
George Washington Birthplace National Monument (Proc. 1944)
George Washington National Forest (EO 5867)
Shenandoah National Forest (EO 5867)
Visas (EO 5226, 5427, 5435)

W

Wabaunce, Elizabeth (EO 5299)
Wabaunce, James (EO 5299)
Wages and salaries
Federal employees
International Joint Commission, American members (EO 5376)
War Claims Arbiter (EO 5267)
Labors and mechanics, regulations for the payment of the prevailing rate of wage for jobs on buildings under Government contract (EO 5778)
Waianae-Kai Military Reservation, Hawaii (EO 5414)
Wales, George R. (EO 5951)
Walker River Indian Reservation, Nev. (EO 5730)
Wamego, Harry (EO 5356)
War, Department of
See also Armed Forces
Assistant Secretaries of War, order of succession (EO 5332, 5371)
Civil service, exceptions from certain requirements (EO 5269, 5285, 5334, 5591)
Civil service rules
Schedule A, positions excepted from examinations (EO 6046)
Schedule B, positions filled upon noncompetitive examinations (EO 5696, 5777)
Lands, transfer of jurisdiction in Wyoming from the Interior Department to (EO 5592)
Military academies, applicants, civil service authorization to test (EO 5918)

War, Department of—Continued
  Military reservations. *See main heading* Military reservations
  Rations (EO 5337, 5952)
  Retirement, compulsory, exemption of certain individuals (EO 5872, 5873, 5896, 5988)
  Transfer of functions performed for veterans to the Veterans' Administration (EO 5476)
War Minerals Relief Act (EO 5830)
Warehouse, bonded (Proc. 1993, 2023)
Warm Springs Indian Reservation, Oreg. (EO 5734)
Wasatch National Forest, Utah (Proc. 1887, 2026)
Washington
  Customs collection district no. 30 (EO 5081, 5206, 5835)
  Double Island (EO 5151)
  Greenleaf administrative site (EO 5976)
  Lands
    Opening to ex-servicemen (EO 5212, 5494)
    Restoration to public domain (EO 5212, 5494)
    Transfer of jurisdiction
      Interior Department (EO 5630)
      Navy Department (EO 5630)
    Withdrawals (EO 5108, 5151, 5244, 5397, 5617, 5818, 5976)
  National forests, parks, and monuments
    Mount Baker National Forest (EO 5634)
    Snoqualmie National Forest (EO 5634)
  Reservoir site reserves
    No. 1 (EO 5532, 5676)
    Wenatchee Lake Reservoir (EO 5532, 5676)
  Sheep Island (EO 5151)
  Trust period extensions on Indian land allotments
    Quinaielt Reservation (EO 5768)
    Yakima Reservation (EO 5746)
Washington, George, Bicentennial of Birth (Proc. 1986)

Washington, Gertrude (EO 5306)
Washington-Alaska Military Cable and Telegraph System (EO 5419, 5450)
Watch-kee, Anthony (EO 5299)
Water reserves, public
  Alaska (EO 5106, 5754, 6006)
  Arizona (EO 5379, 5655, 5780)
  California (EO 5379, 5432, 5478, 5489, 5717, 5902, 5908)
  Colorado (EO 5270, 5379, 5492, 5593, 5672)
  Montana (EO 5293, 5344, 5478, 5534, 5629, 5669, 5907, 6025)
  Nevada (EO 5292, 5344, 5534, 5594, 5496)
  New Mexico (EO 5217, 5272, 5273, 5478, 5597, 5907, 5597)
  Oregon (EO 5344, 5407, 5478, 5650, 5907, 6019, 6040)
  Utah (EO 5274, 5344, 5669, 5780, 6019)
  Wyoming (EO 5245, 5407, 5495, 5594, 5672, 5899, 5907, 6025)
Waterfowl (Proc. 1965, 1989)
Waterton-Glacier International Peace Park, Canada–U.S. (Proc. 2003)
Way me no gwon (EO 5466)
Weather Bureau, Department of Agriculture, Porto Rico (Proc. 1983)
Webb, Ruby Mae (EO 6062)
Weeks of observance. *See main heading* Days of observance
Wells, Hon. Ira K. (EO 5156, 5705, 5842)
Wenatchee Lake Reservoir, Wash. (EO 5532, 5676)
West Indian Islands, appropriations for the Governor of the Virgin Islands to be used for the establishment of a government for (EO 5373)
West ke no (EO 5356)
West Virginia
  George Washington National Forest (EO 5867)
  Shenandoah National Forest (EO 5867)
Western Gas Co., gas pipe line, authorization for right of way across the international boundary strip between the United States and Mexico (EO 5689)

White, Joseph B. (EO 5128)

White, William C. (EO 5742)

White Earth Indian Reservation, Minn. (EO 5768, 5953)

White Mountain National Forest, Maine and New Hampshire (Proc. 1894)

White Sands National Monument, N. Mex. (Proc. 2025)

Whitecrow, Walter (EO 5306)

Whitetree family (EO 5306)

Wichita Indian Reservation, Okla. (EO 5955)

Wide Bay, Alaska (EO 5214)

Wildlife; regulations relating to migratory birds, etc. *See main heading* Migratory birds and certain game animals

Wildlife refuges

Aleutian Islands Reservation, Alaska (EO 5243, 5318)

Bamforth Lake Migratory Bird Refuge, Wyo. (EO 5783)

Bear River Migratory Bird Refuge, Utah (EO 5971; Proc. 2012)

Benton Lake Bird Refuge, Mont. (EO 5228)

Big Lake Reservation, Ark. (EO 5747)

Bird Island Wildlife Refuge, Utah (EO 5349, 5515)

Boulder Canyon Wildlife Refuge, Arizona and Nevada (EO 6065)

Cape Romain Migratory Bird Refuge, S.C. (Proc. 2000)

Cedar Keys Bird Refuge, Fla. (EO 5158)

Charles Sheldon Wildlife Refuge, Nev. (EO 5540)

Crescent Lake Wildlife Refuge, Nebr. (EO 5579)

Fallon Wildlife Refuge, Nev. (EO 5606)

Fort Keogh Bird Refuge, Mont. (EO 5122)

Grand Canyon National Game Preserve, Ariz. (Proc. 1971)

Hutton Lake Migratory Bird Refuge, Wyo. (EO 5782)

Wildlife refuges—Continued

Locomotive Springs Migratory Bird Refuge, Utah (EO 5727)

Long Lake Migratory Bird Refuge, N. Dak. (EO 5808, 5914)

Minidoka Bird Refuge, Idaho (EO 5375)

Nunivak Island Reservation, Alaska (EO 5095, 5470)

Ocala National Game Refuge, Fla. (EO 5814; Proc. 1918)

St. Marks Migratory Bird Refuge, Fla. (EO 5740; Proc. 1982)

Salt Plains Wildlife Refuge, Okla. (EO 5314)

Salton Sea Wildlife Refuge, Calif. (EO 5498)

Savannah River Bird Refuge, S.C. (EO 5748)

Savannah River Wildlife Refuge, Georgia and South Carolina (EO 5748)

Semidi Islands Wildlife Refuge, Alaska (EO 5858)

Tule Lake Wildlife Refuge, Calif. (EO 5945)

Upper Mississippi River Wildlife and Fish Refuge, Miss. (EO 5721)

Wolf Island Wildlife Refuge, Ga. (EO 5316)

Williams, J. Elizabeth (EO 6063)

Williams, James (EO 5416)

Williams, Maude (EO 5232)

Willow administrative site, Ariz. (EO 5726)

Wilson, Sinclair A. (EO 5802)

Wind River Indian Reservation, Wyo. (EO 5768, 5953)

Windows, Utah (Proc. 1875)

Winney, Mary E. (EO 5306)

Winnibigoshish Indian Reservation, Minn. (EO 5768)

Wire, change of duty rate (Proc. 1934, 1940)

Wisconsin

Customs collection district no. 36 (EO 5530)

Lands, withdrawals (EO 5138, 5671, 5796, 5929; Proc. 2035)

Wisconsin—Continued
  Nicolet National Forest, Wis. (Proc.
      2035)
Wish-ken-o, Willie (EO 5299)
Wish kuk ke ash kuk (EO 5356)
Witt, Helen R. (EO 5554)
Wolf, Hon. Adolph G. (EO 5705)
Wolf Island Wildlife Refuge, Ga. (EO
    5316
Wood flour, change of duty rate (Proc.
    1936)
Wool, change of duty rate (Proc. 1996,
    2001, 2023)
World's Fair, Chicago (Proc. 1896)
Wynne, Edward C. (EO 5171)
Wyoming
  Boulder Canyon Project (Proc. 1882)
  Lands
    Opening to ex-servicemen (EO 5090,
        5181, 5183, 5184, 5215, 5411,
        5413, 5679, 5741, 5793, 5884,
        5933, 5935, 5995, 5996)
    Restoration to public domain (EO
        5090, 5181, 5183, 5184, 5215,
        5296, 5411, 5413, 5510, 5679,
        5703, 5741, 5745, 5793, 5795,
        5797, 5884, 5899, 5933, 5935,
        5995, 5996)
    Transfer of jurisdiction
      Interior Department (EO 5592)
      War Department (EO 5592)
    Withdrawals (EO 5085, 5098, 5140,
        5162, 5323, 5354, 5407, 5436,
        5480, 5494, 5595, 5603, 5639,
        5656, 5668, 5671, 5672, 5687,
        5782, 5783, 5886, 5904, 5907,
        5949, 6025)
  National forests, parks, and monu-
      ments
    Ashley National Forest (Proc. 1903,
        2030)
    Hayden National Forest (Proc.
        1888)
    Medicine Bow National Forest
        (Proc. 1888)

Wyoming—Continued
  National forests, parks, and monu-
      ments—Continued
    Targhee National Forest (EO 5296)
    Yellowstone National Park (EO
        5296)
  Power site reserves (EO 5510, 5703,
      5745, 5795)
  Trust period extensions on Indian
      land allotments
    Shoshone Reservation (EO 5768,
        5953)
    Wind River Reservation (EO 5768,
        5953)
  Water reserves, public (EO 5345,
      5407, 5495, 5594, 5672, 5899, 5907,
      6025)
  Wildlife refuges
    Bamforth Lake Migratory Bird
        Refuge (EO 5783)
    Hutton Lake Migratory Bird Ref-
        uge (EO 5782)

Y

Yakima Indian Reservation, Wash. (EO
    5746)
Yakutat Bay, Alaska (EO 5214)
Yankton Sioux Indian Reservation,
    S. Dak. (EO 5173)
Yellowstone National Park, Montana
    and Wyoming (EO 5296; Proc.
    2013)
Yocta, Samuel (EO 5416)
York, Helen Hall (EO 5348)
Yosemite National Park, Calif. (Proc.
    1904, 2005)
Young, Clarence M. (EO 5242)
Young, Downing (EO 5306)
Young, Harry R. (EO 5171)
Young, Solorena (EO 5306)

Z

Zhuck kah o see, Albert (EO 5415)